THE AMERICAN REVOLUTION
AND THE WEST INDIES

Kennikat Press

National University Publications

Series in American Studies

General Editor
James P. Shenton
Professor of History, Columbia University

THE AMERICAN REVOLUTION
AND THE WEST INDIES

Edited by
CHARLES W. TOTH

National University Publications
KENNIKAT PRESS • 1975
Port Washington, N.Y. • London

The editor and publisher acknowledge with gratitude the cooperation of the authors and publishers in permitting use of
the selections herein reprinted. Full bibliographical citation
is given at the front of the first page of each selection.

Manufactured in the United States of America

Published by
Kennikat Press Corp.
Port Washington, N.Y. / London

Library of Congress Cataloging in Publication Data

Main entry under title:
The American Revolution and the West Indies.

(National university publications)
Includes bibliographical references.
1. United States–History–Revolution, 1775–1783–
Addresses, sermons, etc. 2. West Indies–History–1775–
1783–Addresses, essays, lectures. 3. Great Britain–
Colonies–America–Commerce–Addresses, essays, lectures.
I. Toth, Charles.
E263.W5A53   973.3   75-15631
ISBN 0-8046-9110-X

CONTENTS

AFTERMATH

PREFACE

On the eve of the American Revolution, after Boston Harbor had been shut down, John Adams remarked with regard to the West Indian trade that "it was an essential link in a vast chain, which has made New England what it is, the southern provinces what they are, the West India islands what they are." In effect, the trade not only with the British islands, but with the West Indies in general, had become a cornerstone of the American economy well before the colonies had revolted. To quote Adams again, "our trade could not be taken from us, or granted stingily, without tearing and rendering."

A substantial part of the trade with the West Indies was "illicit" in that the mercantilist system restricted (or attempted to restrict) this trade almost entirely within the confines of the British Empire. As Parliament endeavored to tighten this system, the illegalities increased and were ultimately transformed from "economic" questions into fundamental "constitutional" issues.

As will be seen in this selection of articles, the growing anxiety with regard to commerce with the West Indies before the Revolution did not end with the Declaration of Independence; rather it was exacerbated by years of military struggle. And the existence of the West Indies played an important role after the war as the United States attempted to reestablish its relationship both with England and Europe. When the Treaty of Paris (1783) was being drawn up, the American ministers (Franklin, Adams, and Jay) made a strong effort to secure for America a share in the carrying-trade to the West Indies. "The West India commerce," Adams reported to Richard Livingston, "now gives us the most anxiety." When the ministers failed to secure the right for American vessels to enter British ports in the West Indies, Livingston answered that "we are very angry here with Great Britain, on account of her West Indian restrictions." And John Adams, America's first minister to England, took occasion to remark that "they think America may have what she desires except a free trade with the West India islands," and then reflected that "our natural share of the West India trade is all that is wanting to complete the plan of happiness and prosperity of our country." Later, when the Republic was established, Washington was as much concerned, writing to Gouverneur Morris that in any negotiations "let it be strongly impressed on your mind, that the privilege of carrying our productions in our vessels to the West Indies, and of bringing in return the productions of those islands to our own ports is regarded here of the highest importance; and you will be careful not to countenance any idea of our dispensing with it in a treaty."

The Bicentennial will stimulate much writing and editing, and this volume was conceived with the hope that this important chapter in the story of the American Revolution will receive its due consideration. The role of the West Indies in the history of America during the eighteenth century has not been neglected, as will be noted by the materials selected for this volume. But often these items are scattered, or buried in scholarly journals, across the years. Therefore the subject may give the appearance of having been overlooked. The Bicentennial is a convenient time, then, to assemble some of these writings. It is the editor's feeling that the general reader will be more than surprised by the complex relationship which existed between the thirteen colonies on the mainland of America and the islands of the West Indies. An attempt has been made to show the impact of the "civil war" on some of the island possessions of the various powers across the Caribbean.

This is an exciting and marvelous story, full of the history of the eighteenth century, and therefore rich in significance. As always in a volume of this kind, much has had to be omitted. Space was only a partial reason. The attempt to balance meticulous scholarship with the needs and requirements of the general reader has been time consuming. This has demanded the utmost in editing, especially to preserve the integrity of each author's work. Abridgment in a number of selections was a basic requirement to produce a readable book. By abridgment is meant simply that extraneous, repetitious, or extended elaborations were excluded as judiciously as possible. In a few cases the entire work of an author was reduced to a chapter by selections from across the pages of the book. Footnotes, sometimes mountainous since historians also write for historians, had to be considerably reduced and, in a few instances, some of the very pertinent material lifted into the text. As to the listing of sources, the criterion used was the attempt to satisfy the curiosity of the general reader who would like to further pursue a source or subject while, at the same time, to satisfy the interested scholar who would like to carry forward an awakened interest in this area of historical pursuit. A tedious part of the task of editing was the completion of sources cited by the authors, or the correcting of them.

The titles of the chapters were chosen for their descriptiveness and pertinence, but in all cases the reader will conveniently find the original source from which the selection was taken.

A word of thanks to those who provided encouragement in all its forms, including the necessary freedom from some teaching duties: Dr. Luis M. Diaz Soler and Dr. Arturo Santana of the University of Puerto Rico; Professor William Trembley of the University of Guyana for his valuable suggestions of material to consider; David Price for his interest and encouragement. Invaluable were the efforts of Carola Rosa in arranging so many interlibrary loans, since this manuscript was prepared almost entirely while working and living in the West Indies. And to Haydee O'Reilly a special word of thanks for learning to decipher my scribblings in order to type an intelligible text. Finally, this editor was favored in having in Jane Toth a wife who is both a professional librarian and an interested and patient partner in all of life's endeavors.

Charles W. Toth

THE AMERICAN REVOLUTION
AND THE WEST INDIES

It was the best of times, it was the worst
of times
It was the age of wisdom, it was the age
of foolishness,
It was the epoch of belief, it was the epic
of incredulity,
It was the season of light, it was the season
of darkness,
It was the spring of hope, it was the winter
of despair.

Dickens's description of 1775
A Tale of Two Cities

BACKGROUND

"America is the colony of all Europe," cried Tom Paine, and the distinguished historian Samuel F. Bemis, in his classic study *The Diplomacy of the American Revolution,* offered a mountain of scholarship to underscore the fact that it was the bitter international rivalry which ultimately made American independence possible in that the revolt of the thirteen colonies gave all an excuse for war. This bitter rivalry, and its consequences for the New World, is brought out in the following selections. Marshall Smelser traces the development of this rivalry to show how North America increasingly became the stakes of European diplomacy, culminating in the deadly competition for empire and commerce between England and France. As Prof. Smelser pointedly shows, this confrontation "might easily have started at, say, Albamaboe or St. Lucia."

St. Lucia, of course, is in the West Indies, and although one could press the claim that the Seven Years' War resulted directly from the fact that France and England were closing in on the headwaters of the Ohio (the Parliament took Canada instead of Guadeloupe in 1763), the "politics of sugar" was an important ingredient in the rivalry of empires during the eighteenth century. As the selection by Frank Wesley Pitman so clearly shows, although England reduced its empire in the Caribbean in the 1760s, this must be regarded as only a temporary result reflecting the influence of the sugar interests which feared the negative effects of additional islands in the market place. Pitman quotes William Pitt to show that the conflict of empires was still the basic problem for England. Pitt warned Parliament in his opposition to the Treaty of Paris that it appeared to have lost sight of the great fundamental principle "that France is chiefly, if not solely, to be dreaded by us in the light of a maritime and commercial power . . . therefore, by restoring to her all the valuable West India islands . . . we have given her the means of . . . becoming once more formidable . . ."

The suggestion finally underscored by the author is that if the sugar interests had not prevailed, the addition of the French "mercantile gems" in the Caribbean would have legalized the growing illicit American trade in the

West Indies. This, together with the continued presence of the French in Canada, would have prevented the war of independence.

In any case, the Treaty of Paris reflected his Majesty's desire for peace. Allowing France and Spain to keep their "mercantile gems" would not, however, prevent France from growing in power, nor from seizing the right moment to further diminish British power. In the meantime the northern colonies refused to confine their activities "to such produce, trade, and manufactures as are most for the benefit of Great Britain." Thus Charles M. Andrews promoted the view, so lucidly presented in the following pages, that the new realities of the age demanded a modification, or moderation, of the mercantilist system—which system increasingly restricted an expanding merchant class as it sought ever wider markets. The result was not only a growing conflict between the mainland colonies and the mother-country, but with the sister colonies in the West Indies. And feelings were intensified as Yankee ships increasingly frequented foreign ports at the "expense" of the Creole planters.

MARSHALL SMELSER

THE CONTENTIOUS EMPIRES

*The outbreak of the Seven Years' War in 1756 involved more than just
the struggle for power over the map of Europe; it was also a struggle for the
expansion and control of empire across the oceans of the world. With respect to the western hemisphere, a modern geographical and political term
is found in embryo—the "Atlantic Community." The French and Indian
War was an extension of the European conflict in North America, and in the
West Indies the war expressed itself in the attempted conquest of islands.
The sugar islands were considered a great source of wealth, proof of which
is the fact that it took the English Parliament three weeks to debate whether
England should take Guadeloupe or Canada from France in 1763.*

*The author of the following selection has succeeded in showing, with
clarity and perception, the politics of empire-building over the generations,
leading up to the forces and events of the eighteenth century which gave
shape to the struggle for empire in the New World. The thirteen colonies
and, more particularly, the revolt of the colonies, ultimately served as a cat-
alysis for the events to follow. As Samuel Eliot Morison remarks in his fore-
word, the conquest of Guadeloupe "was one of the gayest and most gallant
operations of the war which brought England glory, territory—and a colonial revolution."*

Before the founding of the United States, the five westernmost kingdoms
of Europe were drawn irresistibly to the new world of the Americas. From
the late Middle Ages they had been in a state of almost chronic contention

From *The Campaign for the Sugar Islands.* University of North Carolina Press, 1955.

over religion and over the merits and territorial claims of their several royal families. The revelations of Columbus and his immediate successors made America's affairs immediately the business of European governments and, in time, complicated the existing struggles by adding a new imperialism as an ingredient of the quarrels.

Although the British people came late in the new field, by the seventeenth century they too were deeply involved in the race for dominion and profit in the New World. As decades passed, a sort of elimination tournament brought two nations ever closer to a final contest: Great Britain and France. At the beginning of the eighteenth century it was clear that Spain, Portugal, and the Netherlands had failed to continue their imperial growth and were hardly able to defend what they had, because of a lack of industrial and naval strength. Thus the rivalry of Great Britain and France became the most conspicuous fact of international relations in the first half of the eighteenth century.[1] The empires of the rivals were alike only in external appearance. Actually they were much different. The British empire had been built piecemeal by the expansion of a relatively free society and became a collection of thirty once relatively well-to-do free provinces, while the French empire was unskillfully but minutely regulated from France.[2]

Because religion was no longer the moving force of politics, and liberalism had not yet become its dynamo, the age of Anglo-French imperial rivalry was an age of power politics, pure and simple. The coexistence of national states competing for territory, for power, and for treasure, brought almost continuous war between powers unable to reduce each other to permanent inferiority. In that deadlock they sought a "balance of power," which is to say they hoped to reform the anarchy of international society by balancing the competitive ambitions of the members. But the many wars brought no steady balance; after all, the notion of preserving a balance of power could easily be used as a cover for aggression.

Personally, the policy makers of Europe saw no benefit to them in permanent peace. The continental nobility provided both the diplomatic corps and the military leaders. They had an ancient tradition of personal advancement and fame achieved in warfare. Their monarchs also found victory in battle useful to add luster to crowns. As Walter L. Dorn well said, the recent tendency of historians to minimize war leads them to forget that "war itself became a basic ingredient of European civilization."

Unlike the continental nobility, the British aristocracy was not a self-conscious military aristocracy separate from the other social elements of national leadership. On the contrary, the landed lords and the merchant princes were closely allied by marriage, by social imitation, and by investment. This was an alliance of agriculture and commerce, with commerce being the dynamic partner. Commerce generally favors peace, but Britain was at once commercial and warlike, for commercial men were willing to accept war as part of policy if they were excluded from a field of great promise by some unfriendly foreign government.

In the British Parliament the businessmen, unlike their French commercial rivals, could force the direction of national policy, and they did so in the eighteenth century. French and British imperial competition was therefore a struggle of the French aristocratic and dynastic ambitions, centered on the goals of glory, splendor, and dynastic security, against the British desire to expand the sources of supply, and to find markets to which their productive and growing factories could send their products.

The policy of the British leaders was strengthened by the theory that a nation could only increase its commerce at the expense of the commerce of another nation. If the idea is correct, a nation's prosperity is best measured by the poverty of its rivals. Jean Colbert, the seventeenth-century French statesman, thought the same, but the belief did not appear to govern French policy in the following century. Nevertheless, to some observers, even in France, every nation seemed to get rich by war (except the losers).[3]

Britain and France, poised in precarious balance in the eighteenth century, found themselves pursuing very similar policies for different reasons; the British seeking commercial gain for its own sake, the French hunting profits as a means to strengthen France for reasons of dynastic grandeur, and to fulfill the ambitions of an aristocracy—in short, to get power for power's sake. In both states politics and economic policy were fused and directed toward empire.

The French and British colonies were closely woven into the fabric of their national economies. Much of the prosperity of both nations was derived from their colonies, and their merchants and politicians knew it. The French had a real fear that British competition would be made worse at any time by military action, while the British colonists and traders were persuaded to tolerate some degree of governmental control by fear that otherwise France would win out. They saw the French as the prime miliary power of the world, with a population thrice as great as their own, and a dangerous business competitor in many places because of subsidies, fine workmanship, and low labor costs. If the day should ever come when [the French] could weave wool as well as they raised sugar cane, cured codfish, and made hats, England's basic industry would collapse. The interests of France and Britain collided in four remote quarters of the world, North America, the West Indies, Africa, and India. They were militant rivals in several essential commodities, among them Negroes, sugar, and furs. When "special interests" asked the help of their governments, war could easily follow.

A competition most provocative of complaints occurred in the West Indies where the provision and lumber trade of North America and the slave trade of West Africa converged to support rival sugar plantations. The French sugar islands showed greater profits than did the British, largely, it was thought, because of a lively illegal traffic between British North America and the French West Indies, a trade which seemed a very natural arrangement to those concerned in it. The French West Indies were the richest colonies in the world. Their golden age began at the end of the seventeenth century when French planters switched to sugar cane and began to undersell the British West Indies, just as the British had previously undersold the original sugar planters of the New World, in Brazil. The British West Indian nabobs would have foundered except for the steady expansion of the English domestic market which they monopolized by act of Parliament.

There was no question whether the British would let their Caribbean colonies fail. They must survive. Jamaica alone bought almost as much of English manufactures as Virginia and Maryland combined, and more than any two other colonies of the empire. It was thought that the illegal trade with North America which was carried on by the French islands was a positive danger to a great asset, and complaints were numerous that Americans refused to buy British molasses while consuming a large quantity of French molasses. If the French continued to produce a greater quantity of sugar and to corner the continental European market, as they had done by the aid of their government and the help of Yankee smugglers, the British West Indies might be ruined. It was alleged that the close connection of New England skippers and French planters was deliberately fostered by the French government, in order to hurt the British sugar industry. Plainly the economic interests of British colonists in North America and in the Caribbean were not the same. The French sugar growers had a cheaper supply of labor, greater resources of soil, and a large annual supply of molasses which was barred from France in order to protect the brandy makers but which found a ready market in British North America. From the buyers they received food for their slaves, lumber, and other necessaries. This trade could hardly be broken up by the British government except by severe restrictive action. Such severity seemed, in the 1750s, politically unfeasible.

French competition also brought the slave trade to a crisis. By the 1750s the British slavers seemed to face bankruptcy. If they abandoned their West African stations, the West Indies would have a desperate labor shortage since the life expectancy of a West Indian slave was but seven years [after start of bondage]. From the British point of view the trouble with the West Indian slave traffic was that the French government subsidized their slave traders, and by various aids and credits made it easier for planters to buy land and slaves. Because of government help and a greater volume of sales the French were able to outbid the British on keenly competitive sections of the African coast and, conversely, by unified policy were able to drive purchase prices down wherever the British did not appear. A reorganization of the British trade, by parliamentary action in 1750, staved off ruin but did not give superiority over the French.

Another grievance of British subjects was French supremacy in the European hat trade. During the War of the Spanish Succession the French controlled the beaver catch of Hudson Bay, and their hat makers were never outdone after that. Because of better workmanship French makers sold hats of beaver felt to all of Europe and British hatters were idle. The Hudson's Bay Company, which exploited northern Canada, did not suffer since it reexported its bales of pelts to France at a higher price than British buyers could pay. Only the hatters suffered. The British fur traders generally did better than their French competitors in America because they could offer higher prices and more of the goods the Indian trappers wanted—particularly rum, like as not made in Rhode Island from French West Indian molasses.

Fish dealers were also pained by French competition. By the Treaty of Utrecht the French could use the northern shores of Newfoundland to cure their cod by drying. This was an advantage because that coast is less humid than the southern side where the British fishers dried their catch. British cod, poorly cured, lost ground in the world market.

In another area Anglo-French feelings were heated. The British East India Company had factories from St. Helena to Borneo, from which its officials uneasily watched the rising power and prosperity of French far eastern trade. The officers of the East India Company do not seem to have intended to found an empire, but in the end they and their rivals came to strife in efforts to eliminate each other as dangerous competitors.

The idea that the French were trying to encircle Britain's American colonies was strongly believed by the middle of the eighteenth century. "Encirclement" was not an official policy of the French government but was made in America where local administrators, in an astonishingly swift advance, had linked the St. Lawrence, the Great Lakes, and the Mississippi River system within 110 years of the founding of Jamestown. This linkage was practically complete at a time when Georgia had not yet been founded. While responsible Englishmen were worried about encirclement by their rivals, the French feared that the British would divide Canada and Louisiana and conquer each separately. Knowing that Canada was a drain and not a fountain of wealth, the French motive for defending Canada and underwriting its continuous deficits was political. They hoped the maintenance of Canada as an outpost of France would distract Britain from affairs on the continent of Europe, and when they found it difficult to feed their Canadian garrison, they went so far as to encourage a trade in provisions from New England to Cape Breton Island.[4]

The precise boundaries of French and British America had been long disputed. Each side made demands impossible for the other to accept and during forty years of assertion the disagreement had hardened beyond the possibility of reasonable compromise. While the French were setting up their western chain of posts some English officials thought of doing the same. Said Governor Alexander Spotswood of Virginia, in 1716, "We should attempt to make some settlements on the lakes, and at the same time possess ourselves of those passes of the great mountains, which are necessary to preserve a communication with such settlements." This would have divided Canada and Louisiana, but, lacking such posts (except for Oswego) the British leaned heavily on an alliance with the Iroquois to shield them from French forays.[5]

By midcentury that alliance had weakened. The Iroquois were beginning to compare the disunity of the British colonies with the unity of French policy and were uneasy. In 1754 an attempt at an Albany congress of representatives of the northern colonies to repair this Anglo-Iroquois bond by founding a colonial union failed, although the Iroquois were somewhat mollified by attention to certain of their specific grievances.

This New World maneuvering reflected a feeling in Europe that the balance of power depended for stability upon a balance of colonial power. To the French it seemed that Britain was determined to upset the balance. The upper valley of the Ohio River was a point of collision and British interest in that region seemed indicative of "vast designs on the whole of America."[6]

France and Britain were at war in over fifty of 126 years after 1689, a period sometimes called "The Second Hundred Years' War." Of course, not all of these wars had identical causes, but their results, before 1815, may be stated generally as the temporary reestablishment of a delicate and easily disturbed balance of power. In this violent relationship the British seem generally to have been guided in their diplomacy by two principles: first, opposition to French domination of the continent of Europe as a danger to the security of the British Isles, and, second, opposition to the consolidation of the French and Spanish empires, which would put in hazard Britain's overseas possessions.[7]

The indecisive War of the League of Augsburg (1689-99)—known in America as King William's War—was shortly followed by the War of the Spanish Succession (1701-14)—Queen Anne's War. These wars were fought to prevent the expansion of continental France, and to prevent the union of the French and Spanish crowns on one head. The problems were temporarily solved by the Treaty of Utrecht which established a threefold balance, separating the crowns of France and Spain, guaranteeing the unhappily vague American territorial boundaries as of the reign of the English King Charles II, and establishing a legal but very limited British trade with Spanish America. The balance soon began to teeter dangerously as the legal trade was used as a curtain for illegal trade. For the next thirty-five years European foreign offices concentrated on attempts to frustrate real or fancied disturbances of the balance by colonial expansion, an expansion of Europe which could hardly be prevented under the circumstances. Great Britain was seen to be the most dynamic and the most dangerous to the balance, and in time British leaders deliberately upset the balance, bringing on the war with Spain called the War of Jenkins' Ear (1739) which was soon merged with the War of the Austrian Succession (1744–48)–King George's War. The economic clashes of the rival empires, and the parallel dynastic rivalries which are usefully revealed by the "double names" of this series of wars, effectively make clear the way in which dynastic and economic ambitions were intertwined in the making of policy. When the War of the Austrian Succession came to an end, its Treaty of Aix-la-Chapelle marked only the peace of exhaustion.

Vital issues were left still unsettled. None of the economic pressures of the bitter rivalry had been relaxed; few of the essential political difficulties had been resolved so far as overseas affairs were concerned. After 1748 a common French simile was "bête comme la paix." It is only fair to say that each side wished for peace, but they wished for more than peace with honor; they wanted peace with prestige and profits. When prestige seemed necessaril to require domination of North America there was no restraining the warriors. The best that can be said of the situation after 1748 was that war was not quite inevitable. Commissioners met at Paris to negotiate but, again, impossible proposals were made and peace was not made.[8]

The tensions mounted. Jamaica merchants had profited sixty thousand pounds per annum from legal trade with Spanish America, plus an untold amount from illegal trade with Spaniards anxious to escape the excessive mark-ups of Spanish legal monopolists. After 1748 all of that business was lost except the slave trade, and its troubles have already been described. When the Jamaicans complained, their government took them seriously. War almost started on the west coast of Africa in 1752 when a British naval officer ordered a French squadron away from Anamaboe on the Gold Coast, but the war was postponed when the French chose to obey. In the West Indies the question of the so-called "neutral islands" caused dissatisfactions. St. Lucia, St. Vincent, Dominica, and Tobago had been declared "neutral," although the commissions of the governors of the British colony of Barbados traditionally included jurisdiction over all of them but Tobago. The actual settlers, although few, were mostly French. British officials found the status of the "neutral" islands intolerable because they were dens of smugglers and, in war, could be privateer bases. In North America both powers were closing in on the headwaters of the Ohio. The governor of Canada formally claimed the area in 1749, and, at the same time, the British crown chartered a land company with a tentative grant there. In 1752 the Canadians began to fortify the region and Virginia sent a promising young militia officer, George Washington, to protest. In 1754 Washington was sent back with an armed force. There was a border skirmish, a wilderness siege, a French victory, and another world war had started. That it had started in North America is an accident. It might just as easily have started at, say, Anamaboe or St. Lucia.

NOTES

1. See Walter L. Dorn, *Competition for Empire, 1740–1763* (New York, 1940). Also Charles M. Andrews, "Anglo-French Commercial Rivalry, 1700-1750," *American Historical Review,* XX (1914–15), pp. 539–56, 761–80.
2. Lawrence H. Gipson, *The British Empire before the American Revolution,* I (Caldwell, Idaho, 1936–56), pp. 3–4, 8, 8n, 9 volumes. *Editor's note:* Revised edition published by Alfred Knopf in 15 volumes (New York, 1958-70). Of the British colonies, twenty-one had representative governments.
3. Arthur J. Grant, "The Government of Louis XIV," in *Cambridge Modern History* (London, 1902–29), V.
4. Lawrence H. Gipson, "The American Revolution as an Aftermath of the Great War for Empire, 1754–1763," *Political Science Quarterly,* LXV (1950) pp. 86–104.
5. *Editor's note:* see George M. Wrong, *The Conquest of New France* (New Haven, 1921). See also Albert P. Brigham, *Geographic Influences in American History* (Boston, 1904).
6. Max Savelle, "The American Balance of Power and European Diplomacy, 1713–1778," in Richard B. Morris, ed., *The Era of the American Revolution* (New York, 1939), pp. 157–62.
7. Lawrence H. Gipson, "The Art of Preserving an Empire," *William and Mary Quarterly,* 3rd Series, II (1945), p. 407.
8. Lawrence H. Gipson, "A French Project of Victory Short of a Declaration of War, 1755," *Canadian Historical Review,* XXV (1945), pp. 361–71.

FRANK WESLEY PITMAN

THE PEACE OF PARIS
AND THE POLITICS OF SUGAR

In his speech delivered at the fiftieth anniversary of the American Histor-
ical Association, J. Lowell Ragatz warned historians that, when studying
the American Revolution, they should not overlook the fact that there were
more than thirteen colonies in British America. Most certainly the colonists
themselves were quite conscious of their close interrelationship.

The emphasis in the following selection is upon the fact that the Seven
Years' War showed an increasing incompatibility between American mer-
chants and the West Indian planters just at a time when the West Indies, in-
cluding the non-British, were swiftly becoming a great permanent market
for colonial staples. Therefore, the restrictions on commerce, together with
the decision not to enlarge the West Indian Empire after the Seven Years'
War, led ultimately to the Revolution. As Piers Mackesy wrote in The War
for America, *the Peace of Paris in 1763 "had left England alone in splendid*
but perilous eminence. She had crushed her enemies, but lost her friends."

For the author of the following selection the Seven Years' War marked a
momentous crisis in the history of the empire in that the planter interest
provided the foundation for the great discontent, riding the rails of sugar
and molasses, which culminated in the American Revolution.

On the 9th of December, 1762, when that memorable debate took place
in Parliament on the peace which Bute and Bedford concluded with the
crafty Choiseul, it is recorded that, outside, a turbulent crowd roared in

From *The Development of the British West Indies, 1700–1763.* Yale University
Press, 1917.

concert its disapproval of the treaty. Inside the House of Commons, however, where the treaty was carried by an overwhelming majority, we are told that many gentlemen from the West Indies had seats and that the number of their votes was "very formidable."

The contrast between the popular discontent over the Peace of Paris and the opposition of the powerful West India interest to British expansion deserves some explanation. The English public was keenly disappointed at the almost insignificant additions of territory acquired in the West Indies, in view of the sacrifices borne and the conquests made, which included all the French sugar colonies except Santo Domingo, and Cuba and Manila. Manila, however, had been captured too late (October 6, 1762) to enable the British ministers, even had they been so disposed, to exchange it for Puerto Rico. But there was some talk of exchanging Cuba for Puerto Rico.[1] Nor did the imposing gains in Canada and India compensate for the failure to secure for the British Empire an area adequate to supply its demand for sugar. The failure of the peace in this respect is the more to be regretted, for it is conceivable that a great addition to the empire in the West Indies, say of Guadeloupe and Martinique, would have legalized much of the illicit commerce from North America, the control of which was a contributing cause of the American Revolution.

In the clauses of the treaty relating to the West Indies, Bute and his colleagues let slip the opportunity of relieving England of one of its heaviest economic burdens, the exorbitant cost of sugar, and lost the possible chance of preserving an empire. Cuba was exchanged for Florida, Martinique and Guadeloupe were returned to France, and England renounced all claim to the strategically important island of St. Lucia, receiving instead the little islands of Dominica, St. Vincent, Grenada, the Grenadines, and Tobago. The total area acquired was about 700 square miles, or about 448,000 acres, the majority of which land was too mountainous for sugar culture.

The planting interest opposed the acquisition of Guadeloupe, unless sugar from the old British islands was given a preference in British markets. Such an extension of power in the West Indies as the public of England needed and expected could not have been made without the support of British sugar planters. There was, on the other hand, an increasing number of Englishmen with some capital who were desirous of establishing new sugar plantations. The inordinate prices of 1750 could hardly have acted otherwise than to invite new capital and labor into the sugar industry. But either the British sugar islands were completely cultivated, or, as in the case of Jamaica, the arable land was nearly all monopolized. Aspiring planters were tempted, therefore, to acquire plantations in foreign islands in the expectation, probably, that they might smuggle their sugar, as so many were doing, into the British market. Thereupon, the old planters were aroused to destroy this menace to their monopoly.

The popular impression, however, that Great Britain was supporting the burden of a sugar monopoly was not to be overcome. In 1754 there appeared in London a very able pamphlet entitled *A Short Account of the Interest and Conduct of the Jamaica Planters.* The author asserted that the interests of the planters were opposed to the interests of Great Britain. The planters really objected to the development of Jamaica, whereby the price of sugar would be lowered, and their power in Parliament blocked any attempt to relieve England of the burden of monopoly. He then described in detail the futile efforts to settle Jamaica and the existence there of one million acres of arable land, all patented but neither occupied nor cultivated. The data on this situation had been made public by the parliamentary investigation of the preceding year. The writer's conclusion, in spite of his exaggeration of certain charges, appears to have been well founded. "The personal interest of a rich planter at Jamaica," he said, "is contrary to the interest of every true Briton, whether in a national or personal light."[2]

With the opening of the French War in 1756 [Seven Years' War], the agitation temporarily subsided. It was naturally expected that the results of the war might bring relief from the sugar monopoly by the acquisition of one or more of the larger French islands. In his *Scheme for the Taking of Santo Domingo,* Thomas Cole stated that that island produced nearly as much sugar as all the English islands put together. Besides, there was an enormous commerce between Santo Domingo and British North America, which the conquest of that island would legalize. When, in 1759 and 1760, the success of the British seemed assured, public feeling toward the planters again found expression through several pamphlets by the economist Joseph Massie. In one of these he maintained that the profits of the sugar planters were twice as much per acre as landholders in England received, and that during the preceding thirty years the kingdom had suffered vast losses through the sugar colony trade. The loss to Great Britain, in the year 1759, through such excessive profits, Massie put at £840,000, which would more than pay and clothe for one year an army of 40,000 foot soldiers. Massie supported his charges with other broadsides during the following year.

Thus the conviction grew that Great Britain was suffering a great and unnecessary annual loss through the limited area of sugar culture and the conditions of monopoly surrounding the sugar trade. A most reasonable remedy, the apparently inescapable answer to public demands, lay in a substantial expansion of British dominion in the West Indies. It would seem that the arguments presented to Pitt in 1760 for the acquisition of Guadeloupe were unanswerable. From the standpoint of the British public it is difficult to understand how Canada could in any sense have been regarded as of equal value with the sugar islands. Guadeloupe, it was pointed out, could produce at least 100,000 hogsheads of sugar annually, or nearly as much as all the British islands put together. The reply that Jamaica could, if properly cultivated, afford more sugar than England wanted, was unconvincing, for England had waited thirty years in vain for the theory to be put in practice. The planters' opposition to Guadeloupe was in the interest of the British sugar monopoly.

The unwarranted assumption existed that *both* Canada and Guadeloupe could not be taken, that a *choice* between them must be made. That furs were as important as sugar could hardly be maintained; "the consumption of sugar is daily increasing both in America and Europe, and become one of the necessaries of life." Furs, moreover, would never give rise to as much shipping as sugar. The greater strategical value of Canada was, however, more difficult to disprove: "acquiring Canada, dazzles the eyes, and blinds the understandings of the giddy and unthinking . . . yet it is easy to discover that such a peace might soon ruin Britain," for the withdrawal of the French would promote the independence of America.

On the other hand, it was perceived that an increase in the number of sugar islands would solve the most vital commercial need of North America as well as of England; the northern colonies would get access to a far more adequate tropical market and England would obtain sugar enough for herself and, possibly, for export. It would give the British Empire in America a proper balance between temperate zone and tropical colonies; heretofore the empire had been overweighted on the temperate zone side. As William Pitt remarked, "It is our sugar islands that raise the value of North America, and pour in such wealth upon the *mother-country*. The more we have of those islands, America becomes from that cause the more important and valuable, and England the richer."[3]

The arguments in favor of the retention of Canada and the return to France of the sugar islands appeared in a number of pamphlets. Reasonable as many of the advocates for Canada were, they failed to recognize what must have seemed to the majority of Englishmen a very tangible need, a radical reduction of the price of sugar and the recovery for England of some share in the European sugar market. Thus a pamphlet, attributed to the Earl of Bath, urged the retention of Canada as the only basis for a durable peace, and regarded the West Indies as insignificant compared with such security as Canada would bring. In a reply, William Burke suggested that security was illusory if it facilitated, as he believed it would, the independence of America. A greater degree of security in both America and the West Indies would result from leaving to the French a Canada bounded by the St. Lawrence and the lakes, and retaining Guadeloupe. Such an arrangement would also answer infinitely better the economic wants of both England and the northern colonies.

Benjamin Franklin's answer to Burke, emphasizing America's need of

Canada in its inevitable expansion—and discounting the apprehensions of the rise of manufactures and independence—paid slight attention to the condition on which temperate zone settlement would for a long time depend, namely, access to adequate markets. In reply to Franklin, another pamphlet, attributed to William Burke, declared that the political advantages of having Canada were illusory, whereas the release of the sugar islands involved the sacrifice of a substantial trade, which the French had regarded as the most valuable branch of their commerce. While the importance of the West Indies as producers of exports to England was recognized, Burke endeavored to correct the impression that they did not create markets for manufactures, by pointing out that, as a market for slaves and for produce from the northern colonies, it was really the West Indies that enabled Africa and North America to purchase British goods. In his comparison of the colonies north of Maryland with the West Indies, he showed the former, by their tendencies to compete with Great Britain, to be of doubtful value, while he thought the latter group were ideal colonies.

These views of the superior value of sugar colonies to the empire at that time were supported also in memorials from Barbados and St. Christopher (St. Kitts). "St. Christopher is by far the best [British] Sugar Island, both for the Quality of the Sugar, and the Quantity it produces in Proportion to Extent; but it is very small indeed, and not one Inch uncultivated, and must wear out." The author also observed that the French islands produced a greater variety of products than the English islands. He advocated British expansion in the West Indies.

Another memorial urged that, although Guadeloupe should not be retained in preference to Canada, the neutral islands ought unquestionably to be retained: (1) because of the validity of England's claim; and (2) because "The English want more sugar land to plant not only to supply foreign markets, but also to encrease the quantity for home consumption, and thereby reduce the price of a commodity now become of general and necessary use."

It is clear from the foregoing evidence that there was a widespread and well-founded belief in England that the empire was in pressing need of more sugar colonies. Whatever else peace might bring, the public was justified in expecting a substantial expansion of British power in the West Indies. Had Pitt remained in control of the negotiations, it is incredible that he would have disregarded this expectation of the nation. That Bute and Bedford sacrificed one of England's most vital interests, by returning Guadeloupe, Martinique, and St. Lucia to France, seems explicable only by their subserviency to the powerful planter class of Great Britain. Consistent with their policy of the previous half century, the aim of which was to perpetuate monopoly prices for sugar in England, the British planters as a class opposed the acquisition of any considerable area of sugar land. The retention of Canada, on the other hand, offered the pleasing prospect of an enlarged colonial market for sugar.

In the debate on the treaty in Parliament, December 9, 1762, Pitt in the Commons made a scathing criticism of the Bute ministry. "They seem to have lost sight of the great fundamental principle," he said, "that France is chiefly, if not solely, to be dreaded by us in the light of a maritime and commercial power. And therefore, by restoring to her all the valuable West India islands, and by our concessions in the Newfoundland fishery, we had given her the means of recovering her prodigious losses, and becoming once more formidable to us at sea."

Since the Peace of Aix-La-Chapelle, France had gained a decided superiority over England in West India commerce. The advantages to be gained in the West Indies were not conjectural but certain and immediate. Pitt insisted, furthermore, upon the benefits that would accrue to the North American and African trades through an enlargement of the British West Indies, all of which trades would center in Great Britain. But, if the French islands were restored, he gave warning that a revival of illicit trade between America and the French islands would result, and the British would lose a great part of the benefit of their colonial commerce.

It was said in defense of the treaty [of 1763] that France would never be brought to any considerable cession of the West Indies, and that her power and increase there could never become formidable, because the existence of her settlements would depend more than ever upon trade with British North America. But the fulfillment of this ministerial hope rested upon the ability of England to restrain by the Sugar Act of 1764 America's trade with the French—a policy of coercion that led straight to revolution. In losing something of the sugar trade, it was claimed that England lost little else than a luxury. But this view was contrary, as we have seen, to the facts as stated by many contemporary writers. At last the Treaty [of Paris] was approved by the Lords and, in the Commons, by the overwhelming vote of 319 to 65.[4]

Associated with the feeling of disappointment at the insignificant area acquired was a desire to make the most of the ceded islands. But the ceded islands, in fact, offered few opportunities to newcomers or to experienced planters seeking relief from soil exhaustion and exorbitant land values in the older islands.[5] Unfortunately the sugar lands obtained by the Peace of Paris were altogether too limited to offer such planters adequate relief under the British flag. The aspirations and interests of this class had little or no weight with the rich proprietors who guided West India policies.

The Peace of Paris marked a momentous crisis in the history of the empire. Through it the planting interest came triumphant. Its position of monopoly was practically undisturbed; Great Britain and America were still exposed to exploitation by an interest whose aims were well understood.

The opportunity of adjusting a balance in the American empire had been thrown away, and the means of reducing the exorbitant cost of sugar ignored. Colden had officially declared, in 1760, that it would be difficult to confine America to the British West India markets while the people believed that "The Sugar Islands have gained a preference inconsistent with the true interest of their mother country." But his warning went unheeded. The Treaty of Paris, the Sugar Act of 1764, and the administrative reforms of Grenville revealed a firm determination to restrict America to the same old markets which time and again had been proved inadequate for either England or America. It is not surprising that murmurs about "the inconvenience of being British subjects" grew louder in the northern colonies. The West India planting interest had laid substantial foundations in the realm of economic life for that great discontent which culminated in the American Revolution.

NOTES

1. *Editor's note:* On the question of Puerto Rico in the politics of empire during the eighteenth century, see Arturo Morales-Carrion, *Puerto Rico and the Non-Hispanic Caribbean* (Rio Piedras, P.R. 1952).
2. *Editor's note:* West Indian remonstrances are excellently summarized in George L. Beer, *British Colonial Policy, 1754–1765* (New York, 1907).
3. See John Almon's *Anecdotes of Pitt*, III (London, 1792), pp. 211–12.
4. *Editor's note:* See the excellent article by William L. Grant, "Canada vs. Guadeloupe, an Episode of the Seven Years' War," *American Historical Review*, XVII (1912), pp. 735–43.
5. *Editor's note:* The ceded islands were Grenada, the Grenadines, Dominica, St. Vincent. Collectively they were referred to as the Windward Islands.

CHARLES M. ANDREWS

CREOLE vs. YANKEE

As the islands in the Caribbean sought protection from England for their economic well-being, their support of a strong mercantilist policy produced a serious conflict of interest as the northern colonies sought a wider trade in the foreign islands of the West Indies. Yet the British islands depended not only on the mainland markets, but became increasingly dependent upon the American colonies for many of their basic staples.

Those who supported a relaxed mercantilist policy argued that strict laws in trade could only endanger the commercial life of all the colonies. But the sugar colonies accused the mainland of lacking the vision to see that the West Indian view was far from selfish. As the respected eighteenth-century historian, William Robertson, expressed it, in reality the problem was the existence of "a great contest between England and France over who should be mistress of the foreign sugar trade."

Intensity of feeling continued through the 1760s with both the northern colonies and West Indian islands representing their own economies as languishing as a result of the prosperity of the other. In 1762 Jamaica took unilateral action in declaring the importation of all foreign rum, sugar, and molasses as a felony punishable by death (which was fortunately disallowed by the Privy Council).

As the eve of revolution arrived, colonial merchants in America continued to challenge mercantilist laws with a growing "unlawful" trade demanded by its dynamic growth. During the Seven Years' War this "unlawful" trade had produced the famous writs of assistance, *justified perhaps in at-*

From "Anglo–French Commercial Rivalry, 1700-1750." *American Historical Review,* XX, 1915.

tempting to halt American trade with the enemy, yet pregnant with a signif-
icance that led John Adams years later to remark that "there and then the
child of independence was born." Edmund Burke expressed it differently.
"America," he said, "is singular; it is grown up to a magnitude and impor-
tance within the memory of man; nothing in history is parallel to it. The
question is, not whether their spirit deserves praise or blame, but—what in
the name of God, shall we do with it?"

Before 1700 the problem of French competition with England in the commercial world of the West had not become sufficiently prominent to demand a solution, but in the eighteenth century important changes took place which materially altered the situation. The area of the French sugar-producing colonies was enlarged by the addition of new territory, notably a considerable portion of the island of Santo Domingo or Hispaniola, where the soils were "new, vastly extended, incomparably more fertile, and easier of cultivation than any other Sugar Country in the World." The French government at home gave renewed encouragement to its sugar colonies, transported planters and aided them to subsist, paid the salaries of their governors, and took care to strengthen and secure their settlements against attack. By new edicts it permitted the colonists to carry their sugars direct-ly to Spain, thus ensuring further shipment to Italy and even to Turkey. In consequence, the French output of sugar and its by-products was doubled and trebled and the demand of the French colonies for lumber, livestock, and provisions became correspondingly great. Until this time the northern British colonies had been accustomed to send their surplus products to the southern continental colonies or to the British West Indies, thus fulfilling their mercantilist function as purveyors of supplemental staples to the Brit-ish tropical and semitropical colonies. But this carefully adjusted equilibri-um could not be maintained, as colonial conditions refused to remain sta-tionary and the northern colonies refused to confine their activities to "such Produce, Trade, and Manufactures as are most for the Benefit of Great Brit-ain" or to be diverted from raising more "of Cattle and Provisions than are needful or convenient for themselves."[1] The growth of the northern Brit-ish colonies and the increase in production of lumber, livestock, and provi-sions destroyed the balance, and the rise of new economic conditions and trade requirements rendered inevitable the overthrow of this part of the mercantilist scheme. The surplus products of New England, New York, and Pennsylvania had to find a wider market and as they were not wanted in

England, it is hardly surprising that the quick-witted traders of the North should have discovered the profitable opportunities that the needs of the French sugar colonies furnished.

According to every contemporary account all the British sugar islands, except Jamaica, were declining, and their demand, which even in times of prosperity would not have been sufficient to take off the entire output of the northern colonies, was unable to keep pace with the supply. The New Englanders could sell to the French more cheaply than could the merchants of France and had a monopoly of the trade as long as the French island market was not glutted.[2] On the other hand, they could buy more cheaply in the French and Dutch West India market, where the foreign planters, with only a one percent export duty to meet, were better off than the English with their eighteen pence per hundred plantation duty of 1672 and their four and a half percent export duty of 1663, and where French sugars were rated from twenty-five to thirty percent cheaper than were those of Barbados and the Leeward Islands. Molasses, too, they could obtain for about what they were willing to pay, as it was a commodity practically worthless to the French. The value of this trade, in which the French could undersell the British planters, was so great that the governors of the French islands were authorized to issue at their discretion permits for trade to masters of colonial and British vessels, purchasable at prices dependent on the value of the cargo.

Despite the agreement entered into in 1686 between England and France that the subjects of the one were not to frequent the ports of, or trade with, the other, or in any manner to interfere with the commerce belonging to the subjects of the other, this trade attained large proportions. We hear of "unlawful trade with the French" as early as 1700, and so zealous were certain of the island governors to observe and execute the instructions given them in this particular that they even caused British ships trading with the French islands to be seized and condemned. At the same time, whenever the French islands found themselves sufficiently stocked with staples from the north or the wheat harvest in France was sufficiently bountiful, they were wont to seize vessels from Ireland and the northern colonies in order to check what they called, when it was advantageous to do so, a contraband trade. This trade customarily took two forms. The northern colonists might sell their produce to the British West Indies for cash and passing on, purchase their return cargo from the French islands, a traffic estimated at one-third to one-half of the whole; or they might carry their horses, building materials and provisions, and other plantation necessities directly to the French or other foreign islands and there exchange them either for cash or more frequently for sugar, molasses, and rum. In either case, the loss fell on the British West Indian planters, denuding them of their coin, of which they had none too much, or cutting into their market for sugar and depriving them of their needed supply of provisions and lumber. The situation was a very undesirable one from the point of view of the British sugar planter, and equally unsatisfactory from the point of view of the British customs, for all "dead" commodities exported from the French islands to the northern British colonies meant to the British exchequer a loss by just so much of the four and a half percent and the plantation duties.[3]

The growth of this trade from 1713 to 1730 became so rapid as to alarm the British merchants and planters, particularly in Barbados, the center of resistance to the French encroachment. The attention of the home authorities was called to the calamitous condition of the planters, and in 1724 the Privy Council ordered the board of trade to prepare a full state of the sugar and tobacco trades. Four years later it instructed the same body to consider "what Laws it may be reasonable to pass in the Severall Plantations for restraining his Majesty's Subjects from Importing into the British Plantations such products of the French Plantations as may interfere with the British Trade." In the meantime the Barbadians had begun a determined campaign of their own. They formed an organization, raised funds which they transmitted to London, and despatched representatives to act there in conjunction with the agents of the colony. They invited the planters of the Leeward Islands to join in the movement, offering to meet all expenses. In 1730 and 1731 the matter was brought to the immediate attention of the Privy Council in a series of petitions from the "Planters, Traders, and other Inhabitants" of Barbados and the "several Merchant Planters and others interested in and trading to His Majesty's Sugar Colonies in America." At the same time agents and representatives of the northern British colonies appeared to defend their side of the case. The borough authorities of Liverpool upheld the cause of the sugar colonies, while the merchants of Dublin naturally took the part of the northern colonies. Exasperated by frequent postponements of the hearing before the Privy Council, and convinced that the sugar colonies were "engaged in a mortal Combat with those of Foreign Nations" and that no "quacking and palliative Medicines" would suffice, the Barbadians and their allies finally decided to seek directly the aid of the British Parliament. On March 30, 1731, they withdrew their petition to the king, announcing that they had made application to Parliament for relief "in the Matters complained of in their said Petitions." In so doing they expressed not only their discontent with the procedure of the Privy Council, but also their agreement with a rapidly growing conviction in England and the colonies that an act of Parliament was a more "certain and effectual" means of gaining relief in matters colonial and commercial than was an order in council, which could do nothing more than authorize the passing of remedial legislation by the colonies themselves.

The appeal to Parliament was at first unsuccessful. The government, with manifest reluctance and a lively realization of the issues involved, brought the matter before the House of Commons in the form of a bill for securing and encouraging the trade of the British West Indies. This bill was planned as a blow at the French sugar trade, and was designed to check and turn back if possible the French invasion of the British colonial market. . . . As a prohibitive measure, this bill was a true mercantilist device, for though the merchants and planters were ready to present a dozen minor remedies for the relief of the sugar trade, they were all agreed that complete prohibition was the only certain method of attaining the desired end. On the plea of their own necessity and the welfare of the mother-country they sought to control by means of parliamentary legislation a course of trade that was the natural and inevitable outcome of the agricultural and commercial life of the northern British colonies.

The struggle that followed was exciting. The supporters of the bill declared that the British sugar islands were in a languishing condition, their export of sugar diminished, their duties high, their plantations understocked, their planters poor, their soil worn out, and their fortifications destroyed. They acknowledged that the French islands contained fresher sugar land than the British, were more fruitful, better inhabited, paid less duties, and had greater encouragement from the home country. But, they maintained, the British islands were a source of great profit to England and must be protected, else they would steadily deteriorate and might eventually pass into the hands of the French themselves. For, as Robertson expressed it, "this Contest is not as some weak People imagine and some selfish People would have us all to think, a Contest between the British Southern and Northern Colonies, but between Great Britain and France, which of the two shall be Mistress of the Foreign Sugar Trade." "We are contending," he continued, "with the united Forces of our Nation's Rivals in the Sugar Trade and the Practices of our too selfish Sister Colonies on the Continent."

On the other hand, the opponents of the measure asserted that the passage of the bill would ruin the bread colonies by diminishing the supply and raising the price of tropical staples desired by the New Englanders, and by cutting off the market for the northern staples would glut the demand and lower the price in the West Indies. Should the bill pass, they insisted, the northern colonies would certainly suffer in their wealth and prosperity, would become the slaves and bondsmen of the sugar colonies, and be reduced to the status of purveyors without independent economic and commercial life.[4]

Turning on the supporters of the bill, they declared that the present situation was due not so much to the decline of the islands as to the sumptuous and extravagant habits of the planters, and to the fact that owners of plantations resident in England, a number far too large for the good of the colonies, wished to continue the large profits that enabled them to play the part they desired in English social and political life.[5] In other words, they said, the British West Indian sugar planters asked to be favored at the expense of the remainder of the colonial world, and if they were so favored then England would lose the bread colonies as a vent for her manufactures, because the latter would have no money wherewith to buy English goods.

To the last group of arguments the mercantilists replied with equal spirit. . . . They insisted that the northern colonies were in fact what the tropical colonies were falsely said to be, very rich, and that the conduct of the latter in "dissembling what they are has perhaps turned as much to their private advantage, as our folly in boasting of what we never were, has injured both us and our Mother Nation." . . . And as to favoring one part of the colonial world more than another, the bill was designed to benefit the commerce of Great Britain and to advance the welfare of the colonies that were of most importance to her, and no one could deny that in this respect the sugar trade and the sugar colonies were deserving of greater attention than the provision trade and the bread colonies.[6]

The literature of this discussion, both in print and in manuscript, is very extensive, but the arguments are often far from convincing. "In each case," to quote a comment made on trade quarrels in England at an earlier date, "both parties had an interest in representing their own trade as languishing through the prosperity of their opponents, while the opponents retorted that they themselves were not half so prosperous as was made out." All of these pamphlets were written to uphold or oppose the bills of 1731 and 1733, but later letters and papers, issued during the continuance of the controversy, 1733–63, repeat many of the same arguments.[7]

The bill of 1731, though passed by the House of Commons and debated in the House of Lords, was finally dropped altogether. This event is a landmark in the history of the relations not only between England and France, but also between England and her continental colonies in America. It marked the first important failure of that phase of the mercantilist policy which rated the colonies furnishing tropical products more highly than those taking off manufactured articles, and it began the tilting of the balance in favor of the bread colonies, a movement slow in its consummation and not completed till 1763 when Guadeloupe was returned to France and Canada retained. . . .

In 1733 the planters returned to the attack and this time they were successful. The new measure, endorsed by a special representation sent from the board of trade to the House of Commons, was accepted by the House of Lords, because it omitted the objectionable features of the first bill, and finally became a law. Thus, after a discussion lasting not less than ten years, the famous Molasses Act of 1733 came into existence. But it was, from the standpoint of the true mercantilist, an emasculated measure, in that it conceded the very principle which the bill of 1731 had denied, the right of traffic between the British bread colonies and the foreign sugar colonies. Sugar, rum, and molasses, under heavy duties, might be imported into the northern continental colonies, and horses and lumber might be exported without restraint into the French, Dutch, and Danish West Indies. It is true that the duties imposed were judged to be tantamount to a prohibition, so that even in its modified form the measure was a blow aimed at the commercial encroachments of the French, but the act did allow the northern colonies to export all but the enumerated commodities to the foreign West Indies, thus favoring these colonies as far as possible. At best it was but a half-way measure, unsatisfactory to the mercantilists, because it was not prohibitory, and burdensome to the northern colonies, because it restrained, or tried to restrain, their freedom of commercial intercourse. . . . It failed to answer the needs and expectations of the British West Indian planters because it did not go far enough. And, finally, it checked but slightly the export of French sugars to the northern British colonies because it was consistently evaded from the first.[8]

The sequel demonstrates the truth of these conclusions. The effects of the act were slight. Conditions after 1733 were but little changed from what they had been before. The West Indian planters were not satisfied with the terms and demanded further concessions. They sent in petitions to the board of trade, wrote pamphlets, encouraged lobbying by the colonial agents, and made the Jamaica Coffee House, Cornhill, the center of an active propaganda. . . .

The matter came up in Parliament in 1739. The West Indian planters recommended the passage of a bill allowing general and free exportation, reductions of duty and excise, remission of the four and half percent direct trade with Ireland, and further relief in the reexporting of refined sugar. But it was manifest to all that no bill could pass embodying such terms as these. . . . The bill as finally passed permitted West Indian planters to send their sugar, but sugar only, to foreign ports south of Cape Finisterre, in ships built in and sailing from Great Britain and navigated according to law. As by this bill sugar was placed in the same class with rice, we have here another instance of the gradual breaking down of the strict mercantilist policy in favor of the northern colonies. But the measure as a whole was so clogged with restrictions as to be of little benefit to the sugar planters. . . . The chief grievance, however, was the confining of the foreign market to the least desirable parts of the European world. The best sugar markets were in the north, not in the south where the French and Portuguese had control of the trade. . . . During the decade that followed but two concessions were made by the

British Parliament to the continued demands of the Sugar Islands. In 1742 colonial-built ships were admitted to the privileges of the act of 1739, and in 1748, the drawback on sugar, refined in Great Britain and exported to the Continent, was increased, a measure manifestly passed quite as much in the interest of the sugar refiners as of the sugar planters.

The situation in 1750 was to the mercantilists no better than it had been in 1731. The latter were ready to prove that the British traders in North America had for years carried on a large and extensive trade not only with the foreign colonies in America but with the French and Dutch in Europe directly; that they imported vast quantities of sugar, rum, and molasses yearly from the French and Dutch sugar colonies into the northern British colonies in direct violation of the Molasses Act, and had carried this trade to such a height as to purchase vessels destined for this trade only, of which there were three hundred employed annually, and to settle correspondents and factors in the French islands to facilitate this commerce; that they carried on this trade with and for the benefit of France, to the injury of the British sugar colonies, draining them of their money which was spent in the foreign colonies for tropical products, or for European and East Indian commodities that should have been obtained only through English ports; and lastly, that they went so far as to lend themselves to the corrupting influence of the foreign planters and to become instruments for introducing foreign sugars, under the denomination and disguise of British, into Great Britain itself. In 1750 the assembly of Jamaica sent a remonstrance to England against this trade. In February 1752, a committee of eight, representing a group of merchant planters in England, appeared before the board of trade and at the same time sent a petition to the Treasury, asserting that there was then under seizure by the custom house officers at the port of Bristol sugar entered as British from New York, that was really and bona fide from the French colonies. These men begged that a bill be presented in Parliament for the purpose of prohibiting entirely this traffic, thus reverting to the purpose of the measure defeated twenty years before. But the effort failed. The Privy Council ... contented itself with writing a circular letter to all the governors of the sugar colonies directing them "to use their best endeavours to procure the passage of [colonial laws] containing regulations for preventing this illicit and clandestine traffic." It was an innocuous and nerveless device for evading responsibility, and to the West Indian planters it must have seemed but the "palliative cure" of which they had been afraid in 1731.

* * *

The act of 1733 and the supplemental measures that followed from 1739 to 1752 were weak and impotent blows at a powerful enemy, whom all the mercantilists characterized as England's greatest rival in the commercial world. Though the pamphleteers greatly exaggerated the menace of French competition, which was actually dangerous only in the sugar trade, their writings were influential at the time and served to spread the belief that France was outfooting England in nearly all parts of the world, was in control of the best markets, and was threatening British commercial leadership in America, the West Indies, Africa, and India. To these men it seemed a crime against England that the French should be aided in their race for commercial supremacy by the northern British colonies, which continued without cessation their practice of importing sugar, rum, and molasses from the foreign colonies and of exporting these foreign staples to England as if they were British products. It was inevitable that continued advance on the part of the French, either real or apparent, should lead to arms, just as a similar advance on the part of the Dutch had ended in war a century before, and that something stronger than legislative enactments should be resorted to, in order to break the hold that France, to all appearances, was gaining on the territory and trade of the western world. The commercial conflict, which had known no truce in the years from 1700 to 1750, merged almost imperceptibly, but none the less certainly, into that great military and naval struggle known as the Seven Years' War.

NOTES

1. It is, of course, well known that the board of trade made many efforts to persuade the northern colonies to produce the staples desired by the mercantilists.
2. One of the objections raised by the northern colonies to the first Molasses Bill, that of 1731, was that if the French were prevented from trading with these colonies as the bill proposed, they would build up Canada and Cape Breton as provision and lumber supplying regions, and in so doing strengthen French control in Canada to the serious danger of the British colonies to the southward.
3. This trade in all its manifold aspects is discussed at length by the pamphleteers of the period. One of the fairest and least contentious of the writers is Robertson, a planter of Nevis.
4. Herein lay the crucial point of the dispute. The mercantilists who upheld the cause of the Sugar Islands saw in an independent economic life for the northern colonies a menace to the prosperity of the mother-country. In this particular, at least, the views of the disputants were irreconcilable. The danger to England of foreign success in the race for territory or the race for markets is a factor to be reckoned with in our colonial history.
5. More important was the question of absentee planters. This question was deemed so vital to the welfare of the colonies that from 1730 to 1764 acts were passed, notably in Jamaica, but also in Antigua and St. Christopher, imposing a double tax on absentees. The Board of Trade recommended that these acts be disallowed as unjust and improper.

6. The only British colony in the West Indies that was able to obtain a sufficient stock of good slaves was Barbados. The Leeward Islands and Jamaica were always understocked, and even in Barbados it was claimed that the best Negroes went to the French and Spanish plantations, partly because the French controlled the richest areas of supply and partly because the French and Spanish were able to offer better prices on account of the steadily increasing demand. Furthermore it was reported that the soil in Hispaniola was so rich that the planters could do more with one slave than could be done with four at Jamaica.

7. *Editor's note:* An excellent resumé of the arguments is given in Thomas Salmon, *Modern History,* III (London, 1736–38), pp. 624–32. 4 volumes. An expanded edition was published in 3 volumes (London, 1744–46).

8. *Editor's note:* For a good collection of remonstrances, see *Caribbeana,* especially volume 2 (London, 1741). 2 volumes.

PRELIMINARIES

Horace Walpole, writing in 1739, remarked that "it has always been a maxim with me to encourage the trade of the American colonies *in the utmost latitude.* Nay it has been necessary to pass over some irregularities." Walpole was not alone in recognizing that the famous Molasses Act of 1733 was a dead law, but after the Seven Years' War, with His Majesty's Exchequer growing ever hungrier, an attempt was made to revive it. In American history this new molasses act is known as the unpopular Sugar Act of 1764. This was followed by other legislation which sought not only new revenues, but also to strengthen the mercantilist system which English leadership still considered essential to the well-being of the British Empire. Yet as Claude Van Tyne emphasizes in the following selection, the growth of a clandestine trade over more than a generation was "happily enlarged," so happily that the author suggests that John Adams did not blush to confess that "molasses was an essential ingredient in American independence."

By the eve of the American Revolution the "pampered Creolians" of the West Indies and the "selfish colonists" of the mainland were drawn closer together as each saw themselves sharing the negative effects of the *new imperialism* which emerged after the middle of the eighteenth century. Reflecting the renewed struggle for supremacy, this "new" imperialism, as Charles Andrews so ably describes in this section, demanded increasing financial and military contributions from all the colonies in the New World. Although not exploiting the colonies as did some of England's contemporaries, there was a distinct departure from what is sometimes referred to as "salutary neglect." To quote Andrews: "It was inevitable that Great Britain should build up her system on the widely accepted principle that colonies were desirable only as far as they were useful to the states from which they took their origin."

The economic interdependence of the British colonies in the western hemisphere, therefore, could only assure that imperial policy as it was expressed after 1763 would make both Yankee and Creole increasingly aware of certain burdens held in common. This interdependence is brilliantly described, in all its complexity, by Richard Pares. In the process, Pares suggests that a certain imperial preference for the West Indies over North Americans may have predisposed the latter to eventually seek independence. Yet it was something more fundamental, more far-reaching, something far more pervasive than "imperial preference" or "predisposition." It was the importance of the overall trade between the mainland colonies and the West Indies. As Pares remarks: "Without it the sugar colonies could not have existed and the North American colonies could not have developed."

As for North America, this commerce facilitated the payment of debts to England "and so lubricated the trans-Atlantic trade." This resulted in the search for expanded commerce across the Caribbean and in the search for the formation of capital to further "lubricate" the lanes of trade. But such activity increasingly defied the navigation laws which sought to regulate the empire in the interest of England.

CLAUDE H. VAN TYNE

"IN RECEIPT OF HIS MAJESTY'S EXCHEQUER"

One of the most distinguished historians of colonial America, Charles M. Andrews, summarized a lifetime of study with the remark that to discover the meaning of the Revolution required not only an intimate knowledge of the colonies, but also an insight into the many and varied aspects of the relations existing between them. This would include, also, the colonies in the West Indies.

Benjamin Franklin, as colonial agent in London, largely reflected the protest of men such as the Boston merchants who, after the passage of the Sugar Act of 1764, bitterly remarked that "it was pressured by the interest of the West India planters, with no other view than to enrich themselves, by obliging the northern colonies to take their whole supply from them." Perhaps this issue of the 1760s has best been expressed by Sir Lewis Namier (England in the Age of the American Revolution) *in describing what the colonists on the mainland could not entirely comprehend at the time—that in reality the influence of some twenty West Indian votes in the House of Commons meant less than the fact that their commercial demands were in accordance with the mercantilist doctrine of trade. Thus the colonists would continue to refer to the West Indians as those "pampered Creolians."*

But as the policy of Grenville and his successors persisted, it became increasingly obvious that more was involved than West Indian influence. The point of no return finally arrived with the provision that all duties be paid into the receipt of His Majesty's Exchequer—in gold and silver. But gold and silver were largely obtained from the growing illicit trade, especially the French, "our best customers, our good friends, the enemy."

From *The Causes of the War of Independence.* Houghton, Mifflin Co., 1922.

33

*On the eve of the Revolution smuggling had become the rule rather
than the exception, and the chief issue became the manner of supporting
the entire imperial establishment. Would only that Lord Shelburne had
had the opportunity to introduce those modifications to the laws of navigation so essential by the middle of the eighteenth century. In the meantime the "pampered Creolians" were forgiven as it became obvious that
the history of the West Indies in the late eighteenth century became, in
the words of Frank Wesley Pitman, "wrapped in an atmosphere of pathos."*

In a passage of the *Confessions* of St. Augustine, that worthy post-Nic-
ene father discourses on the rashness of those who inquire what God did before He created heaven and earth. It may appear a like temerity to have
gone back to the days of Edwin Sandys, William Bradford, and John Win-
throp to seek the causes of American independence. One would not need
to be unduly disputatious to argue that all of the "fundamental causes"
might have led merely to the creation of a different variety of English-speak-
ing people than that produced by the environment and experience in Corn-
wall or Northumberland or London. One might point to Canadians, Austral-
ians, and the English colonists of Cape Town, as examples of people radical-
ly changed by a new environment into a race quite different from the English who stayed at home, but a race which, nevertheless, had retained loyalty to the British Empire. The rebuttal, however, would emphasize the fact
that before any of the other overseas colonies of England had attained the
strength that America had gained in 1775, the British government had learned not to allow its relations with them to become strained, but to yield, if
not gracefully, at least in time to keep their allegiance.

After the Treaty of Paris (1763) British imperial affairs seem, to one
looking backwards, to have been at the crossroads where one turning would
lead to the political Delectable Mountains, and the other to the Slough of
Despond. The British Ministry then met a great problem, and a new one,
because the vast domain in Canada and the Mississippi Valley had been tak-
en from France during the momentary triumph of a new theory as to the
value of colonies. William Pitt, after wondering which he should be "hanged
for not keeping," decided to keep Canada, rather than Guadeloupe, and his
judgment was accepted by the makers of the Peace of Paris. That decision
became the star which pointed out the course of British colonial policy for
a decade thereafter. It was plain that the hour had struck when the British
government must decide and apply its policy to its western dominion, or

else resign that region forever to the capricious wills of the several colonies.[1]

Both the hour and the man were at hand. When Lord Bute resigned in 1763 as the head of the ministry, and selected his own successors, Lord Shelburne was made president of the board of trade and sat in the Cabinet, where he was entitled to equal weight with the secretary in colonial matters. Indeed, he came to manage American affairs as an independent department. Though he was a believer in the free-trade ideas of his friends, Adam Smith and David Hume, yet his conception was a free trade between colony and mother country so managed as to be of value to both. Thus modified, his economic theory would not make him intolerable to George Grenville and Lord Halifax, his colleagues in the ministry, both of whom he disliked and to whose plans he was lukewarm. His catholic taste and wide intellectual interest brought him into friendly relations with the greatest minds of his time, Dr. Johnson, Oliver Goldsmith, Price, and Priestley, and from all he took his toll of ideas. William Pitt was his idol, and he often consulted with Benjamin Franklin. This man in his strength and his weakness was destined to affect deeply the fate of America.[2]

On taking office, Shelburne began with characteristic thoroughness to make a complete study of the whole matter of the western policy. He sought advice from every source whether there should be a contribution by the colonies for the support of the imperial establishment. Such a contribution by the colonies was to be as little "burthensome and as palatable to the colonies" as possible. Of this plan even Edmund Burke, "friend of the colonies," and later repealer of the Stamp Act, approved "when a more calm and settled season comes." William Pitt, too, seems to have approved. This carefully conceived plan of Shelburne's was prevented by factional politics from ever coming to full fruition, but it had great influence upon all later actions of the government.

It seems a pity that Pitt's genius could not have been summoned to his country's service at that critical moment. That spirit, supported by fleets and armies, which in Barré's phrase, had "set Great Britain at the head of the world," might have knit its scattered provinces together. All efforts to surround Pitt with obedient colleagues failed, [and] the king in desperation was finally obliged to dismiss Lord Bute in order to gain the Duke of Bedford's aid in forming a new ministry. Thereupon George Grenville was enlisted, and the Grenville-Bedford régime, with its fatal consequences for the British Empire, began its course, vain of its power, but soon distrusted by the king—and that at a time when England was laboring under a war debt of nearly £130,000,000. Having taken one step [to support the military establishment proposed for the western posts], the Grenville Ministry was pledged to the next, and that implied the acceptance of Shelburne's plan to raise the money needed for imperial expenses in America from the American colonies themselves. Unfortunately this plan was not to be carried out by Lord Shelburne, whose liberal mind conceived of a system which would give all of the colonies as much self-rule as was enjoyed by Connecticut, but was to be jammed through by the Bedford faction, which believed in the complete subordination of the colonies.

The Molasses Act of 1733, which was about to expire, had been devised to force New England distillers and sellers of rum to buy their molasses and sugar from British sugar planters, and to keep colonial traders out of the French and Spanish West Indies. It seemed to the colonists a bad piece of class legislation, seeking to enable "a few pamper'd Creolians" to "roll in their gilded equipages thro' the streets" of London, at the expense of two million American subjects. Smuggling, on such a scale that it was the rule rather than the exception in colonial trade, had made the statute a dead-letter.[3]

Urged on by the sugar planters of the British West Indies, whose political influence was fairly proportioned to their wealth, an act was passed which aimed to make perpetual "the old Molasses Act" (1733) and to prevent "the clandestine conveyance of goods to and from the said colonies," so "happily enlarged by the recent peace." The duty on French and Spanish molasses was reduced from six pence to three pence that the profits of evasion might not offer so great a temptation to the smuggler. New duties, also, to be collected with the utmost rigor, were imposed upon wine from the Azores and Madeiras, and upon white sugar, coffee, pimento, and indigo from the foreign islands of the West Indies.[4]

The greatest burden of all, as colonial agitators interpreted it, was a provision that all duties and forfeitures were to be paid into the "Receipt of His Majesty's Exchequer." This was asserted to mean silver and gold, which would thus be drained from the colonies. To pay for all the manufactures of Great Britain, the New England provinces had long depended in part for the requisite gold and silver upon an illicit trade with the French and Spanish islands. The Puritan provinces had no staple like tobacco or rice or indigo with which to pay for their English-made glass and locks and hinges, or the manufactured finery with which they were clothed. To take away their molasses trade or to burden their slave trade, in which rum was an essential item, was to take away the balance in gold and silver or bank exchange, with which they gave satisfaction to their English creditors. John Adams, years after, did not blush to confess that molasses was an essential ingredient in American independence.[5]

Although the southern colonies, with bountiful staple products to exchange for British goods, were little injured by the Sugar Act, the middle colonies felt its effect only less than those of New England. They had enjoyed devious ways of getting hard money with which to pay for English manufactures. Their merchants carried their lumber, wheat, and meat to the West Indies, and exchanged them there for cotton, indigo, and sugar, which were good as gold for remittance to their English creditors.[6] Rum and molasses got in the Indies were by the alchemy of trade turned into gold and silver to the same end. The fur trade, too, furnished exchange welcome to the English merchant. To limit their trade, as the Sugar Act intended, to the British sugar islands, would woefully cut down their market for lumber and foodstuffs. This would reduce greatly the supply of silver needed to square accounts in London. Finally, it was maddening to colonial vanity to have the interests of a small coterie of West Indian sugar planters made an object of greater concern to Parliament than the interests of the thirteen colonies of the Atlantic seaboard.

All the colonies north of Virginia were suffering a real blow to their economic well-being. Though many laws in earlier days might have been burdensome if enforced, their ill-effects had been nullified by individual enterprise joined with a moral obtuseness to the crime of smuggling. Though illicit trade had always been common, and though it was smuggling that lost Massachusetts her charter as early as 1684, yet in the general colonial import trade there had not been a serious amount of contraband trade, [and] that in colonial exports was very small also.

It was the Molasses Act which had created the greatest incentive to illicit trade. The great mass of contraband trade was in molasses, rum, and sugar. From the French and Spanish West Indies, and therefore paying no duty, came 11,500 hogsheads of molasses out of the 14,000 imported into Rhode Island every year. Indeed, the entire output of the British islands would not furnish two-thirds of the quantity imported into Rhode Island, and, moreover, the British planters asked a price more than twenty-five percent higher than the foreign islands. It was estimated that the loss each year to the English treasury, due to the success of the New England smugglers, was not less than £100,000.[7]

There is no doubt that this illicit trade maintained the prosperity of the individual colonies, but its effect on British national welfare was demoralizing. This evil was at its worst during the Seven Years' War, when the colonial smugglers, especially those of Pennsylvania and New York, neutralized the advantage of British naval supremacy by supplying the French colonies with flour, beef, and pork, the very articles of trade which the navy's activity aimed to cut off. Flour concealed in claret kegs, or carried under flags of truce—flags sold even by colonial governors for twenty pounds sterling—"nourished and supported" the French enemies.[8] Yet when the colonists were reproached for this treasonable trade, they asked how they were to pay their share toward the support of the war without money gained from commercial dealings with their best customers, their good friends, the enemy.[9]

The Livingston family of New York were said to have made a fortune out of this trade, and many fortunes in New England and New York and Pennsylvania were reputed greatly swollen by this illicit trade. The colonial conscience omitted smuggling from the catalogue of crimes. John Hancock was no less respectable because he was suspected of smuggling. Indeed, this suspicion was only an ornament of his respectability. So common was the crime that all distinction between a merchant and a smuggler was lost. Smuggling and respectability went hand in hand in the market-place. In the colonial mind, in fact, "smuggling" was not a well-chosen word to describe evasion of the trade laws, which was, after all, only a defiance of the British sovereignty by the individualist colonist. The acts of smugglers refusing obedience to the trade and navigation laws, and rhetorical defiance by Patrick Henry and James Otis, were only preludes to ultimate defiance by all the American colonists. Like any laws which do not appeal to the understanding and sympathy of the honest citizens of a state, the trade laws which ran counter to the interests of the colonial merchants were not enforceable.[10] Burke could have had little understanding of these conditions when he declared that "the Acts of Navigation attended the colonies from their infancy, grew with their growth, and strengthened with their strength. They were confirmed in obedience to it, even more by usage than by law." The only element of truth in his assertion was that the colonists did not object to them, if they were not enforced in such parts as opposed colonial interests.

NOTES

1. *Editor's note:* The excellent and exhaustive study of this whole subject is Clarence W. Alvord, *The Mississippi Valley in British Politics* (Cleveland, 1917). 2 volumes.
2. This attempt to portray the character and personality of Shelburne is based upon Lord Edmund Fitzmaurice, *Life of Shelburne* (London, 1875–76). 3 volumes. Second revised edition (London, Macmillan & Co., 1912). 2 volumes.
3. Arthur M. Schlesinger, *The Colonial Merchants and the American Revolution, 1763–1776* (New York, 1917), pp. 42–43.
4. There were certain provisions meant to help the colonial trade. Some duties were repealed and bounties granted to that end.
5. See Herbert C. Bell, "West Indian Trade Before the Revolution," *American Historical Review*, XXII (1917), for an excellent detailed description of trade with the West Indies.
6. This was their chief market, for the importation of grain and meat into England had been prohibited during the reign of Charles II (1660–85).

7. George L. Beer, *The Old Colonial System, 1660–1754.* 2 volumes. (New York, 1912) II, p. 269.
8. George L. Beer, *British Colonial Policy, 1754–1765* (New York, 1907).
9. See Hubert Hall, "Chatham's Colonial Policy," *American Historical Review,* V (1900), pp. 659–75.
10. William S. McClellan, *Smuggling in American Colonies at the Outbreak of the American Revolution* (New York, 1912). *Editor's note:* This volume was printed by Moffat, Yard & Co., for the Department of Political Science at Williams College. The study was written with special emphasis on the West Indies trade.

CHARLES M. ANDREWS

YANKEES AND CREOLES
vs. ENGLAND

As the competition for empire reached a climax in the middle of the eighteenth century, the cross-currents made for an erratic relationship between England's colonies in the western hemisphere. The West Indies, on the one hand, sought protection from England for their economic well-being as expressed in the most advantageous aspects of mercantilist policy. On the other hand, the West Indies depended not only upon the mainland markets, but also upon basic imports from the northern colonies which proximity made more accessible and often less costly. Thus, as the continental colonies sought wider markets across the Caribbean, the West Indians could remark that "we are contending with . . . the practices of our too-selfish sister colonies on the continent"; yet there was less hostility than concern involved since they also believed strongly that "this contest is not a conflict between southern and northern colonies, but between Great Britain and France."

In spite of a growing anxiety as American vessels increasingly sought out non-British ports in an ever-expanding trade, by the eve of the Revolution the West Indians already shared one thing in common with the colonies to the north—the ever growing reality that the mercantilist system increasingly sacrificed the welfare of the outlying parts in the interest of the mother country. As the author concludes, it was inevitable that merchants and planters, West Indian as well as continental, should have taken the measure of British regulations and have determined in a critical spirit the disadvantages imposed. Some colonies took the measure more rapidly and England

From *The Colonial Background of the American Revolution.* Yale University Press, 1931.

swiftly lost thirteen of its thirty-three colonies, thus bringing the so-called First Empire *to a close.*

In tracing the course of British colonial policy from 1713 to 1763, we are obliged to consider special features of the history of Great Britain and her colonies during this period of half a century. In the first place, the British colonial world was steadily growing larger and more complex. From one colony in 1607 it rose to twenty-five after 1713, and thirty-three after 1763; and as these colonies advanced rapidly in wealth and prosperity, they formed habits of self-reliance and developed methods of government that were in many ways more free, more individual, and less stereotyped than were those prevailing in the mother country at the same time. Secondly, in her foreign relations Great Britain was confronted with a constantly shifting international situation that presented new obligations and new perplexities, and demanded frequent enlargements and alterations of policy to enable her to meet, with efficiency and despatch, the various emergencies that arose. And, thirdly, the British constitution itself was undergoing far-reaching changes in form and spirit: much that was old was giving way to much that was new, old powers became vested in new hands, and authority in matters that concerned administration and control was often transient and uncertain. It is not sufficiently recognized by writers on our colonial history that during our colonial period the foreign and colonial policies of Great Britain passed through several clearly defined stages, and that her political and social order underwent a noteworthy and remarkable transformation.

The history of Europe from the sixteenth to the eighteenth centuries was strongly monarchical and national, in contrast to its imperial and unified status during the Middle Ages. The centralization prevailing under pope and emperor, never complete and rarely effective, met its doom in the rise of the maritime states of the West, among which territorial and commercial rivalry was a conspicuous factor. England's maritime rivals were first Portugal and then Spain, the former a negligible competitor, the latter the great colossus of the western world. Hostility for Spain, arising in the religious conflict of the Elizabethan era, continued down to the very eve of the Restoration, a century later. In order to loosen the hold that Spain had acquired on the West, English seamen sailed boldly into Spanish waters, capturing towns and galleons, planting settlements upon islands in the very heart of the Caribbean, and endeavoring to promote commerce in a region which Spain had claimed as peculiarly her own. Trading companies sent out ships laden with colonists and supplies, hoping thereby to obtain those tropical commodities—drugs, dyes, spices, cloths, and fruits—that the Englishmen of the day valued as scarcely inferior to gold, silver, and precious stones. In this period of western enterprise, England was not seeking empire or promoting colonies for the purpose of territorial increase. She was giving vent to the bitterness of her hatred against Spain, and at the same time was pressing for a share of those raw materials which only the warm countries of the earth could furnish abundantly, or which the cold countries could supply, but only at the cost of an unfavorable exchange either in goods or money.

Portugal as a competing rival was eliminated by means of a series of treaties with England and by the terms of the marriage settlement between Charles II and Catharine of Braganza, which reduced that country to a position of commercial vassalage. Spain finally was rendered harmless by her own administrative inefficiency, bankruptcy, and naval deterioration. But Holland, who had already crowded out Portugal from many of her points of vantage in the East and in Brazil, now entered the field, and for three-quarters of a century remained the mistress of the carrying trade in the eastern and western seas. Outmatched by the superior naval and mercantile skill of the Dutch people, England was compelled to adopt new strategy and to widen the scope of her naval and commercial policy. Where the Tudors, in order to avoid the decay of national shipping, had groped uncertainly toward the establishment of sea-power, the Stuarts founded and developed it and made it an aggressive instrument in British hands for the overthrow of a resourceful rival. England's organized method of extending her sea-power is seen in the famous navigation acts of 1651, 1660, 1663, and 1673, and the various regulations and appointments that accompanied and followed them, whereby her own people became the sole carriers of British commerce and appropriated and secured for England and her subjects all the emoluments arising from the trade of her own colonies. By such means she sought to wrest from the Dutch their control of sea-borne trade, and by monopolizing the colonial output she was able to add to the national stock of raw materials and to confine the importation of European goods into the colonies within routes that passed through her own ports. All the while she was striving to increase her customs receipts; to ensure the proper collection of all the royal revenues in the plantations, by extending her audit system; to augment the profits from her fisheries; and to enlarge the navy and strengthen the merchant marine, by adding to the number of seamen and multiplying the tonnage of ships. It not infrequently happened, as early as the seventeenth century, particularly in the religious Puritan commonwealths of New England, which did not want to have anything to do with the British system, that in her attempts to meet her impelling needs—as during the Andros administration—England ran athwart colonial practices and aspirations, thereby producing much friction and an enduring ill will.

After 1675, when the Dutch monopoly of the carrying trade was a thing of the past, England seemed to be advancing successfully on her way toward commercial independence and leadership. But already girding herself'for the lists was a greater rival—France—who differed from England's earlier opponents in that she, as well as England, was aiming at colonial and commercial supremacy, and was dominated by an overpowering ambition to become the leading state not only in Europe but upon the ocean also. She was enlarging her territory by planting settlements for profit in the West Indies; rooting herself firmly in Canada, where the seignorial system, with its strong peasant farming stock, gave substantial body to the military régime: and finding lodgment in Louisiana and up the Mississippi to the Illinois country, which, though organized on a trading and military basis, was to no small extent a region of villages, farmers, and wheat fields. She was chartering trading companies for carrying on the slave trade and the establishing of colonies; and with nervous energy was building a merchant marine that she might be as powerful on the sea as she had been already on the land. She aspired to be what England was fast becoming—a trading nation, owing its wealth, freedom, and power to the industry of the people at home and the extensive commerce that this industry enabled it to carry on abroad. That she might realize her desires, she was putting into operation a scheme of trade which, though more artificially fostered, and differing in some important particulars from that of England, was, in many of its features, identical with that of her great antagonist. She was a rival ready to compete with England at every point of her widening sphere of activity and to put to the hardest test her growing powers. Thus the eighteenth century shows us two well-matched contestants, actuated by similar aims and purposes, eagerly extending their colonial area in the interest of trade, shipping, and manufactures, and seeking the welfare, wealth, and power of their respective kingdoms. Seemingly, in the first encounter, France more than held her own, for in 1745 an English mercantilist pamphleteer could say with concern that "the French commerce and colonies, from being inferior to ours, have risen to a dangerous superiority over us in less than half a century."

But in several fundamental respects these two antagonists were dissimilar. France was an absolute monarchy, the executive powers of which were highly developed and excessively centralized, but whose law-making functions, which were exercised by an estates-general, corresponding to an English parliament, remained dormant for another century. As far as its form of government was concerned, this unified French state continued unchanged during the whole of our colonial period, and because it was free from the distracting interference of a parliament or other agency limiting the prerogatives of the crown, it was admirably fitted to take prompt and

efficient action in any struggle for supremacy with England. This centralized control, uniformity of plan, and unrestricted royal authority sometimes induced excessive paternalism—particularly in matters of military
defense and direct supervision of the domestic concerns of her colonies—
but it also made possible relief in the form of gifts, loans, land grants, and
other varieties of state aid during the period of emigration and settlement,
and great generosity in times of stress, when fire and hurricane destroyed
houses and crops. France introduced no "enumeration" clauses into the
royal arrêts and decrees which determined her commercial policy, and imposed only moderate duties on imported colonial products. The French
islands of Guadeloupe, Martinique, Marie Galante, and Hispaniola were alike
more fertile and less liable to exhaustion than were the British islands, and
because the French African Company—unlike the Royal African Company
of England—had a monopoly of the slave business, could count on a cheap
and continuous supply of Negro labor. Nevertheless, advantageous as the
French system seemed and was, it had evil consequences, for the islands always lacked the spirit of independence and self-reliance which characterized
the British islands, and never became anything more than plantation colonies growing tropical produce by means of slave labor.

On the other hand, conditions in England and her colonies were exactly
the opposite of those in France. England imposed heavier customs duties
at the home ports, but she interfered rarely in the internal affairs of the colonies and concerned herself scarcely at all with matters of emigration, state
aid, and maintenance. She expected the colonists to stand on their own
feet and to support themselves. In 1742 she laid down the principle that
not only the royal colonies, but also those with special rights under their
charters, should realize that they had obligations to meet, as well as rights
to enjoy, the most important of which was their own defense. Under this
somewhat rough and ready method of treatment, which was not at all what
Burke called it, "salutary neglect," but rather the mercantilist's idea of how
a mother country should guide her colonies, the English colonies in America
became self-reliant, self-governing, and self-supporting groups, possessed of
a spirit of independence and of confidence in their ability to manage their
own affairs that made for steady growth and permanence.

It is not surprising that the new British customs officials, whose jurisdiction covered the proprietary and corporate colonies as well as those that
were royal, should have met with many discouragements, and have been
looked upon as meddlers and busybodies. They in their turn were vocal in
their comments on the treatment they received. Even when the system
seemed fairly well established, the authority of the royal governors, as expressed in their instructions from the crown, the operations of the vice-admiralty courts and customs officials, and the commercial restrictions—nota-

bly those imposed by the Molasses Act of 1733—were subject to dispute, and, at times, to evasion and complete nullification. Such opposition was no part of a deliberate purpose on the part of the colonists; it was inherent in the process of adjustment to a new relationship which was forced upon them and in which they found much that seemed ill adapted to the conditions of growing communities. British rulings often showed complete ignorance of colonial business methods and of colonial conditions generally, and attempts to enforce these rulings, particularly after 1763, disclosed, as never before, the difficulties of applying the British system as defined by the revenue and navigation laws.

In fact, the period from 1713 to 1763 was one of transition, always disturbing to men's minds. By increasing her colonies and strengthening her control, Great Britain gradually widened her horizon and attained a status that was imperial in form. Changes took place also in popular thought and terminology. True the word "empire" had been frequently used by pamphleteers and letter writers as early as 1685, when "R. B." employed it in his little volume, *The English Empire in America,* but with no other meaning than that implied by Raleigh, when a century before he wrote of "rule and empery," or by Thomas Pownall, in his *Principles of Polity, being the Grounds and Reasons of Civil Empire,* published in 1752, wherein he speaks of the "empire of government," "imperium, the power of government," and the "empire of the State." However, in the first half of the eighteenth century it was beginning to connote something more specific than "rule" and "power," and it was used to describe the self-sufficient empire of the mercantilists, the empire of the seas, "that dominion which nature designed us," the maritime empire of the elder Pitt. It can hardly have meant to the men of the early eighteenth century what Milton saw in his prophetic vision, that is, England "with all her daughter lands about her"—a great oceanic, imperial state, a mother land presiding over subordinate communities subject to the will and authority of king and Parliament. It may well be doubted if there were many, even among the leaders themselves, who foresaw the imperial form that the greater Britain was to take after her long and successful struggle with France for colonial and commercial supremacy. Such a conception of empire was only vaguely, if at all, a part of the common consciousness until after 1763.

To aid in her struggle for supremacy England needed all the help the colonists could furnish, not only in the form of direct contributions, but even more in the indirect advantages that they might offer as sources of supply and revenue. The rule that each colony should be self-supporting and bear the burden of its own maintenance was fundamental to the mind of the mercantilist, whose system of public economy was at that time in the ascendant; and, except for the expenses of naval and military protection in all the colonies, and the charges for a part of the administration of Nova Scotia and Georgia, this rule was, at the cost of considerable trouble, consistently adhered to. Unlike the colonies of France, those of Great Britain before 1763 imposed upon the mother country but a slight and constantly diminishing financial obligation—an advantage that was not trifling to a heavily burdened exchequer. More positively advantageous were the contributions that the colonies made of men and material in times of war on colonial soil. Between 1689 and 1763 Great Britain was engaged in four wars with France, each of which was fought in part in America with the cooperation of the colonists, and one with Spain, to which the northern and southern colonies contributed a considerable number of men. This military aid was not always as timely or as enthusiastically rendered as it might have been, and sometimes was prompted by motives of self-interest quite as much as by a desire to help the mother country in her hour of need.

But of greatest value in the eyes of Englishmen, both statesmen and merchants, were the indirect benefits that the colonies conferred, the most profitable of which was colonial trade. England, influenced by the economic views of the time, deliberately discouraged importations from France, "the dangerous and inveterate enemy of Great Britain," and rejected a French trade which, had it been reciprocally pursued, would have permitted a turnover of business capital many times a year. In its place she cultivated, and greatly overvalued, the trade of her own colonies, where the returns from invested capital could not be assured within less than from one to four years. France retaliated, particularly after the outbreak of the Spanish War in 1701, and in the later readjustment duties, estimated by Adam Smith at seventy-five percent of their value—an amount equivalent to absolute prohibition—were imposed by England on French goods and maintained until 1786. Though the official balance was probably in England's favor, the total trade was inconsiderable, and smuggling increased so enormously that the illicit importations exceeded those that were regularly entered. The policy was damaging for both countries; but the fact that of the two France suffered the more, made it possible for England to profit from her colonial trade. It was inevitable, therefore, that Great Britain should build up her system of colonial control on the widely accepted principle that colonies were desirable only as far as they were useful to the states from which they took their origin, and were useful only as far as they procured for those states new advantages and solid means of extending their commerce. But she did not exploit her colonies as France did hers, for the latter made little effort, by means of bounties on colonial materials, by the granting of a monopoly of the home market to colonial staples, and by the admission of colonial ships to the advantages enjoyed by those of the mother country, to favor the colonies, as Great Britain was wont to do, and so to render the colonial relationship as far as possible mutually advantageous.

Thus during the earlier part of the colonial period, at least until the middle of the eighteenth century, Great Britain valued the plantations not as aggregations of people only or as accretions of territory to be used as homes for an overflowing population from England; for the mercantilists held that a territory larger than could be adequately settled or defended, or economically maintained, was a liability not an asset, a burden not a benefit. Rather did she expect them to produce those raw materials that would contribute directly or indirectly to the success of the mother state in its contest with other nations for the supremacy of the seas and for leadership in the commercial and colonial worlds. Therefore, when rating the colonies as British assets, Great Britain valued New England and the middle colonies much lower than the southern and West Indian colonies, not only because the former furnished little that could not be as well supplied by Ireland and even by England herself, but also because they had an almost complete monopoly of the provision trade with the tobacco and sugar plantations in America. The most useful colonies to the mother country were the British West Indies with their sugar, and the southern colonies with their tobacco, rice, indigo, and naval stores; and in order that these commodities should redound to the advantage of Great Britain rather than to that of her rivals, certain staples, such as sugar, tobacco, cotton, and dyewoods had been "enumerated" as far back as 1660; that is, they could be shipped, in vessels British built, owned, and manned, to England only. Later, as other products gained value in British eyes, the list was very considerably extended.

Now, as the colonies increased in number; as colonial trade became more varied, complex, and profitable; and as the menace of French commercial aggression aroused in England a greater interest in the plantations overseas, these ideas regarding the colonies were elaborated and given more articulate and coherent form. British policy became colonial as well as commercial in character—colonial, that is, as far as Great Britain ever had a colonial policy, properly so called, before the nineteenth century. The doctrine of "the self-sufficing empire"—a well-turned phrase but one never used contemporaneously—describes a policy which the mercantilists of the period before the Revolution used to support both argument and action. According to this doctrine, the mother country, the sugar and tobacco colonies, the provision or bread colonies, the fisheries, and Africa formed a single economic and commercial whole, made up of mutually sustaining parts, each of which contributed something to the strength and profit of the entire group.

The mercantilists valued the northern or bread colonies because they could supply the sugar, tobacco, and rice colonies with bread, flour, meats, fruits, vegetables, houses, horses, sheep, pigs, pipe-staves, headings, and lumber that the latter could not sufficiently produce for themselves. The southern colonies, also, provided some of these things, and the West Indies raised for the maintenance of their Negroes, to a larger extent than is commonly supposed, what were locally known as "ground provisions," thereby often lessening the demand for outside bread and flour, and driving the captains and super-cargoes from the bread colonies to seek markets elsewhere, particularly among the French, Dutch, and Spanish islands. But the British West India planters made no effort to supply all that was needed for the up-keep of their tables, houses, and plantations, and consequently the northern colonies found in the islands of the Caribbean their most lucrative market. As early as 1709 the board of trade could report that the British islands in the West Indies would "not be able to carry on their trade, or even to sub-sist (especially in time of war) without the necessary supplies from the north-ern plantations of bread, drink, fish, and flesh of cattle and horses for cul-tivating their plantations, of lumber and staves for casks for their sugar, rum, and molasses, and of timber for building their houses and sugar works." That the arrangement was satisfactory from the British point of view ap-pears from the remark of a contemporary pamphleteer that "our sugar col-onies could hardly subsist without the assistance of those on the continent, and those upon the continent thrive and grow rich by this commerce with our sugar islands, but it is Great Britain that reaps the benefit of both, for all their gains centre here." Thus the New England and middle colonies, though considered by the mercantilists a detriment rather than a benefit to Great Britain, found themselves necessary though subordinate factors in the general commercial scheme.

During the first half of the eighteenth century, the sugar and tobacco colonies played their part in this "self-sufficing empire" as exporters to Great Britain of their leading staples; while the bread colonies, though send-ing to the mother country a few products, such as naval stores, furs, flax-seed, whale oil, and—when Great Britain allowed it—grain, corn, and salted provisions, served as secondary and contributory factors, chiefly useful be-cause of the bread and provisions they sent to the southern and West Indian colonies. France was valuing her colonies in precisely the same way, but without the heavy customs dues and the restrictive features—such as the "enumeration" and the requirement to import manufactured articles through the home ports; and because she had no bread and provision colonies—for neither Canada nor Louisiana could match the British northern colonies in this respect—she offered a tempting opportunity to the merchants and sea captains of Pennsylvania, New York, and New England to carry their sur-plus products to her West Indian islands and so to break through the re-straints of the British mercantile system. The frequent glutting of the Brit-ish West Indies with northern goods which resulted in a dull market; the high prices of return freights of rum, sugar, and molasses; the scarcity of money and bills of exchange which rendered payment of debts uncertain; and the frequent complaints of the inferior quality of the colonial staples— all these things drove the northern colonies, in the interest of their own prosperity, to find a market where they could. But because this trade between the British northern colonies and the French and other foreign colonies in the West Indies was contrary to mercantilist principles and to the ends sought in the self-sufficing empire, Englishmen, both at home and in the West Indies, became alarmed. They declared that British subjects in North America were serving themselves with foreign sugar, rum, and molasses, and by so doing not only were transferring to foreigners the benefits of a trade that in its original channel belonged to Great Britain, but also were enriching the foreign sugar colonies and impoverishing their own. In fact, neither Great Britain nor France ever attained or could have attained that condition of commercial equilibrium which the mercantilists desired, for the theory did not allow for the natural growth in population and resourcefulness of the colonies themselves, nor did it take into account the fact that the time would come when the northern colonies would demand, in some measure, an independent commercial life of their own.

Mercantilism was essentially a nationalistic policy, selfish as all nationalistic policies are selfish. It fomented war in provoking an economic struggle among the commercial and industrial nations for place, power, and wealth, and sacrificed the welfare of the outlying and dependent parts of a state in the interest of the dominant portion.

Historically considered, mercantilism was the materialistic, self-protective philosophy of a growing state that was striving to win for itself a place of superiority among the nations. It was a doctrine of exclusiveness and self-sufficiency, opposed to cosmopolitan cooperation and to any form of international control.

Of all the staples that Great Britain obtained from America, by far the most important were sugar and tobacco. To British administrators and traders these were the leading commodities, and so valuable were they and so prominent a place did they hold in the esteem of the mercantilists that their influence in shaping British policy toward the colonies was probably greater than even that of politics, war, and religion. They brought increased business to the shippers, freight carriers, and insurance writers of the time, and they made large profits not only for planter and merchant in America, but also for every wholesale and retail dealer, manufacturer, and sugar refiner in England. The merchants and capitalists of the eighteenth century considered these two commodities so much the mainstays of British prosperity that they constantly appealed to the board of trade, the Privy Council, and Parliament for favorable action in their own behalf and almost invariably succeeded in having their complaints heeded and their petitions met. The British government as well as the British merchants rated these commodities as assets of tremendous consequence, because the duties received from therh bulked largest in the customs returns of London and the outports, and so contributed to swell enormously the sum total of the British customs receipts.

From the beginning the colonies lay outside the barriers of the British fiscal system and were obliged to pay heavy duties in England on their own exports, in addition to whatever similar duties they chose to levy on the same commodities at their own customs houses in America. A planter in Barbados and the Leeward Islands had to pay the four-and-a-half percent export duty on sugar and other "dead commodities" at the time of their shipment from the West Indies, and another considerable duty on the arrival of the commodity at London or one of the outports. He might have to pay also the "plantation duty" imposed by the act of 1673, in case he wished to carry his "enumerated" commodity to another plantation. A planter in Virginia or Maryland had to pay a two shilling a hogshead export duty in the colony and an import duty in England, and he might be liable also for the "plantation duty" of a penny a pound on tobacco. Many illustrations could be given of the exceedingly heavy duties actually levied on colonial exports at the port of London, amounting after 1750 to more than sixty percent of their selling value....

Before 1750 the colonies exported more than they imported and received cash in return, but after 1755 their imports from Great Britain began to exceed their exports, until the balance in Great Britain's favor amounted to nearly two millions in 1760 and nearly three millions in 1770. Thus the business of exporting manufactured goods to America was advancing by leaps and bounds, and after the failure of the non-importation movement in 1769–70, British merchants indulged in what has been called "a mad mercantile speculation," in which trade was being built up on capital borrowed in England and Scotland and on a system of long-term credits in America, extended, as Governor Bernard said, "beyond all bounds of prudence." This inflation of credit had been carried dangerously far in the years immediately preceding the Revolution, for it seemed unlikely that the colonists could ever pay so huge an indebtedness either in cash or commodities. For want of a sufficient medium of exchange they were always cramped in their trade and were never able to do the business they might have done had England been willing or able to find a remedy or offer some kind of monetary relief.

Nevertheless, to all outward seeming the colonies throve and prospered. Their apparent wealth increased, imports became more varied in kind and luxurious in quality, and conditions of life and standards of taste, particularly in the towns and on the large plantations, mounted steadily in the scale of comfort and elegance and even of extravagance. Much of the prosperity was illusory, for it was based on credit inflation and excessive issues of paper currency. Hard money became exceedingly scarce, and the necessity of meeting colonial indebtedness resulted in a persistent drift of that money toward Great Britain. To many observers, even as early as 1774, a financial crisis in the business world seemed much more imminent than a break with the mother country....

There was another side to colonial trade, "a precious commodity," as one merchant called it, "but subject to many casualties." At best it was always uncertain, and those who had a part in it were often anxious and full of foreboding. Some years were notorious for their tedious and irregular returns. The year 1736, for example, was reported as "intollerably bad, sales very slack, and prices much too low for their costs," though why this was so is difficult to discover. In the eighteenth century the British merchant became less and less inclined to receive raw materials, particularly the heavy staples from the northern colonies which were troublesome to handle and hard to dispose of. He preferred to send over manufactured goods and receive his remittances in money, but coin was always difficult to obtain in America and expensive to ship, and bills of exchange were the usual medium. Often and bitterly did the British merchants complain of the failure on the part of the American merchants and planters to settle their accounts, and many a one, who not infrequently was doing business on a very narrow margin himself, was compelled to carry a burden of credit far greater than his own capital would bear while for two, three, and even four years he waited to get his pay for goods he had sent to America. In rapidity of payment the colonies differed greatly, the northern colonies being much less dependable than the West Indies. In the eighteenth century the West India planters presented a balance against Great Britain, but they spent their cash or their accumulated credits, not in the islands where they made their money, but for houses, lands, and political and social positions in the mother country. The continental colonists, availing themselves of this practice of the West India planters, were always glad to use their own credits acquired in the West India traffic to obtain there bills of exchange with which to pay their British correspondents....

To the colonist the trade was always more or less of a gamble. What he wanted was a good market and a quick return; what he frequently got was a poor market, where sales were slow, debts difficult to collect, and bills of exchange impossible to obtain; where either there was no return at all or where a return was secured but at so high a price as to leave no profit. Yet even an unsatisfactory freight was better than a return empty or in ballast, for to come back "dead freighted" was usually accounted a disaster. It was this need of a profitable return that led many ship captains, who arrived early at a British West India market and sold promptly, to go on to the French islands, where the cost of a return freight was frequently lower on account of the favorable climatic and agricultural conditions and the greater cheapness of slave labor. . . .

Despite all these drawbacks, the trade flourished and was profitable to all, particularly to Great Britain. Whatever might be the various balances of trade existing among the continental American colonies or between the continental colonies and the West Indies—and to have a favorable balance of trade was the object of every colony in its relations with the others—the eventual balance was, after 1755, favorable to Great Britain, at least on paper. The goods that were exported to America from the mother country were more than sufficient to pay for the staples that the colonies furnished; and consequently Great Britain, in her eighteenth-century dealings with the colonies, began her career as the creditor nation of the world. But credit without assurance of payment is hazardous and in the long run destructive of confidence. There was scarcely a large merchant or planter or storekeeper below the Pennsylvania-Maryland line who was not in debt to his correspondent in England or Scotland. There are exceptions to this statement, particularly among the merchants of Charleston and the planters of the West Indies, who were generally able to meet their trade balances and so to keep out of debt to England, though not out of debt to the northern colonies, whose chief supply of hard money came from their favorable balance of trade with the South and the West Indies. But taking the American trade as a whole, the exports from Great Britain far exceeded the imports, and the balance of cost had to be made up in coin, bills of exchange, or drafts on the Bank of England. The colonists met their balances fairly well, despite the great scarcity of hard money, until 1770, when what would seem to have been an orgy of buying in the colonies and of selling in England sent the indebtedness up to nearly three millions of pounds, and ushered in a brief period of extravagance and inflation. . . .

Then there were the absentee planters from the West Indies, who like the nabobs of India, dissipated the profits of their plantations in efforts to obtain political and social preferment and, as is often the case with the *nouveaux riches,* scattered their wealth with a prodigality out of all proportion to the success attained. But they served to counteract whatever disadvantage might occur from the unfavorable balance of trade with the West Indies, for they brought their wealth with them to England and so retained their character as Englishmen, giving to the traffic with the West Indies the nature of an internal rather than a foreign trade. . . .

It was inevitable that members of growing communities with interests of their own—merchants and planters, West Indian as well as continental—should have taken the measure of the British regulations and have determined in a critical spirit the disadvantages that resulted from the commercial restrictions imposed upon them by the mother country. Just as the English mercantilists, at the beginning of the century, expressed their admiration for the French system of colonial control, so the merchants and planters in America deemed the British regulations far less liberal than those of France, where there were only light duties, no "enumeration," and no restriction upon their field of purchase. Self-interest underlay their criticisms as it underlay the policy of the mercantilists in England. Each group was consulting its own wishes and catering to its own needs, and out of the irrepressible conflict thus provoked arose that century-long activity in smuggling and illicit trade which marked the effort of the colonists to attain commercial freedom and to develop their own independent commercial life. How extensive such smuggling was, in proportion to the whole volume of colonial trade, it is impossible to say, but it went on in some measure wherever an opportunity offered—in Newfoundland, along the Atlantic coast from Maine to Georgia, and notoriously in the West Indies. . . .

The business of those in England concerned with colonial affairs was to adapt the varying needs and circumstances of the colonies to the superior rights and privileges of the mother country and to the prerogatives of the crown. British officials watched with care to see that the colonies did nothing to hamper British colonial trade or discriminate against the activities and interests of those engaged in it; and Parliament passed many laws dealing with debt, bankruptcy, coinage, and paper currency that were designed to protect the British merchant doing business with America, sometimes, undoubtedly, at the expense of the colonists themselves. There are many orders in council and many acts of Parliament that can be understood only in the light of this policy, which was born not of British willfulness or desire to tyrannize or even to meddle, but of a conviction, deeply entrenched in the British mind, that the moment a colony attempted to act solely for its own benefit and without regard to its proper status as a dependent and sustaining member of the British oceanic world, it ceased to fulfill the duty incumbent upon it. This conviction, fashioned in the hard school of experience, widely prevailed in the eighteenth century, particularly before 1763, and was maintained the more strictly because of the Britishers' respect for precedent and tradition.

RICHARD PARES

BOSTON TO BARBADOS: THE ECONOMICS OF INTERDEPENDENCE

A New England sea-captain, James Brown, noted with pride that he carried with him all his life an atlas purchased in Boston (The English Pilot), *which described the navigation of the West Indies whether one started from Hudson's Bay or the Amazon. One fact was clear by the eve of the Revolution: all of the West Indies were only irregularly supplied from Europe. Not surprisingly, enterprising Americans were quick not only to develop trade with the sister colonies in the West Indies, but with the foreign islands as well.*

Frank Wesley Pitman has expressed the conclusion of a number of historians that for Americans the West Indies "was a great and permanent market for all their staples, and the wealth of the West Indian trade underlay [America's] prosperity and civilization." The author of the following selection has endeavored to describe in detail this West India commerce as a means of fully understanding the economic relations—both in terms of profit and loss. He is not as ready to conclude as some historians that the vital interests were such as to lead straight to revolution; but he does feel that imperial preferences in legislation "may have predisposed" the Americans to take the course of independence. As John Adams remarked years later, "molasses was an essential ingredient in American independence."

And so the sloops and schooners spread out across the West Indies, to the extent that their captains had committed their atlases to memory, or enlarged upon them. In a single generation this expanded trade literally turned Baltimore from a village to a bustling town. This trade involved

From *Yankees and Creoles.* Longmans, Green, 1956.

ships traveling first to the Madeiras for wine, or the African coast for slaves, not to mention the rivalry between the colonies on the mainland, nor an active coastal trade which contributed to the intricacies of exchange and commerce with the islands of the Caribbean.

Historians of the British Empire have long recognized the importance of the trade carried on before the American Revolution between North America and the West Indies. Without it the sugar colonies could not have existed and the North American colonies could not have developed. The balance between the tropical and temperate zones within the empire was a matter to be considered when peace treaties were negotiated; and the preference for the West Indians over the North Americans which the imperial Parliament showed, perhaps unfairly and injudiciously, in its legislation may have predisposed the latter to revolution.[1] But, although much has been written of this conflict of interests and its influence on policy, much less is known of the trade itself—of the way in which it was carried on. Nearly forty years ago Professor Herbert Bell wrote an excellent short article on the subject; but perhaps a study of a somewhat longer period, drawn from a rather wider range of sources, may throw some new light on the people who conducted this trade, the purposes for which they conducted it, and the methods by which they did so.[2]

The first founders of the English colonies did not distinctly mean to establish complementary sources of supply. They knew what they wanted, and they mostly wanted the same things—wine, oil, sugar, silk, and other products of warm climates for which the Englishman had (or so he thought) to pay through the nose to foreigners. But they did not know where they would ultimately find these things: thus, they would have grown sugar in Virginia if they could have done so, and they grew tobacco in Barbados before they found that sugar would answer better. Only after some years of trial and error did the familiar pattern of American trade become clear. The colonies north of the Mason-Dixon line had few staples of any value in the European markets but a permanent surplus of food and lumber; the West Indies, just the contrary; and the hybrid colonies from Maryland to Carolina produced both staple crops and a less important surplus of certain kinds of food. This differentiation of products first became important from about 1640 to 1650. The end of the immigration boom in New England must have made food and lumber available for export, and forced the colonists to find new methods of paying their debts in England. About the same time the beginning of the sugar boom in the West Indies increased purchasing-power and accentuated the temptation to sacrifice food production to the dominant cash crop.

The differentiation of products was obvious, for it created the trade between North America and the West Indies. But other differentiations were no less important.

In the first place, the two groups of societies differed more and more from each other. It may seem obvious to us that this must always have been so, but it was less obvious to the first adventurers. There may have been puritan colonists who never wished or hoped to found plantations (in the modern sense of the word), but there was no necessary antithesis between puritanism and plantations: elements which, at any rate, passed for puritan were strong in the early history of Virginia and Jamaica, and the puritan syndicates interested in the tropical colony of Old Providence and in the far from tropical colony of Saybrook, Connecticut, had more than a little in common with each other.[3] Some personal links between the northern and the sugar colonies survived until the Revolution: the Redwoods of Newport, the Livingstons of New York, and the Dickinsons of Philadelphia continued to hold West India property, and the descendants of other West Indian families—Searles, Silvesters, and Morrises—lived in the northern colonies. The islands also contributed less valuable elements to the North American population, for their parochial poor relief often took the form of paying a passage for North America.[4] Visits were also exchanged by the sickly in search of health: Barbados sent Philadelphia her hard drinkers, with their "carbuncled faces, slender legs and thighs, and large, prominent bellies," and young Major George Washington accompanied his ailing brother in 1751 to 1752 to Barbados, where he commented, with an emphasis surprising in a Virginian, on the planter's indebtedness. But in spite of these feeble links, society developed on different lines in the West Indies and in North America.

The active merchant class, whose business I have been describing, was located at a dozen or so of seaports up and down the coast, of which Boston, Philadelphia, New York, and Newport were easily the most important by 1740—the ascent of Providence and, later, Baltimore only became visible shortly before the Revolution, and neither Charleston nor even Salem quite rivaled the four big ports in this trade. Of these, Boston was the oldest and for a long time the greatest: it was described in 1675 as "a magazine both of all American and Europian commodityes for the furnishing and supplying of the severall countreys," and Edmund Randolph, who doubtless exaggerated the illicit prosperity which he envied and wished to destroy, described the merchants of New England as trading generally with most parts of Europe, exporting colonial produce and bringing back European goods which they distributed among the West Indies. They Bostonians themselves preserved into the eighteenth century a tradition of this preeminence; but in fact they began to lose it after the Peace of Utrecht, if not before.

The relative decline of Boston resulted, in part, from natural causes—above all, from the extension of settlement eastwards and, still more, southwards. This extension required, in the first place, the felling of trees along thousands of miles of sea-coast and river-bank, which released staves and other lumber from new areas for the West Indies. The deforestation was followed by the cultivation of new staples, or of the old staples over again, and this produce too was ready to be carried to the islands from ports further and further removed from Boston: Virginia and Carolina pork might not be as good as Burlington pork, nor Baltimore flour as good as New York flour; but they were good enough for the West India market....

The cargoes in this trade were exceedingly various. The list includes the natural products of more than a thousand miles of coast; it is no wonder that the range is great. But even a single vessel of less than a hundred tons might carry a cargo, less various indeed than that of a whole continent, but diverse enough. To take an example chosen at random: the Sloop *Mary Ann*, owned by the Browns of Providence, Rhode Island, sailed for Surinam in October 1766 with the following cargo: 100 hogsheads tobacco, 122 boxes spermaceti candles, 1,975 staves, 433 hoops, 4,000 bricks, 1,700 feet heading, 8 horses with awning (and hay, oats, and water for their use), 3,500 bunches onions, 35 wood axes, 62 shaken hogsheads, 9 2/3 barrels beef, 5 2/3 barrels pork, 7 cwt. ship bread, 3 firkins butter, 30 oars, 12 barrels flour, 25 barrels tar, 8 barrels oil, 3 "shotes," and 50 kegs oysters. Even if she shook hogsheads and some of the lumber was for the cooperage of the return cargo of molasses, and the beef, pork, bread, and "shotes" were ship's stores (which may well be, for there is no account of their sales), this is a mixed cargo; and more extreme examples could have been found.[5]

There were good reasons for such variety. As I have already suggested, it might insure the shippers against the risk of glutting the tiny markets of the islands with any one article. It also resulted, in part, from the haphazard way in which these export cargoes were collected—a point to which I shall have to return shortly. It was more noticeable in some ports than in others. The example I have quoted comes from Rhode Island, a colony with only one staple product (horses) and no definite hinterland. The merchants of Rhode Island had to collect the materials for a cargo as best they could from the surrounding farmers, from their own few manufactures, from the fishermen of Nantucket, from any other passer-by or coastwise speculator in goods fit for the West India market. The same thing is true of Boston, a commercial capital whose merchants drew upon the resources of widespread farms, forests, and fisheries. It was even true, though to a lesser degree, of Philadelphia and New York: these commercial centers collected the miscellaneous products of the neighboring provinces, but they also had their own characteristic manufactures of bread and flour, which bulked larger in their West India cargoes than any one thing Boston or Newport had to show. Other ports were still more specialized: some of the Virginia rivers exported very little besides lumber; Piscataqua, Salem, and Marblehead little but lumber and fish. Of course, there was fish and fish: many invoices, especially in the later years, specified mackerel, alewives, menhaden, and so forth. Still, one could not mistake the relatively homogeneous Salem cargoes for the very miscellaneous ones which the Bostonians and Newport men carried to the West Indies.

Not much was said about the competition between different provinces in the production of similar articles. Comparisons were quite often drawn between the flour of Philadelphia and that of New York. The pork of New Jersey and that of the southern colonies were held to compete: the latter was badly prepared at first, and always inferior to the best Burlington pork: but it was cheaper, and thought good enough for the Negroes. The hucksters of the Leeward Islands (who presumably dealt with the Negroes) were said to prefer it to the better article, which was only wanted for the private consumption of the planters' families. But comparisons such as these were not made often. The production of the continent was too little standardized, and the local diversities too slight and indefinable. On the other hand, the planters were, for the most part, supplying their slaves' wants rather than their own, and were therefore the less nice in their choice. They bought from hand to mouth, and if they ever aimed at a bargain in the purchase of these coarse goods, it was price rather than quality that attracted them....

The cargoes exported from North America to the islands were collected in a number of ways. Many of them, especially in the more primitive times and places, resulted from a system of local barter. The exporters of northern produce were also the importers of sugar, molasses, and rum, which they sold to store-keepers or to consumers for "country pay," often of the most miscellaneous character. There was only one way to turn this stuff to account—to export it to the West Indies; and this fact probably explains, better than anything else, the great variety of the outward cargoes to which I have already referred.

In the greater ports, however, the merchants assorted their cargoes somewhat more scientifically. Although their papers reveal more coastwise speculation in West India produce than in goods for the West India market, the latter is not wholly absent. They drew to themselves the lumber and foodstuffs of the adjoining provinces, and this enabled them to assort their West India cargoes not only better but quicker. The governor of Maryland complained in 1762 that much of that colony's wheat and flour was carried to Philadelphia:

... the price there being always higher than in Maryland owing to the vast trade carried on from thence to the West Indies & other parts; as the merchants there can always load their vessels at once they can afford to give more for the cargoes than merchants in this province can give, because ours must be a long time collecting a cargo for even a small vessel there being no town or port in Maryland where any considerable quantity of country produce can be purchased at once or altogether.

This was before the rise of Baltimore.

By no means all the cargoes for the West Indies started from the home port of the ship and her owner. From the first, there were many voyages from New England to Barbados via the wine islands of the Atlantic or the slave coast of Africa, where the most important part of the cargo was picked up. The vineyards offered a market for the New England lumber, also, especially at crop-time, for the New England fish. The same ship would carry forward to the West Indies the inferior wine which nobody but the planters would drink, with the somewhat better qualities which found a market in North America and were said to improve on the voyage. The proceeds of the wine sold in the West Indies would buy a load of rum or sugar at home. A slave voyage had many of the same advantages, though it was not until the eighteenth century that the Rhode Islanders rediscovered for themselves the art, familiar to the Barbadians in the seventeenth, of buying their slaves for the West India market with rum distilled from West India molasses. Lastly, the merchants of the northern and middle colonies sent their vessels to the agricultural South to buy lumber, pork, or Indian corn for the West Indies. Here, too, a *perpetuum mobile* could be established—with the produce of Virginia or Carolina, molasses could be bought, carried to Boston or Philadelphia, there distilled into rum, and returned to Virginia or Carolina to buy another cargo of local produce for the West Indies.

The sales of northern goods in the islands cannot be considered apart from the purchase of the return cargoes. The two operations were inseparable in the merchants' minds, though it was only in the earliest days that they formed part of the same transaction, either by a contract of barter or by the sale of goods for a price reckoned in West India produce as currency. The choice of return cargo varied according to a number of different circumstances. In the first place, it had to depend on what was available; and the several islands varied somewhat in their characteristic produce. This applied particularly to the two great West Indian exports to North America—rum and molasses. For many years—indeed, down to the age of the American Revolution—rum and molasses figured in every kind of barter transaction. Among the articles for which they were exchanged, in whole or part payment, were bread, tobacco, spermaceti candles, head-matter (the raw material of candles), hats, land, ships, and dwelling houses. For any constructional work which required the employment of much labor, rum and molasses necessarily formed part of the payment because the contractor had to dispense these articles constantly to the workmen.

The Browns of Providence paid for a sloop in 1764 in merchantable molasses at 1s. 8 ½d. lawful money per gallon, 300 gallons on demand, 900 gallons on laying her deck, and the rest when she was finished.

Nothing was too large to be paid for in rum and molasses—or too small. Obadiah Brown once paid an insurance premium in molasses, and there exists among the Brown manuscripts the account-book of an apothecary who took West India goods, as well as pepper, iron, hay, and tobacco, in payment for his drugs and prescriptions; some of the West India goods he retailed in smaller quantities. One of the Browns tipped people in molasses for minor services. The general shortage of cash was the chief reason for all this. Far more people on the continent of North America had rum and molasses to disburse than large sums of cash. Conversely, industrialists like the Browns would try to buy West India produce with their own manufactures rather than pay cash for it, even if this meant paying a higher national price: thus, in October 1763 when they wanted 20 hogsheads of molasses, they would rather buy it at 38s. per gallon for payment in spermaceti candles (valued at 56s. per lb.) than get it at 35s. for cash payment in three months.[6]

The complication is increased, for the historian at least, by the fact that the same persons were by no means on the same side of every bargain: thus the Brown brothers, whom the transactions just described reveal as trying to buy molasses and rum with candles, often bought head-matter or tobacco with molasses and rum, and again, at other times, managed to sell molasses and rum for cash which they paid to the tobacco-growers. Their father, James Brown, behaved in just the same way: sometimes he had exchanged country produce for West India goods, at other times vice versa. He may have had a reason for this, besides the general shortage of cash: he was a small, up-country trader, on the very edge of the main commercial current (for Providence was then little more than a village) and he had little capital or knowledge of market conditions; small wonder, then, that he preferred a barter bargain at stated prices to standing the hazard of the Newport or Boston market as buyer or seller.

The decade from 1730 to 1740 was a turning point in the history of European sugar prices: they never returned to the low levels of 1730 until after the Battle of Waterloo. The impulse given to the prices of West India produce in North America was less permanent. In Philadelphia the rise of sugar prices roughly kept pace with that of flour prices until 1763, when the ratio began to fall a little. The same thing is true of molasses and rum, but the fall after 1763 was greater. Probably the earlier appreciation of West India produce was caused not so much by the war as by the discrepancy between the rate at which production expanded on the continent and in the British sugar colonies; the balance was righted after 1748 by the ever-increasing intercourse between British North America and the French sugar colonies, which provided new markets for northern produce and new supplies of sugar and molasses.

Much as the profits of this trade must have contributed to the formation of capital, this was not the only part which it played in North American economy. Above all, it facilitated the payment of debts to Europe, and so lubricated the trans-Atlantic trade. Even old colonies and well-established merchants who traded no longer as mere agents of Englishmen but on their own account, found the West India trade, and the trade in West India goods, a very useful, indeed necessary, device for settling the balance of payments between North America and Europe. Bringing West India goods to North America and sending them on to Europe can never have been the most profitable traffic, except at certain emergencies. This was not only a matter of the Plantation Duties, or even of the double freight and risk. It was commonsense and it saved time to consign West India produce straight from the islands in payment of North American debts.

Businessmen continued for several generations to consign ventures upon their own account to the West Indies in order to put money into their London correspondents' pockets by having the proceeds remitted to them in sugar and rum. Samuel Sewall did so via Antigua; Isaac Norris via Nevis, Barbados, and Jamaica.[7]

It was, at best, a clumsy business to send goods to the West Indies and thence forward other goods to London. As time went on and the colonial trade became specialized, the creditors and correspondents of North Americans became less and less qualified to handle consignments of West India produce and less and less willing to receive them. A northern merchant who shipped such produce to England on his own account was liable to make costly mistakes in the choice of a factor to sell it. Moreover, a sugar-factor in the eighteenth century, however willing to advance thousands for a sugar-planter, would not care to give credit even for hundreds to a mere merchant, without any mortgageable property, in a colony of which he knew nothing.[8]

Although remittance of goods and bills of exchange were the methods by which most North Americans used the West India trade in order to pay their debts in Great Britain, they were not the only ways. The earnings of North American shipping could be used for the same purpose. Several things must be distinguished here. Vessels were built in the North American ports to the orders of British merchants, whether for the West India trade or for some other; similar vessels were built on speculation for sale in the islands or, more likely, in England; and these last might well go by way of the islands in order to add to the profit by taking a freight of sugar across the Atlantic.[9]

But besides these, other ships which were not only built but wholly or partly owned in America plied as regular "stationed ships," fixed in the trade between a particular island and Great Britain or (less frequently) in a triangular traffic between Great Britain, North America, and the West Indies.[10] In spite of all disadvantages, vessels built and, in many cases, owned in North America engaged in the trade between the West Indies and Great Britain in such numbers as to nettle by their competition the owners of the regular London-built ships. These owners often warned the planters solemnly against entrusting their property to such inferior shipping. These warnings were sometimes quite sincere.

In many other ways, too, the West India trade and the trade in West India goods played an incidental but useful part in the economy of North America. Some of this is easily discerned—for example, the exports of rum from Boston and Rhode Island to the African coast, where it was bartered for Negro slaves who were later sold in the West Indies for bills of exchange on London or Bristol.[11] No less obvious, as a means of earning money in London, were the exports of rum and molasses to Newfoundland, or to the tobacco colonies, where the fishermen and the planters respectively gave their bills on London in exchange for it. This last trade was a standby, not only for New England ship-owners who wanted to keep their crews together in the winter but also for merchants whose ships had brought home from the islands more rum and molasses than the local market would absorb, or for sugar-refiners likewise anxious to dispose of their surplus, or even to anybody who wanted to make a little money and was ready to buy West India goods for a venture to the southward. It had its risks, above all that of bad debts: in the tobacco colonies, as in the sugar colonies, neither planters nor merchants excelled in prompt payments, and the ship-owners of Salem or Rhode Island had to caution their masters to sell any debts outstanding at their departure to whoever would buy them up, rather than leave any behind. (Indeed, this was probably one of the reasons why such vessels were more often consigned to the masters than to the merchants of Virginia and Maryland, who made fair proffers and elaborate schemes, but did not even pretend to return the value of the cargo by the vessel: sometimes they got so far behind with their payments that the owners had to send a special agent, as the Browns of Providence had to send Captain Coffin to recover their property from the plausible Messrs. Adams and Griffin of Virginia.) But in spite of these risks the trade was a useful one: when it did not yield bills of exchange, it provided cargoes of farm produce and lumber which might be further used, directly or indirectly, in the West India trade, and so keep the wheels of commerce turning.[12]

Again, the West India trade itself could be used as a means of payment between one part of the continent and another: thus the merchants of

Portsmouth, New Hampshire, who wanted money in Philadelphia ordered their ships thither with cargoes of rum and molasses from St. Kitts or salt from Salt Tortuga; their object was to obtain flour and bread, or to pay for flour and bread they had already received, presumably for their own consumption.

The voyages just described can be explained by the need of merchants in the commercial centers to earn, however indirectly, money in Europe or by the economic diversity of North America whose regions required each other's products and exchanged them by means of West India goods.

In countless ways West India goods and the West India trades helped to keep the wheels of American commerce turning; but it is less easy to be sure how much they contributed to the formation of American capital. Very few of the great mercantile fortunes were built up without the help of the West India trade; but none that I can remember was built up by it alone before the Revolution. The most obvious contribution it made was that of clearing the debts which North America owed to Great Britain for consumer-goods, and so enabling the importers of those goods to use part of the money they received from their up-country customers as the foundation for fresh enterprises. But this contribution can be overrated. "Returns via the West Indies" were not quite so easy as they were believed to be; and, although small men and beginners may have relied on them exclusively, big men do not even seem to have relied on them mainly. Nicholas Brown and Aaron Lopez of Rhode Island both incurred large debts—five or ten thousand pounds—for dry goods to British merchants after the Peace of Paris. Both made West India remittances—Brown in Surinam bills, Lopez in Jamaica bills and in miscellaneous West India commodities such as logwood and mahogany. But neither relied on these alone; their main remittances were the produce of North America.[13] The English capitalist was less directly useful to the trade between the continent and the sugar islands, and above all he had less control over it than in the early days; but the North American entrepreneur would have been hard put to it to do without him.

This is not to say that every North American merchant who dealt with the West Indies was trading on British capital. Many of them, such as the Pepperrells of Piscataqua, Timothy Orne of Salem, and G. G. Beekman of New York, clearly were doing no such thing. These were mostly the smaller men; at least, they imported few goods from Europe, so that the chief cause of indebtedness to British capitalists did not affect them. In their hands the West India business made an original and independent contribution to the formation of American capital. But we cannot identify that contribution. They were jacks of all trades, and few of them kept accounts which show distinctly the profits from any one branch of trade or the uses to which those profits were put. We must be satisfied with the knowledge that more

North American shipping was employed in this trade than in any other, that every North American port and nearly every North American merchant had something to do with it.

NOTES

1. I refer especially to the so-called "Canada-Guadeloupe" controversy of 1760–62. See William L. Grant, "Canada Versus Guadeloupe: An Episode of the Seven Years' War," *American Historical Review*, XVII (1912), pp. 735–43.

2. Herbert C. Bell, "The West India Trade Before the American Revolution," *American Historical Review*, XXII (1917), pp. 272–87.

3. Arthur P. Newton, *Colonising Activities of the English Puritans* (New Haven, 1914). See especially chapter 3.

4. Until about 1720 the authorities of Boston rigorously warned out of the town those who arrived from the West Indies without any visible means of support, but they then became more lenient. Once, at least, they retaliated by shipping to Jamaica two free Negroes who were "old and likely in a short time to become a town charge."

5. *Editor's note:* Shotes are pigs. Shaken hogsheads, or "shook" hogsheads, were terms applied to the staves and heading in bundles before they were made into hogsheads for the packing of products.

6. The difference between cash and barter prices was often much greater than this: Jonathan Dickinson of Philadelphia explained to his West Indian brother-in-law that "We barter goods for staves and hoops but we cannot sell for money unless we would dispose of our goods at the rates of others, not 1/3 so good."

7. Letter Books of Samuel Sewall, I, p. 84. Also Letter Books of Issac Norris, I (Historical Society of Pennsylvania), p. 35.

8. See my book, *A West India Fortune,* pp. 240–42 (London: Longman's Green, 1950).

9. Letter Book of Robert Ellis (Historical Society of Pennsylvania), p. 127. Also Hudson-Rogers Papers (New York Public Library).

10. *Editor's note:* A good survey of this traffic in ships will be found in *Commerce of Rhode Island,* especially volume one (Boston: Massachusetts Historical Society, 1914–15). 2 volumes.

11. More than three-quarters of the rum exported from North America to Africa in 1772 came from Boston and Rhode Island.

12. John van Cortlandt of New York consigned a cargo of rum to Adams and Griffin of Virginia, in order to get a load of peas and corn for Barbados. See John van Cortlandt Letter Book (New York Public Library). For this subject generally, see Arthur P. Middleton, *Tobacco Coast: A Maritime History of Chesapeake Bay in the Colonial Era* (Newport News, 1953).

13. James B. Hedges, *The Browns of Providence Plantations: Colonial Years* (Cambridge, 1952). See chapter 8. See also the letters of Henry Cruger, Jr., to Aaron Lopez in *Commerce of Rhode Island,* I (Boston: Massachusetts Historical Society, 1914–15), pp. 117 ff., 2 volumes.

YEARS OF REVOLT

The previous selections have clearly shown the interdependency which existed between the British colonies in the New World. In a good year on the eve of the Revolution more than 2,000 sail left mainland America for the West Indies (including the vessels of foreign countries). The following selections effectively trace the impact of the war for independence on the island possessions of the European powers, and how they became in themselves the objects of war as the American revolt provided the excuse for another conflict in Europe. In addition the West Indies remained a never-ending source of supply for Americans throughout the revolutionary period, shifting from one island to another as the winds of war blew into the sails of the growing fleet of privateers, merchantmen, and naval craft.

Curtis Nettels relates how the *Association* even before Lexington and Concord took steps to close down trade with the sister colonies, and to expand its "illicit" trade not only with England's adversaries or potential enemies, but with British mercantile interests who sought the profits of war in a disrupted empire. Lowell Ragatz describes effectively the impact of this disruption on the sugar islands, and how "with trembling hands" Jamaica sought to mediate the controversy. As the war progressed and became enlarged the islands increasingly felt the slings or arrows of misfortune—invasions, blockades, and the depredations of privateers. Governor Burt wrote from Antigua that at Montserrat "not a morsel of bread is to be had. Many Negroes have starved, and the same has happened in Nevis. Antigua has lost above a thousand and some whites."

On February 3, 1781, the island of St. Eustatius, which had become one of the great entrepôts of revolutionary contraband, was finally sacked by Admiral Rodney. No one has surpassed the story as told by the distinguished historian, J. Franklin Jameson. "It is a tale worth telling," remarks Jameson, "on account of the important part it played in enabling our forefathers to sustain that difficult and unequal struggle." As Rodney himself remarked, "this rock has done England more harm than all the arms of her most potent enemies."

There were other "rocks" in the West Indies, but none became so exposed as St. Eustatius, Rayford Logan describes the important role of Saint Domingue (Haiti) as the great trans-shipment point not only of French but of European products needed by the Americans during eight years of war. And James Callahan discusses the lesser role played by Cuba, although not without importance since Spanish aid became a reality by the eve of Yorktown. Actually it was Spanish silver from Cuba which helped send the fleet of De Grasse from Saint Domingue to its fateful rendezvous in Chesapeake waters.

Puerto Rico played a strange, and not inconspicuous role, as so ably described by Arturo Morales-Carrion. Although cast in a minor role, the name of Puerto Rico ran the gamut of European diplomatic circles as an international settlement was sought. As King George wrote to Shelburne: "The holding Gibraltar very high is quite judicious and if not taken I should hope Porto Rico may be got for it."

Would that space could allow a chapter for each island to view the impact of both the American Revolution and the European war across the West Indies. Yet the interested reader will find that the selections in this volume range across the islands from Bermuda to Barbados. It is not only the story of the West Indies during the American Revolution, but of the interdependency of all the colonies, north and south, during the dawn of a new age.

CURTIS P. NETTELS

THE FOUNDING FATHERS AND THE WEST INDIES: THE ECONOMICS OF REVOLUTION

The revolutionary phase of the relationship of the colonies in revolt with the West Indies began officially when the Secret Committee, appointed in September of 1775, was authorized by the Continental Congress to export to the foreign islands "such products as it might deem necessary for the importation of arms, ammunition, and saltpetre." One of the central figures of the Revolution, Robert Morris, became the dominant figure in the committee and helped set up a basic trade, through his mercantile connections, with the French West Indies. After the treaty with France in 1778, and with the excellent efforts of William Bingham (agent of the Continental Congress in Martinique), the "foreign" islands in the West Indies not only supplied local products long a part of American commerce, but also served as a point of trans-shipment for so much of the European goods required by the war effort, not to speak of basic consumer necessities. With regard to the latter, in 1779 President Ezra Stiles of Yale notified the students that the shortage of these "necessities" demanded that the vacation "be extended a fortnight."

The Dutch-American commerce must not be overlooked. The role of St. Eustatius became, for the British, an intolerable link between the colonists in rebellion and the European markets—not to speak of the West Indian trade with merchants from the British islands. The story of its rise and fall during the revolutionary period is told elsewhere in this volume. Suffice it to say that midway in the war about 3,000 vessels left this great entrepôt during one year. Today St. Eustatius is a small, sleepy island in the West Indies, and the only one not under the American flag which celebrates the

From *The Emergence of a National Economy, 1775–1815.* Holt, Rinehart & Winston, 1962.

American Revolution annually.

When the famous (or infamous) British Admiral, Rodney, took vengeance on the Dutch and reduced St. Eustatius, Havana became the new focal point of traffic in goods and bullion. The American privateers, of course, supplied the states with an immense quantity of goods, especially after France went to war with England and had to divert its vessels. Much of this privateering, as described elsewhere, took place in West Indian waters, and it was a heroic effort indeed.

During the forty years after 1775, the American people brought forth not only a new nation, but also a national economy. The Revolution began a process of change that modified nearly every phase of American life.

Foreign trade first felt the shock of new forces. After October 1774 the Continental Congress moved steadily toward the goal of freeing the people of the Union from their former dependence on British vessels, merchants, markets, and goods. Congress did this both to weaken Britain and to supply American troops with the sinews of war.

The antecedents of an American commercial policy are to be found in the work of the First Continental Congress. On October 20, 1774, its members signed the Continental Association, seeking thereby to put pressure on the British government, with the aim of inducing it to repeal twelve obnoxious laws. In effect, the association prohibited the importation (excepting Georgia) after December 1, 1774, of any goods exported from Britain or Ireland, any East Indian tea, any slaves, any British sugar, molasses, or coffee, any Madeira wine, or foreign indigo. The association also imposed a ban, to become effective September 10, 1775, on all American exports to Britain, Ireland, or the British West Indies.[1]

But once the fighting had started, in April 1775, Congress quickly adopted more positive measures. On July 15 it authorized foreign vessels to import essential war materials [and] next undertook to engage, in an official capacity, in a limited trade with foreign islands of the West Indies. On September 19, 1775, it appointed a "Secret Committee" and empowered it to make contracts for the purchase of foreign war supplies. Soon afterward the committee received authority to export to the foreign West Indies such American products as it might "deem necessary for the importation of arms, ammunition, and saltpetre."

In France, a zealous friend of the American cause, Caron de Beaumarchais, persistently urged the government to supply the Americans with military stores. These supplies, shipped clandestinely to America, contributed decisively to the great victory at Saratoga in October 1777.[2] That, in turn, inspired the French court to make two treaties with the United States, one of commerce and one of alliance. Thanks to the generosity of France, the United States entered the circle of trading nations as the equal of a great European power, for the French-American Treaty of Commerce (1778) was such as France might have made with Britian or Spain. Each country accorded to its ally the status of a most favored nation in regard to commercial concessions [and] France offered to the United States the use, in both Europe and the French West Indies, of free ports where American products could be imported and disposed of.[2]

Sea-borne trade during the Revolution, carried on largely by armed vessels, was almost as warlike as military operations on land. American ships had to contend with a naval power that menaced them wherever they went. The sea lanes and ports of British-American trade were the scenes of a boundless maritime war. In the Caribbean, six sugar islands—Jamaica, St. Kitts (more formally known as St. Christophers), Barbados, Montserrat, Nevis, and Antigua—contributed more than 9 percent of all Britain's external commerce. All such trades took on an added importance after 1775, by reason of Britain's loss of most of its business with the thirteen colonies—a loss that amounted to about 10 percent of all its commerce overseas. To defend the homeland, to blockade the coasts of the United States, to guard transports and supply ships serving the British army, to convoy merchantmen, and to seize American vessels—such were the duties of the British navy.[3]

In addition to the handicaps that hampered the British navy, the Americans benefited from some positive advantages on the sea. For one thing, they had a large fleet of merchant vessels that were well suited to all branches of maritime commerce—particularly the coastal trade from state to state and the highly important traffic with the West Indies. The mariners who manned such ships knew the principal routes of trade and had learned, during the Seven Years' War, the tricks of privateering and of eluding enemy vessels. In Europe and in the West Indian colonies of France, the Netherlands, and Spain, the states had the benefit of contacts with traders and officials who were either hostile or indifferent toward Britain.

Of economic pursuits during the war, privateering—the operating of privately owned commerce raiders—was the most exciting, dramatic, and colorful. In November 1775, Massachusetts enacted a law which authorized the issuance of commissions to privateers and provided for the establishment of prize courts.[4] Other colonies soon took similar action. In March 1776, Congress empowered the inhabitants of the Union to fit out privateers under its authority and approved the issuing of continental commissions.

Under the dual system for privateers both the states and Congress commissioned vessels. The states provided the prize courts, with right of appeal to an agency of the Union.[5]

American merchants managed the business of privateering. Usually they acted as a group when fitting out a vessel, each purchasing a share or shares, thereby spreading the risk. The privateers varied in size from 15 to 320 tons and were well supplied with guns. The vessels usually set out alone, but occasionally as many as ten or twelve went out together. Almost at will the privateers scoured the seas, haunting the principal routes of British trade. They swept up and down the coastal waters of North America, combed the Caribbean Sea, and seized enemy ships sailing between Britain and the West Indies. In the West Indies, French Martinique served the Americans well. When France and Spain were neutral their port officials often connived in the American operations by judging privateers to be merchantmen or by treating prizes as American ships, thereby permitting them to be sold.[6] It is estimated that 10,000 men served on American privateers in 1778. The fleet of the Salem-Beverly area ranged from 30 vessels in 1777 to 100 in 1782. Salem alone sent out more than 200 ships during the war, a third of which were captured or destroyed.[7]

The outbreak of the war caught the Royal Navy in a state of inefficiency and neglect, with the result that it did not provide adequate protection to British shipping. Later, in 1778, when Britain had developed a system of convoys, France's entry into the war compelled the Admiralty to divert much of its naval force to the defense of Britain's coastal towns, so that American enterprise flourished in the period from 1778 to 1782. The privateering fleet grew larger year after year, reaching its peak in 1781, when 550 vessels with continental commissions were busy. At the end of the war the Americans had acquired many large ships and were profiting by a wealth of experience.[8]

Britain's total wartime losses of £18,000,000 signify that privateering supplied the states with an immense quantity of goods. Altogether, Britain lost 2,000 vessels and 12,000 sailors, including a Quebec fleet worth £500,00(and half of a rich Jamaica fleet, taken in 1776.[9] Franklin cited reports that Britain's West Indian trade had suffered losses amounting to £1,800,000.

The wartime disruption of commerce with Britain forced the states to develop direct trades with France, Spain, and the Netherlands. To retain and to increase long-established trades with foreign islands in the Caribbean was another urgent need. In July and November 1775, Congress authorized a limited trade with the foreign West Indies, for the procuring of arms and ammunition. American vessels were soon importing small shipments. The second stage, beginning in April 1776, when Congress authorized unrestricted foreign trade, lasted until about the middle of 1778. During this period,

France supplied large quantities of goods by way of New England or the West Indies. France was then a neutral, and Britain shrank from seizing French vessels trading with the West Indies. Consequently, the United States had to keep open only the trade routes that linked its ports with the French islands. Small American vessels could elude British cruisers by sailing close to the continent and by darting into the numerous ports and inlets that dotted the coast from Savannah to Maine.

The foreign trade of the states reached its high point in the period from the middle of 1778 until 1782. Britain's military and naval tasks multiplied to the point where she could not maintain a tight blockade of the American coast. The trade of the Union with Europe and the non-British West Indies flourished, supplying an abundance of European goods and West Indian products.[10] However, during the last full year of the war, 1782, the states suffered heavy losses. By that time Britain had abandoned important military operations in America and had concentrated on attacks on American shipping. Entrenched at Savannah, Charleston, and New York, the Royal Navy sent cruisers that seized American vessels trading with the West Indies.

The merchant who best illustrates the wartime commerce of the states was Robert Morris of the Philadelphia firm of Willing and Morris. Well established in foreign trade by 1774, Morris, in December 1775, became a member of the Secret Committee of Congress, which he soon dominated. The Secret Committee made contracts with firms and individuals who undertook to supply it with military stores. Morris exposed himself to criticism because —while he was a member—the committee entered into contracts with his firm and because he enlisted agents of Congress overseas to participate in his private ventures. Such affiliations greatly increased his reputation and prestige abroad. His principal associates were Silas Deane at Paris and William Bingham at Martinique, a Philadelphia merchant who went there on government business in 1776.[11]

Willing and Morris sent flour, tobacco, and rice to Bingham, who exchanged them in Martinique for French goods, rum, sugar, molasses, and coffee, that were shipped to the partners in Philadelphia. Bingham forwarded the tobacco and rice to Silas Deane in Paris in payment for French goods that he had dispatched to Martinique. Willing and Morris disposed of the French products they received from Bingham either by general sales or by fulfilling contracts with Congress.[12]

Soon after the war began American merchants and Dutch traders mutually solicited business. Dutch-American commerce produced one of the striking features of the war—a lively trade carried on at St. Eustatius. Located about 180 miles southeast of Puerto Rico, that little island was so convenient a link between North America and Europe that the Dutch made it an open port where all nations might trade freely. Americans sought out the Dutch there at the start of the war. Trade grew steadily until, midway in the conflict, 3,182 vessels left the island during a period of thirteen months. Baltimore's ships sailing to the Dutch West Indies in 1780 totaled 4,900 tons. As an arsenal of the Revolution, St. Eustatius figured in Britain's decision of December 1780, to go to war against the Netherlands. The first important fruit of that decision was the conquest of the island, February 3, 1781, by a British fleet under Sir George Rodney. He found in the harbor a swarm of American privateers, captured British vessels, and American merchantmen, along with 2,000 American merchants and sailors. The British conquest, which netted between £2 million and £3 million in goods and vessels, ended the glory of this mecca of American commerce.[13]

Trade with the Dutch had yet another angle. It opened a channel by which Americans could import British goods when that importation was forbidden both by Britain and by Congress. A British publicist, Lord Sheffield, asserted that during the war large quantities of British goods reached the states via the West Indies and Nova Scotia. When Rodney occupied St. Eustatius he seized from British merchants there a large stock of goods on the assumption that they had come from or were bound to the states. Bermuda and the Bahamas were also intermediaries in a British-American trade.[14]

In 1780 Spain permitted the states to trade with her colonies in the West Indies. During the next two years, Philadelphia and the Chesapeake area exported large quantities of flour to Havana, the focal point in the traffic. Sugar, military stores, and coin came back in return. Baltimore merchants, it was said, got rich by selling flour at Havana for nine times as much as it had cost them. In 1780 they sent to Havana vessels aggregating only 100 tons; in 1782 the figure was 6,800 tons.[15]

The question now arises: how did the states find the means for paying for a large inflow of imports during the war? Before 1775, the thirteen colonies had always imported goods and services of a money value in excess of the value of their exports. Their difficulty of finding adequate means of payment for imports had long been at the root of their most acute problem of foreign trade. The Revolution intensified this problem, for the states experienced more difficulty in carrying on an export trade than in obtaining imports.

The states lost the services of British vessels that had previously transported most of their produce to Britain. In addition, privateering absorbed shipping that otherwise might have been devoted to an export trade. The states also lost their onetime highly important market in Britain for American-built ships. Thus vanished a principal source of New England's buying power abroad. In addition, the war prostrated the New England fishery, long a leading supplier of export products—fish for Spain, whale oil and whalebone for Britain, and fish for the West Indies, where the colonists had obtained money and produce that could be used for purchases in Europe.[16]

One American export—tobacco—towered above all others. Prewar shipments to Britain had amounted annually to about 100,000,000 pounds, four-fifths of which was re-exported, mainly to Europe. Northern merchants obtained tobacco by supplying the planters with European goods and West Indian products. The state governments of both Virginia and Maryland exported the staple in order to buy arms and powder. At St. Eustatius in 1777, tobacco alone would bring cash. Rodney seized much of it there in February 1781.

In the face of inadequate exports, the United States had to seek other sources of income in Europe. Relief came in three forms: subsidies, loans, and expenditures of the French forces in America. Thus the funds advanced by European countries helped to finance their exports to the Union and brought them its trade, at Britain's expense.[17] Maritime activity during the war invigorated the commercial life of the states. Many towns made notable progress. Baltimore's shipping to the foreign West Indies jumped from 4,500 tons in 1780 to 15,000 tons in 1782. So potent were the merchants who prospered during the war that they were able to exert a powerful influence in national politics between 1785 and 1800.

NOTES

1. Worthington C. Ford, et al, *Journals of the Continental Congress, 1774–1789*, I (Washington: GPO, 1904–37), pp. 76–77. 34 volumes.

2. Claude H. Van Tyne, "French Aid Before The Alliance of 1778," *American Historical Review*, XXXI (1925), pp. 20–40. *Editor's note:* Much of this material was transshipped through St. Domingue (Haiti).

3. *Editor's note:* See Robert G. Albion & Jennie B. Pope, *Sea Lanes in Wartime* (New York, 1942). Also French E. Chadwick, "Sea Power: The Decisive Factor in our Struggle for Independence," *Annual Report* (American Historical Association, 1915). (Washington, 1916).

4. Gardner W. Allen, *Massachusetts Privateers of the Revolution* (Cambridge, 1927). This is volume 77 of the Massachusetts Historical Society *Collections*.

5. See Sidney G. Morse, "State or Continental Privateers?" *American Historical Review*, LII (1946).

6. James Duncan Phillips, *Salem in the Eighteenth Century* (Boston: Houghton Mifflin Co., 1937), pp. 392–442; Helen Augur, *The Secret War of Independence* (New York, 1955).

7. Robert A. East, *Business Enterprise in the American Revolutionary Era* (New York, 1938), pp. 159–61.

8. William M. James, *The British Navy in Adversity* (London, 1926), pp. 415, 424–25.

9. Francis Wharton, ed., *The Revolutionary Diplomatic Correspondence of the United States*, II (Washington: GPO, 1889), pp. 262–63. 6 volumes.

10. James B. Hedges, *The Browns of Providence Plantations* (Cambridge, 1952), pp. 239, 251. *Editor's note:* See also Kenneth W. Porter, ed., *The Jacksons and the Lees* (Cambridge, 1937). 2 volumes. This work is volume 3 of the *Harvard Studies in Business History.*

11. Clarence L. Ver Steeg, *Robert Morris, Revolutionary Financier* (Philadelphia, 1954), pp. 10-20. *Editor's note:* See the early, sympathetic, biographical material in William G. Sumner, *The Financier and Finances of the American Revolution* (New York, 1891). 2 volumes.

12. Margaret L. Brown, "William Bingham, Agent of the Continental Congress in Martinique," *Pennsylvania Magazine of History and Biography,* LXI (1937).

13. Edward Channing, *A History of the United States,* III (New York: Macmillan & Co., 1905-1925), pp. 323, 325. 6 volumes. *Editor's note:* See also J. Franklin Jameson, "St. Eustatius in the American Revolution," *American Historical Review* VIII (1903), pp. 683-708.

14. *Editor's note:* For the workings of this trade, see Susie M. Ames, "A Typical Virginia Business Man of the Revolutionary Era: Nathaniel Savage," *Journal of Economic and Business History,* III (1931).

15. Robert A. East, *Business Enterprise in the Revolutionary Era* (New York, 1938), pp. 39, 59-63. *Editor's note:* Valuable information will be found in Emory R. Johnson, et al, *History of the Domestic and Foreign Commerce of the United States* (Washington, 1915). 2 volumes.

16. *Editor's note:* See especially Samuel E. Morison, *The Maritime History of Massachusetts* (Boston, 1921).

17. Rafael A. Bayley, *The National Loans of the United States, 1776-1880* (Washington: GPO, 1881).

LOWELL J. RAGATZ

THE SUGAR COLONIES DURING THE REVOLUTION

The intimate relationship of England's colonies in the western hemisphere has been explored during peace and international war. And then civil war. For such was the revolt, to a considerable extent, that broke out on the mainland. Even after Lexington and Concord many Americans, such as Governor John Trumbull, hopefully felt that "British supremacy and American liberty are not incompatible with each other." Historian Bryan Edwards, who spent a lifetime in Jamaica, expressed the view of one faction, similar in tone to that of an Otis or Jefferson, that West Indians were no less Englishmen than those living in England—and with a birthright which included the right of revolution. And they petitioned in support of their sister colonies to the north. Renny, in his History of Jamaica, *noted that the petition sent had a surprising boldness in asserting "that the colonists are not the subjects of the people of England, and consequently insist on their own right of legislation." But another historian of Jamaica (Reverend George Bridges) also noted that Jamaica offered this petition "with trembling hands of fearful impotency."*

The Jamaican petition reflected an apprehension felt throughout the British islands in the West Indies, especially after the decision by the Continental Congress to halt exportation to the islands after September 1775. The House of Commons demanded "proof" from the West Indian interests in London that acute distress would follow if concessions were not made and harmony restored. Parliament finally rejected the role of the "pampered Creolians" to attempt any sort of mediation.

From *The Fall of the Planter Class in the British Caribbean, 1763–1833.* The Century Co., 1928.

Suffice it to say that the depredations of the privateers, the eventual entry of France and Spain making war very immediate for so many of the islands, and the resultant scarcity of foodstuffs (exacerbated by a series of violent hurricanes) brought misery to most West Indians. This included the slave population, of which an estimated fifteen thousand died directly or indirectly from starvation. Truly, it could be said that the revolt of the mainland colonies gave all the European powers an excuse for renewed war, and most of their possessions in the western hemisphere could not escape the consequences. In the British islands the planter class did not fall, but in spite of Rodney's great victory over the Comte de Grasse in the famous Battle of the Saintes (1782), the plantation system, although it did not die with the so-called "First Empire," was rapidly expiring as the eighteenth century came to a close.

The planter and merchant interests in England and residents of the British West Indies followed the ominous course of the controversies between the home government and the mainland trans-Atlantic possessions after 1763 with growing apprehension. The threat of the latter to cut off commercial relations with Great Britain and her Caribbean holdings unless grievances were promptly adjusted changed their fear to open alarm. "Without frequent Supplies of Biscuits, Wheat Flour, Rice and Indian Corn from the Continent of America," wrote Sir Ralph Payne, governor of the Leeward Islands in June 1774, "the Inhabitants could not subsist." It was believed, however, that even if a policy of non-intercourse were officially adopted, enforcement would be impossible because of the number of Americans interested in the West India trade.

The decision of the first Continental Congress to close the ports of the thirteen colonies to British Caribbean produce from December 1, 1774, and to stop exportation to the islands after September 10, 1775, if its demands had not been met, adopted in September of the former year, roused both the West Indians and groups in the home country to action.

The Jamaican assembly took the remarkable step of championing colonial rights in general and of approaching the Crown as suitor in behalf of the North Americans. A petition voted at the close of its session in December 1774, professed profound loyalty to the king and denied the slightest intention of offering resistance to the British government, but held it to be an established principle of the Constitution that no part of His Majesty's subjects could legislate for any other part and that no law could bind Englishmen unless it had received the assent of their representatives. Parliament's claim of the right to legislate for the colonies was denied. The assembly lamented the exercise of such power in the past and, while accepting laws regulating the external commerce of the island, demanded that none injurious to its constituents' interests be enacted and forced upon them in the future. It furthermore stoutly declared that depriving colonials of equal rights with Englishmen at home dissolved their dependence upon the parent state and appealed to the sovereign to mediate between his British and his American subjects.[1]

This celebrated memorial was the work of the radical mercantile element from Kingston and was kept secret until the business of the session had been largely completed and conservative rural members from outlying parts of the island had left St. Jago de la Vega, the capital, in order to reach their estates before the opening of the holiday season during which Negro insurrections were always feared. It was presented when but twenty-six of the forty-three assemblymen were present, was passed despite the opposition of the speaker, and was sent to the governor for transmission but a few hours before prorogation.

Its arrival in Great Britain occasioned a storm. The Earl of Dartmouth, secretary of state for the American Department, fulminated against the "so indecent, not to say criminal conduct of the Assembly" and held that dire consequences would follow. The house of representatives of Connecticut and the Continental Congress on the other hand extended votes of thanks to the Jamaicans for their efforts in the cause of peace.[2]

A general meeting open to all persons having relations with the Caribbean colonies was held in the London Tavern, Bishopsgate Street, on January 18, 1775, to consider what measures should be taken for the preservation of common interests in the existing crisis. A petition to Parliament was determined upon, subscriptions to meet the expense attending it were called for, and copies were presented to the two houses early in February. These set forth the alarm felt over the late step taken by Congress, declared that British property in the West Indies valued at £30,000,000 sterling and shipping worth many millions more employed in trading with them would be endangered if free access to North American supplies were ended, predicted acute distress in the Caribbean coupled with a heavy falling off in the national revenue if the American agreement stood, and prayed for the adoption of such measure as would avert the threatened evil and restore the old harmony.

In the House of Commons, the matter was referred to a committee and, some weeks later, the West Indians were called upon to submit evidence in support of their contention that the sugar colonies were altogether dependent upon the thirteen mainland ones for supplies. Their memorial to the Lords fared worse. The Marquis of Rockingham sought to lay it and others

77

from North American traders before the upper chamber but was interrupted by the Earl of Dartmouth who desired the floor. Then followed a long and acrimonious debate on a point of order which became involved with the question of whether or not the Lords should support the Commons in an address to the throne on affairs in America declaring rebellion to exist there. At length the Marquis moved that the grievances be considered and, when a division was taken in the early hours of the morning, the motion was lost, 104 to 29. Immediately after, by an affirmative vote almost as large, it was decided to join in the address. Eighteen members protested against the refusal to hear the petitioners but to no avail. The commencement of hostilities shortly after brought to an end all hope of a settlement through West Indian intervention.

The military and naval events in the Caribbean during the period of the Revolution are in themselves of less consequence for our purpose than are the results which flowed from them. Throughout the war, considerable difficulty was experienced in getting the Jamaican assembly to meet the expense of quartering troops. That body steadily refused to provide new barracks and showed great resentment over the frequency with which the militia was called out. Barbados possessed a turbulent lower house which was constantly challenging the governor's authority in an effort to get power into its own hands and numerous untoward incidents occurred. But all of the British islands remained loyal to the mother country.

During the first phase of the struggle, the sugar colonies were in no actual danger from aggression. A Negro insurrection in Jamaica was nipped in the bud and thirty blacks were executed as an example. The foolhardy proposal of Silas Deane, to further incite the slaves of the island to rebellion and to stir up the Caribs of St. Vincent, was fortunately barren of results. But the war was felt from the first; heavy loss and expense attended the depredations of privateers swarming in the Caribbean; and hardships and even suffering arose from the shortage of supplies.

To reduce captures under letters of marque, the Society of West India Merchants arranged with the Lords of the Admiralty for the convoying of both outward-bound and incoming merchantmen. Notice was given traders and ship owners of the appointed places and dates of departure, protection was afforded from the Downs to Caribbean waters and return and losses were thus reduced to a minimum. . . .

The quantity of mainland supplies in the sugar colonies at the outbreak of the war was large and prices were low. "Provisions of all kinds from the continent of America are cheaper and more plentiful than they have been in the memory of man," declared Governor Payne of the Leewards. Governor Hay of Barbados reported them never so cheap as in May 1775 and wrote a year later "It is wished to talk of Famine, in the most plentiful Island of all the West Indies, and where I, who have no plantation and must buy all the provisions for my Table, can assure your Lordship that scarcely One Article of provisions and live Stock of the Island has varied in price for near these three Years that I have been here." Barbadian warehouses were "crammed full" a short time after. Grenada, too, was well supplied with beef and flour. Several vessels arriving there in the fall of 1776 soon departed in search of better markets. Dominica, on the contrary, suffered from scarcity as early as the beginning of that year. However, highly favorable as conditions in general were, the entire cutting-off of shipments from the principal source of supply made an ultimate widespread shortage of plantation stores inevitable.

That it was not more immediate was due to several causes. An act of Parliament prohibiting intercourse with the rebellious colonies and formally closing the mainland-West Indian trade was accompanied by elaborate regulations governing the condemnation and sale of captured ships in Caribbean vice-admiralty courts. These provided a fairly regular means of supply for some time, especially after the opening of commercial relations between the United States and the foreign tropical American possessions by resolution of Congress in October 1775 in an attempt to secure ammunition and guns.

Distress was also to some extent averted by the local cultivation of ground crops, by increased importations from Great Britain and Ireland, and by the development of commercial relations with the French and Spanish Caribbean. From the first, considerable tracts normally employed in cane growing were turned to the production of foodstuffs. The act providing for the sale of prize cargoes in the sugar colonies was followed by another authorizing the sending out of 100,000 quarters of wheat and its products from London, Bristol, Liverpool, and Glasgow to them during 1776. This was subsequently renewed annually.

But the relief thus afforded did not meet expectations. The assembly of Barbados declared with its customary querulousness in the fall of 1776, "Whatever may have been the provident care of his Majesty and both Houses of Parliament, in the prohibitory act in our favour, yet we are not sensible that the inhabitants of this Island have actually received the least benefit from such indulgence; and from the other act, to allow the exportation of wheat from England to the East and West Indies, the benefit is yet to be received."

Representations of Barbadian planters to the British government, made late in 1777, that famine loomed, accompanied by loud calls for aid, resulted in the sending out of a provision fleet to the island by the Lords of the Treasury with directions that the supplies be disposed of by the governor and council at prime cost with no freight charge. Six vessels with cargoes of flour, beans, and peas, accompanied by two laden with fish, arrived early in 1778.[3] . . .

The removal of restrictions on the trade of Ireland with the West Indies in 1778, whereby the direct exportation of Irish produce and of most kinds of manufactures was authorized and Irish woolens were placed on a footing with British ones, tended to increase the supply of provisions in the sugar islands.[4] The first year that the new regulations were in force they depended solely on Ireland for salted meats. The freeing of the Spanish trade in 1778 likewise, for a short time, gave the British planters further access to stores. Unfortunately for them, the declaration of war between Great Britain and Spain almost immediately thereafter once more closed the ports of Cuba, Puerto Rico, and the Main to them.[5]

But the opening of such new sources of supply in no way compensated for the cutting off of the American trade, and a shortage of provisions and lumber was evident by the close of 1776. A temporary embargo on exports of mainland produce was laid in St. Kitts in December 1775; this was made permanent five months later, and the exportation of Negro clothing and woolen goods was soon similarly prohibited. A fire which consumed Basseterre in 1776 destroyed most of the stores in the island and, because no relief could be secured from the nearby colonies, an appeal for assistance was sent to the Crown.

The situation throughout the Leewards became critical; actual famine set in. In a private letter to Lord Germain, Governor Burt wrote from Antigua at the close of 1777, "At Montserrat they were reduced to such distress that not a Morsel of Bread was to be had in the Island for a Day or two. Luckily a Sloop went from hence with Flower, since that they have scarcely had from hand to mouth. Many Negroes have Starved, the same has happn'd in Nevis. Here & at St. Christophers we have not been so Bad but in great Want. . . ." In another letter, written from St. Kitts in the following spring, "From the best information I have been able to collect, The Island of Antigua has lost above a thousand Negroes, Montserrat near twelve Hundred, & some Whites—Nevis three or four Hundred, & This Island as many from the Want of Provisions. . . . during our Distress I received from Montserrat Intelligence they had not a Morsel of Bread in that Island and that for three Successive Days Hundreds of People came to Town in Search of it & returned Empty."

The scarcity of supplies in Barbados brought to a head differences which had been brewing between Governor Edward Hay and the assembly since soon after his arrival. The lower house of the legislature contained a number of assertive individuals; the governor was a willful and self-centered official with little knowledge of colonial affairs and with but slight understanding of the Caribbean viewpoint. When Captain Payne, a British officer, arrived soon after to purchase provisions and livestock for the consumption of royal forces at Boston, he was allowed to draw on stocks as he saw fit. This occasioned great resentment among the Barbadians. . . . The Negroes and poor whites even then on the point of starvation [were] compelled to plunder and pillage for the means of subsistence while all were facing the immediate future with alarm.

* * *

The increased cost of supplies and of marketing bore heavily on the Barbadians. In 1778 the colony was "decayed and impoverished," credit had ceased and trade was very low. "The inhabitants," wrote Governor Hay, "seem to be much in a desponding way. . . . Many others are much involved." During all this time, the conflict between governor and assembly grew more bitter; it was ultimately carried to such lengths that the popular body steadfastly refused to reform the militia and to provide fortifications and the conflict ended only with Hay's death in 1779.[6]

In Jamaica the situation was less critical though there, too, the scarcity was severely felt. An embargo on the exportation of provisions was already in force in January 1776, and the request of the Count d'Ennery, governor of St. Domingo, to be permitted to purchase stores in the island was courteously but firmly refused. But two years later provisions were more plentiful. The mercantile class then petitioned the governor to remove the embargo and this was subsequently done.

On the whole, the experience of the first period of the war demonstrated the truth of the planters' claims regarding their dependence upon free access to American supplies, and facts were against those few individuals who still professed to see no ground for serious alarm in a derangement of the old relations with the mainland.

The entry of the French into the war in 1778 as allies of the Americans and the outbreak of hostilities between Spain and England a year later greatly changed the British planters' position for the worse. Hitherto in safety in a military sense, they were now directly attacked; and food and lumber from the French and Spanish possessions, which had alleviated their distress in the past, were at the same time cut off.

It was the foregone conclusion that the conflict would be carried to the Caribbean. The Continental Congress had authorized its commissioners seeking an alliance with France to promise that power [France] any British sugar colonies which might be captured by Franco-American action. A proposal made to the West India merchants of London that they interest themselves in a separate neutrality for the islands, was met with the declaration that this was impracticable. Early in 1778 confidential information that war seemed unavoidable was sent to the British governors, and they were directed to prepare in every way possible for the defence of their territories.[7]

Few of the West India islands were in any position to resist attack. On September 7, 1778, Dominica, lying between Guadeloupe and Martinique, protected by only forty-six regulars including officers and 150 militia men with almost worthless weapons, and weakened by the presence of a considerable number of French planters, capitulated to an expeditionary force from the latter island. A few months later, St. Lucia fell before the British whom it served as a naval base throughout the war.[8] The conquest of St. Lucia was one of the few British successes in the war. In 1779 both Grenada and St. Vincent were lost.

Without access to stores in the French and Spanish Caribbean, the Leeward Islanders' distress became acute. "Previous to the arrival of the Cork Fleet on Wednesday last . . . there was not one Barrel of any kind of Salted Meat for sale," declared the legislature of Antigua to Governor Burt in April 1779. Long-continued lack of rain rendered the situation of the Antiguans even more deplorable than the mere scarcity of supplies would have.

A disheartening series of natural disasters in 1780 and 1781 brought widespread ruin in its wake. In the autumn of the former year two terrific hurricanes, an earthquake, and a tidal wave ravaged the West Indies; another tropical storm in 1781 was almost as destructive. Jamaica and Barbados were especially hard hit. Losses ran into the millions sterling. In Barbados alone deaths exceeded 3,000; Bridgetown was all but totally destroyed. Starvation was averted in that island and in St. Lucia only by the timely arrival from the Leewards of 1,300 barrels of the flour sent by the Crown to relieve Antigua.[9] In Jamaica, surplus military stores were placed at the planters' disposal and rice and corn were imported from Georgia and South Carolina, but, to add to the misery of the residents, fire destroyed much of Kingston and a good share of the supplies there, causing a further loss of £400,000 sterling. Famine soon made its appearance and some thousands of Negroes perished of starvation.[10]

Early in the war, St. Eustatius had become an entrepôt for supplying the Americans with manufactured goods and military supplies while the British planters received from there at greatly enhanced prices a considerable part of the mainland provisions and lumber which reached them. The trade carried on in the Danish Virgins was insignificant by comparison, yet the Danish West India Company, trading to them, declared repeated 100 percent dividends in the period of the Revolution.[11]

* * *

The seizure of St. Eustatius was followed by one of the greatest auction sales in history. Naval stores were sent to Antigua, provisions to Jamaica, and West Indian and American produce to the home country, but all goods of European origin were put on the block. Under the promise of protection and clear title to purchasers of all nations, British Caribbean merchants and agents representing French and American buyers flocked to the island. So great was the quantity of commodities offered that there was little competition between bidders and lots on the average sold at one fourth of their value. Supplies became more plentiful throughout all the British colonies than they had been at any time since the outbreak of the war.[12]

* * *

The outcry raised against Rodney and Vaughan in the British Caribbean was tremendous. A resolution before the assembly of St. Kitts sought to bring their action to the king's attention. The West India merchants in London likewise took a hand in the matter and presented a remonstrance to the Crown. In May and again in December 1781, Burke moved the opening of a parliamentary inquiry into the confiscations made, declaring them to have been contrary to the law of nations and holding that, in consequence of the sale, the enemy had been provided with much-needed supplies at low cost. Making use of the loss of the island to the French in November 1781, he accused the commanders of having wasted their time in commercial operation instead of having followed up their military success and charged them with having profited personally thereby.

The position of the French by the close of 1781 thoroughly alarmed the West Indians in Great Britain. The government was repeatedly called upon to provide naval and military reinforcements sufficient to defend properly the colonies and a similar address was made to the Crown. Nor were these fears without foundation. The first quarter of 1782 saw a continuation of French successes. The inhabitants of St. Kitts capitulated in February after a spectacular defence of their fortress-citadel, Brimstone Hill;[13] Montserrat and Nevis fell shortly after. All of the Leeward Islands, excepting Antigua alone were then in the hands of the enemy, as were St. Vincent, Grenada, and Tobago. Demerara, Essequibo, and Berbice were lost. Attacks on Antigua, Barbados, and Jamaica by the united Franco-Spanish sea forces were momentarily expected; the outlook for the British planters was dark indeed when, on April 12, a victory by Rodney over the French fleet commanded by de Grasse suddenly turned the tables.

This celebrated marine battle (Battle of the Saintes), fought between Martinique and Guadeloupe, introduced a new maneuver made possible by a sudden shift of wind, "breaking the enemy's line" instead of engaging the foe in the traditional mere artillery duel. It at the same time reestablished British naval supremacy and saved her sugar colonies to Great Britain. Largely in consequence of Rodney's memorable success, his country secured the restoration of all her captured colonies but Tobago, while she returned St. Lucia to France upon the reestablishment of a peace a year later.[14]

At the same time that they were being plunged into acute distress by the lack of supplies, by increased costs of marketing, by natural disasters, and by enemy successes, the British planters suffered yet further misfortunes through increased customs charges being laid against produce entering the mother country and from their increasing inability to dispose of crops there for lack of carriers. . . . The closing of American markets and the departure of a smaller number of freighters for Great Britain each year made it impossible for the planters to place all of their produce and worked great hardships. A large share of the annual production of rum and molasses had been regularly sold in the thirteen colonies but from the outbreak of revolution their exportation was authorized only under license and then merely to the few ports in British hands. As Lord Howe soon complained that the rebels were being supplied through improper use of such papers, no further permits were issued except to contractors supplying the king's forces and sales fell off sharply. Even though the clearing out of rum for the use of civilians in occupied territory was later authorized, following representations on the subject by the West India traders in London, only a fraction of what had once been shipped was sent to the mainland after 1776.

NOTES

1. "Memorial from the General Assembly of Jamaica Relative to the Present State of American Affairs," in *The Gentleman's Magazine*, Supplement for 1775, pp. 617, 618. See also the summary of a thesis by J. W. Herbert, "Constitutional Struggles in Jamaica, 1748–1776," in *Bulletin of the Institute of Historical Research* (June 1928), pp. 36–39.
2. Peter Force, ed., *American Archives*, 4th series, II, 1891 (Washington, 1837–53), p. 108. 9 volumes.
3. *Editor's note:* John Poyer, *The History of Barbados* (London, 1808).
4. For the nature of the Irish-West Indian trade see *Debates Relative to the Affairs of Ireland, in the Years 1763 and 1764* (London, 1766), pp. 769 ff. 2 volumes.
5. Ricardo Levene, "Comercio de Indias, Antecedentes Legales (1713–1778)," in *Documentos para la Historia Argentina*, V, xxvi–xxxv (Buenos Aires, 1915).
6. John Poyer, *The History of Barbados* (London, 1808). See pp. 372 ff.
7. The matter of keeping war out of the two groups of West India colonies had been under frequent consideration since earliest days. See index to Charles S. Higham, *The Development of the Leeward Islands under the Restoration, 1660–1688; a Study of the Foundations of the Old Colonial System* (Cambridge, 1921). *Editor's note:* See also Charles S. Higham, *History of the British Empire* (London, 1931). 4th edition revised and enlarged.
8. For the importance of this colony from the French point of view, see Daniel Chardon, *Essai sur la Colonie de Saint-Lucie* (Neuchatel, 1779). *Editor's note:* See also Colin Lindsay, "Narrative of Events in the Island of St. Lucie," in

A Military Miscellaney, II (London, 1793), pp. 441–83. 2 volumes. Also published in Alexander Lindsay's *Lives of the Lindsays*, III (London, 1840), pp. 195–235. 4 volumes.

9. See Anonymous, *Dreadful Effects of a Hurricane Which Happened at Barbados in 1780* (London, n.d.). "Brief Account of the Desolation Made in Several of the West India Islands by the Late Hurricanes," in *The Gentleman's Magazine*, Supplement for 1780, pp. 620–23. Anonymous, *A History of Jamaica and Barbados, with an Authentic Account of the Lives Lost, and the Damage Sustained in Each Island, by the late Hurricanes* (London, 1781). Mr. Fowler, *A General Account of the Calamities occasioned by the Late Tremendous Hurricanes and Earthquakes in the West-India Islands* (London, 1781).

10. Report of a committee of the assembly of Jamaica, quoted in Edwards, *History*, II, p. 413.

11. Thomas Southey, *Chronological History of the West Indies*, III (London, 1827), p. 6. 3 volumes.

12. J. Franklin Jameson, "St. Eustatius and the American Revolution," *The American Historical Review*, VIII (1903), pp. 683–708.

13. The story is well told in Algernon Aspinall's *West Indian Tales of Old* (London, 1912).

14. The maneuver "breaking the enemy's line" gave rise to a discussion which was the occasion for an acrimonious pamphlet war half a century later. One of the finest accounts of this battle is to be found in Alfred T. Mahan's *Major Operations of the Navies in the War of American Independence* (New York, 1913). A good popular account is in W. Adolphe Roberts' *French in the West Indies* (Indianapolis, 1942). *Editor's note.*

J. FRANKLIN JAMESON

ST. EUSTATIUS IN THE AMERICAN REVOLUTION

No collection of essays on the subject of the American Revolution and the West Indies would be complete without the seminal work of one of America's most distinguished historians, J. Franklin Jameson, which appeared in the American Historical Review *early in this century. No scholar has quite repeated this masterpiece on the role of St. Eustatius during the war for independence. Modern scholars would do well to use a similar approach with respect to the interplay of forces after 1775 with respect to other areas of the West Indies. With reference to St. Eustatius, in the words of Jameson, "It is a tale worth telling . . . on account of . . . the important part which it played in enabling our forefathers to sustain that difficult and unequal struggle."*

As the reader will surmise, St. Eustatius not only played a vital role in bringing help to the colonies in revolt, but also became the excuse for England to finally declare war on Holland. Some historians stress the fact that when the English fished the secret documents of Henry Laurens out of the Atlantic waters (on his way to Holland to arrange a treaty for aid), war was precipitated. Actually the Laurens fiasco simply ignited the fuse which had been set when Holland gave John Paul Jones the freedom of its ports after his depredations in the waters around England.

Admiral Rodney had no illusions as to the value of St. Eustatius to the enemies of England. "This rock," declared Rodney, "has done England more harm than all the arms of her most potent enemies." In addition it had the reputation of having been the first to salute the thirteen stripes

From "St. Eustatius in the American Revolution," *American Historical Review*, VIII, 1903.

when the Andrew Doria *arrived in November of 1776. And had not Captain Isaiah Robinson been "most graciously received by all ranks of the people."*

Rodney's blow, as he expressed it, "was as sudden as a clap of thunder." 'Statia never recovered, and today lies in green quiet off the beaten tracks of the West Indies. Yet it is the only island not under the American flag to annually celebrate the American Revolution—not on July 4, but on November 16, the day the thirteen stripes of the Andrew Doria *were saluted. And in the era of the Bicentennial there are mothers who still handle their naughty children with the threat that "Rodney will catch you if you don't behave."*

Some islands are, because of their geographical situation, destined by nature to be permanently the home of extensive commerce. Such are Manhattan, Hong Kong, and Singapore. Others are so placed that political circumstances may for a brief period, or during the continuance of a particular war, elevate them into sudden commercial greatness and give them a short but picturesque career of prosperity, while ill winds blow on harbors usually more favored. A familiar example is that of Nassau during the American Civil War. But seldom has an island port had a more meteoric career, or shown a more striking contrast between insignificance in time of peace and resounding prosperity in war-time, than that presented by the little volcanic island of St. Eustatius. Its tale is worth telling, partly on this account, partly on account of the close association of its fortunes with those of the American Revolutionary War, and the important part which it played in enabling our forefathers to sustain that difficult and unequal struggle.

St. Eustatius is a small rocky island near the northeast corner of the West Indian chain. It is neither large nor fertile. Its area is less than seven square miles; and at the time of the Revolution it did not produce more than six hundred barrels of sugar a year. It had but one landing place, and its fortifications had never been important. But its relative position was such as to give it, in the hands of the Dutch, exceptional advantages. . . . Under the old system of colonial management, typified by the Navigation Act, each country persisted in the endeavor to monopolize to itself the commerce of its colonies, whether continental or insular. But the Dutch had early been converted to the principles of colonial free trade. Accordingly St. Eustatius, a free port belonging to a highly commercial nation and set in the midst of English, French, Danish, and Spanish colonies, then rich and prosperous, but managed on the restrictive system which prevailed before Adam Smith, had even in times of peace the opportunity to become an important mart of trade.

... There can be no better description of its rise than that which Burke gave in the House of Commons. The island, he said, "was different from all others. It seemed to have been shot up from the ocean by some convulsion, the chimney of a volcano, rocky and barren. It had no produce.... It seemed to be but a late production of nature, a sort of *lusus naturae,* hastily framed, neither shapen nor organized, and differing in qualities from all other. Its proprietors had, in the spirit of commerce, made it an emporium for all the world; a mart, a magazine for all the nations of the earth.... Its inhabitants were a mixed body of all nations and climates; not reduced to any species of military duty or military discipline. Its utility was its defence. The universality of its use, the constant neutrality of its nature, which made it advantageous to all the nations of the world, was its security and its safeguard. It had risen, like another Tyre, upon the waves, to communicate to all countries and climates the conveniences and the necessaries of life. Its wealth was prodigious, arising from its industry, and the nature of its commerce."

... Let us go back to the beginning of the war, and especially to the days before the French alliance, when as yet the contest was merely one between Great Britain and her revolted colonies and had not widened into a European war. On the whole the best source for a knowledge of doings at St. Eustatius during those early days is the correspondence of Sir Joseph Yorke, British ambassador at The Hague, with the secretaries of state and other officials in London. A large mass of copies from that correspondence is to be found among manuscripts of Jared Sparks in the library of Harvard University, and another among the papers of George Bancroft at the Lenox Library.... His letters, when combined with such materials as we may obtain from other sources, afford a striking picture of the use made of St. Eustatius by the Americans, and must, I think, convince us that the island played a far greater part in the economy of the Revolution than most persons suppose.

In the first place, the war, and the non-importation agreements which preceded it, had cut off at one blow the supply of British manufactures to the American colonies. It was true that the native American inventiveness would in time supply their place. The mute inglorious "hired man," who could do anything with a jackknife, the versatile Jonas of Mr. Abbott's fancy, would blossom forth as the Yankee inventor. But this would take time; and in the meanwhile it was very convenient to have in the neutral islands of the West Indies a means of temporary supply and a market for American exports. The trade ventures of states as well as of individuals were often carried on this way. As early as March 1776, we find Abraham van Bibber, agent of the state of Maryland at St. Eustatius, taking care of cargoes sent or underwritten by the state. In the archives of Virginia there are letters from him, addressed to the Virginia Committee of Safety. In June of the same year Van Bibber of St. Eustatius and Richard Harrison of Martinique announce that they have formed a partnership, and solicit from the Virginia committee a portion of their custom.

After France entered into the war, French carriers and French islands like Martinique became ineligible and the position of the Dutch neutrals became doubly profitable. Merchants of the neighboring British islands tried to keep their goods safe in case of French attack by storing them on St. Eustatius. John Adams, writing to the president of Congress in 1779, after his return from his first mission to Europe, mentions the growing trade through that island as a reason which may justify the attempt to cultivate closer diplomatic relations with the republic of the United Netherlands, relations which he afterwards did so much to promote. The close diplomatic intimacy between Great Britain and Portugal enabled British armed vessels, secure of a shelter in the ports of the latter country, to cruise off the Azores and in other situations well adapted for checking the voyages of French and Spanish vessels to the West Indies; which of course threw West Indian commerce more and more into the hands of the Dutch and of St. Eustatius. A Dutch rear-admiral, who spent thirteen months there in 1778 to 1779, reports that 3,182 vessels sailed from the island during the time of his stay. A careful English observer declared that in 1779 some 12,000 hogsheads of tobacco and 1,500,000 ounces of indigo came to it from North America to be exchanged against naval supplies and other goods from Europe. British traders, too, under the guise of voyages to St. Christoper, embarked in ventures to the neighboring Dutch emporium, careful however to take out separate policies of insurance on the two voyages from England to St. Christopher and from thence to St. Eustatius. Indeed, in 1780 an act was passed encouraging in some particulars the trade with the neutral islands, though of course not purporting to countenance in any way the trade thence to the revolted colonies.

* * *

But such shifting of trade routes is a part of the ordinary fortunes of war. The enrichment of the Dutch West Indies would not necessarily have been a great grievance to the British mind. What excited the English administration to a violent pitch of resentment against St. Eustatius was the fact that it was made the means of an enormous export of military supplies to the American armies, and later of naval supplies to the maritime forces arrayed against England in the Caribbean. It was true that, as early as March 20, 1775, the States General of the United Netherlands, at Yorke's instance, had issued a proclamation, following upon the British Orders in Council of the preceding October, forbidding the exportation of warlike stores of ammunition to the British colonies in America, or to any place without permission of one of the Colleges of Admiralty. But even before the earlier, or British, prohibition, and before the meeting of the first Continental Congress, the movement had begun. By the end of the year 1774 it was noted that there had lately been a prodigious increase in the trade from St. Eustatius. ... It is familiar to what straits the Continental army was often reduced for want of gunpowder, and how Congress, in October 1775, recommended the assemblies and conventions of the states to export provisions to the foreign West Indies in order to get arms and ammunition.

Early in March 1776, a merchant at Campveere writes Yorke that a favorite way in which to take ammunition to the Americans is to load for the coast of Africa but then go to St. Eustatius, where, says he, "their cargoes, being the most proper assortments, are instantly bought up by the American agents." Yorke writes to Lord Suffolk, the secretary of state, later in the same month, that the high price of powder is proving a great temptation to the Dutch merchants. ... In April the profit on gunpowder at the island is reported as one hundred and twenty percent. Lord Suffolk writes to the ambassador that Isaac van Dam, a merchant of the island, is the principal agent of correspondence with the rebels, and that recently, having procured from a trader in Martinique and from a smuggling vessel belonging to Antigua more than 4,000 pounds of powder, he had forwarded it to North Carolina in a Virginian vessel. Afterward he had sent £2,000 to France to buy more powder, to be sent out to North America by way of his island. A little later Van Dam is reported as having said, before his death, that he had carried on this trade on behalf of Frenchmen. The Rotterdam merchant already mentioned reports to Lord Suffolk that the last powder sent out ... is sent disguised in tea-chests, rice barrels, and the like; and that, according to what he hears, eighteen Dutch ships had already gone out this year (this was in May 1776) with powder and ammunition for the American market. Harrison sends 6,000 pounds from Martinique, and then slips over to St. Eustatius and sends 14,100 pounds more. ... Later a single vessel is reported as taking out 49,000 pounds.

Evidently no inconsiderable portion of the powder which the American army shot away, to more or less purpose, in this memorable year 1776, came into its hands in the devious way which has been indicated. In short, Yorke writes to William Eden in this same month of May, St. Eustatius is the rendezvous of everything and everybody meant to be clandestinely conveyed to America. It is easy to get oneself carried thither, and military adventurers of all nations have congregated at the island. ...

It is not to be supposed that the ambassador permitted these underhand dealings to pass unchallenged. ... But the constitution of the Dutch Republic was incredibly complicated, and its system of legislation and execution was so cumbersome and dilatory that hardly by anything short of miracle was it possible to get anything done. Moreover, while most people, he thought, condemned the trade, large numbers were interested in it, the great city of Amsterdam especially so; and Van Berckel, the pensionary of Amsterdam, a statesman of great influence, constantly exerted himself to thwart the ambassador of Great Britain.

The Dutch prohibitions, such as they were, expired in the autumn.... The States General issued a proclamation forbidding, under the same penalties as before, for one year from October 10, 1776, the exportation of warlike stores or ammunition to the revolted colonies, or in British ships to any place. But that no great things were expected from this decree, or achieved by it, is evident from Suffolk's suggestion, soon after its passage, that no larger amount of military stores be allowed to be sent to the Dutch West Indies than the average annual export in years before the war.... Yorke writes in a tone of constant exasperation. The trade goes on, mostly in ships lightly armed, with twelve or fourteen guns and from eighteen to twenty-four men and boys, just enough to gain the favor of the underwriters, for they could beat off a small privateer, though not the least of the British sloops.

* * *

The governor of the island, thought by the English to favor the smugglers, was replaced in the middle of the year by the secretary, Johannes de Graaff; but the new governor did no better. The port was opened without reserve to American ships. Van Bibber writes to the Maryland Council of Safety November 5, 1776, urging them to send all their vessels to St. Eustatius rather than to any other island, "as the Dutch have discover'd that their laws when put in force must ruin their Merchants. I am on the best terms with His Excellency the Governour and have his word and Promise relative to some particulars that gives me great Satisfaction and puts much in our powers. I was not so happy some time agoe, and every bad consequence to apprehend on our new Governour's taking the Command, but we are as well fixed with him now as we were with the former." Two weeks later he writes: "Our Flag flys current every day in the road. The Merchants here are always complaining of Government untill they would give as much Protection and Indulgence here to us as the French and Spaniards do.... The Governour is daily expressing the greatest desire and Intention to protect a trade with us here. Indeed they begin to discover their Mistake and are now very jealous of the French's running away with all their trade."

Between the dates of these two letters an event occurred which raised

91

British exasperation to the highest point. On the sixteenth of November, 1776, a vessel of the infant Continental navy, the *Andrew Doria,* Captain Isaiah Robinson, flying the flag of thirteen stripes, dropped anchor in the road of St. Eustatius and saluted Fort Orange with eleven guns; and the salute was returned. This has been claimed as the first occasion on which the American flag was saluted in a foreign port. But a letter written from the Danish island of St. Croix to Vice-Admiral Young, on October 27 preceding, after mentioning the departure of an unnamed American schooner with a small cargo of powder two days before, adds: "But my astonishment was great to find such a Commerce countenanced by Government here. The Vessel went out under Amer[N] Colours, saluted the Fort and had the compliment returned the same as if she had been an English or Danish ship."[1]

But the incident at St. Eustatius was more conspicious. The *Andrew Doria* was a Continental vessel. Van Bibber reported that her commander was "most graciously received by his Honour and all Ranks of People. Its esteemed here by the first Gentlemen a favour and Honour to be Introduced to Capt. Robertson. All American Vessells here now wear the Congress Coulours. Tories sneak and shrink before the Honest and Brave Americans here." Whatever effect may have been produced on Dutchmen or on Tories by the arrival and the reception of the *Andrew Doria,* it roused the president of St. Christopher to vivid indignation. Summing up in one angry remonstrance the various violations of neutrality which he had observed from his neighboring island, and commenting with especial severity upon the salute, he sent the document solemnly to De Graaff by the hand of a member of his council. At the same time he sent indignant representations to the secretary of state in London, fortified by affidavits.[2] . . .

President Greathead also commented severely on the open encouragement and protection which the rebels received at the Dutch island, the constant equipping and fitting-out of privateers to prey on British commerce, and especially on the incident of the sloop *Baltimore Hero,* said to be half-owned by Abraham van Bibber, and flying the flag of the Continental Congress, which on November 21, almost within range of the guns of Fort Orange, had taken a British brigantine and then returned to the road of St. Eustatius, with flag flying, and there received every sign of aid and protection.

But after all, the greatest offense was the salute, or as Lord Suffolk put it, the honor paid to a rebel brigantine carrying the flag of the rebel Congress, and the governor's insolence and folly in replying to the remonstrance of the president of St. Christopher that he is "far from betraying any partiality between Great Britain and her North American colonies." Such conduct from the representative of a state allied to Great Britain by several treaties was not to be overlooked. The secretary of state sent over to Sir Joseph Yorke a memorial which was forthwith presented to the States General, but which was conceived in a peremptory style not usual in the mutual communications of friendly states. . . .

In fact, the measures deemed appropriate had already been taken. Six days before the memorial had been presented at The Hague the lords of the admiralty had been instructed to order the commander-in-chief on the Leeward Islands station to post cruisers off the road of St. Eustatius, search all Dutch ships for arms, ammunition, clothing, or materials for clothing, and send those ships which were found to contain such things into some port of the Leeward Islands, there to be detained till further orders; and these injunctions were maintained for six weeks.

But the Dutch Republic . . . was in no condition to resent effectively the tone of English memorials. Their reply disavows their governor's actions in so far as they might seem to imply a recognition of American independence, and they required him to come home and explain his conduct. He was more than a year in coming, pleading age, the fear of seasickness, the recent illness of his family and himself; and meanwhile the salutes went on. . . .

In July 1778, De Graaff at last reached home. Called upon to defend his whole course as governor, so far as it related to the North American colonies, he presented in February a verbose *apologia pro vita sua,* in which he endeavored to clear himself of all the accusations raised by Greathead and Yorke. He declared that he had never connived at trade in munitions of war . . . that the salute of the *Andrew Doria* had, by his orders, been returned with two less guns than she fires, that this was the usual return-salute to merchant vessels, and implied no recognition of American independence . . . that it had been his custom to require incoming American vessels to give bonds for due observance of neutrality while in the port; that he had compelled all persons on the island possessing gunpowder to take oath that they would not export it to North America.

A committee of the directors of the West India Company, appointed to hear his defense, reported to the States General that it was perfectly satisfactory, and that the facts which he had adduced showed that there was ground of complaint rather against the British commanders for their conduct toward the Dutch settlements and subjects in the West Indies than against the latter. De Graaff went out again as governor, and conducted himself so acceptably to the Americans that two of their privateers were named after him and his lady; and his portrait, presented sixty years afterward by an American citizen grateful for the "first salute," hangs in the New Hampshire statehouse.[3] Of his defense no more need now be said than that an observance of neutrality which gave to the one belligerent such absolute contentment and to the other such unqualified dissatisfaction can hardly have been perfect.

Accordingly, when Sir George Rodney, sent out to command on the Leeward Islands station, arrived in the West Indies in the spring of 1780, the situation was still exceedingly strained. . . . He seems at that time to have conceived a deep feeling of hostility against the island. "This rock," he afterward declared, "of only six miles in length and three in breadth, has done England more harm than all the arms of her most potent enemies, and alone supported the infamous American rebellion." In August, after he had sailed to New York, Captain Robinson, one of his officers, seized several American vessels under the very guns of the fort on the Dutch part of the little island of St. Martin, and threatened to burn fort and town if any resistance were made. De Graaff represented that the loss would be great if the English persisted in the new stringency which Rodney seems to have introduced; and private letters from St. Eustatius said that numbers of the Americans settled there had left the place for fear of being seized, the governor declaring that he could not protect them. John Adams thought that the amount of American property remaining on the island at the time of its capture was not great. Then came the great hurricane of October 1780, which destroyed between four and five thousand people and nearly if not quite all the dwelling-houses in the town.

But the time had now come when the Dutch West Indies were to be drawn, even more intimately than hitherto, into the widening circle of the European war. The feeling between England and Holland, owing to the position of the Dutch as the chief neutral carriers during the war which England was waging against France, Spain, and the United States, and to the inevitable disputes as to the doctrine that "free ships make free goods"—a doctrine here complicated by treaty stipulations between the two states—was rapidly growing worse and worse. At the same time the Armed Neutrality of 1780 was arraying the northern powers of Europe in diplomatic hostility against England. The Netherlands government seemed likely to accede to it. . . . At this juncture the capture of Henry Laurens and the discovery among his papers of a projected Dutch-American treaty afforded a pretext for forcing hostilities. The paper was but a draft, unexecuted and unauthorized; but it was signed by an agent of the Continental Congress and an agent of the hated city of Amsterdam. Two peremptory memorials were presented to the States General by Sir Joseph Yorke, demanding a formal disavowal of the conduct of the magistrates of Amsterdam, "a prompt satisfaction, proportioned to the offence, and an exemplary punishment on the pensionary Van Berkel and his accomplices, as disturbers of the public peace and violators of the law of nations." . . .

The disavowal was promptly forthcoming. . . . Their reply to the demand for satisfaction and punishment was deemed so dilatory and evasive that the British ambassador was ordered to quit the Hague, and on December 20, 1780, his government, justifying itself in a bold manifesto, declared war against the Netherlands. So rich a nation, with a constitution so little adapted to rapid and effective preparation for war, afforded an easy prey; before Yorke had left The Hague two hundred Dutch ships had been seized, with cargoes valued at fifteen million florins.[4]

But even before he had presented his first memorial he had directed the attention of the secretary of state to the rich opportunity afforded by the Dutch colonies in America. On November 7 he wrote to Lord Stormont: "But it is in the West Indies that the most immediate reprisal might be made, and which would affect them the most, because it is the golden mine of the moment, and in the working of which the greatest numbers are actually employed. It is sufficient to cast an eye upon the Custom House lists of the Rebel Ports in North America, to see what is carrying on through St. Eustatius, Curacao and other Dutch settlements, but above all the former. . . . As these places, but St. Eustatius in particular, are the channels of correspondence and connection with North America, the conduct of Amsterdam upon the present occasion, after the proofs produced of its treachery, seems to justify the taking possession of it as a dépôt, declaring not to mean to keep it, or prevent the lawful trade between the place and the mother country, but only to cut off the intercourse between Amsterdam and His Majesty's enemies and rebellious subjects, till satisfaction is given for the past, and security for the future." . . .

The ambassador's hint was not lost upon the secretary. The portion of his letter relating to St. Eustatius was forthwith transmitted to the admiralty for their guidance. On the fifth of December Stormont informs Yorke that he is preparing "to send secret orders to seize the Dutch settlements in the West Indies." On December 20, 1780, the same day on which war was declared, orders were sent to Rodney and to Major-General Vaughan, commander-in-chief of the land forces in the West Indies, to make immediate conquest of the Dutch islands, beginning with St. Eustatius and St. Martin.[5] How great an importance was attached to the matter may be seen from the declarations of Lord Stormont in the House of Lords a few weeks later, during the debate on the Dutch war. After dwelling upon the enormities of the illicit trade, he said that the Dutch had supplied the rebels with the means of continuing their resistance till France, and afterwards Spain, took a public part in the quarrel, and he declared that "he was persuaded, upon the best information, that we should never have been in our present situation, were it our good fortune that St. Eustatia had been destroyed or sunk in the ocean." . . .

Rodney had left Sandy Hook in the middle of November, and arrived at Barbados on December 6. During his absence and after his return the control of neutral commerce was vigilantly maintained. In October an English privateer, after a half-hour's flight, took an American vessel out of the road of St. Eustatius. Early in January three others seized ten vessels laden with sugar and coffee and cotton, which were sailing from the French islands to St. Eustatius and St. Croix under the convoy of a Danish frigate. . . . At Barbados, on January 27, [Rodney] received the declaration of war and his secret orders. Embarking the troops under Vaughan, he sailed from St. Lucia on the thirtieth. After a feint at Martinique, he appeared before St. Eustatius on February 3 and demanded the instant surrender of the island and all that it contained.

The blow, as Rodney said, "was as sudden as a clap of thunder," and wholly unexpected. A Dutch frigate, which had arrived but two days before, had brought no news of war. As a naval exploit the capture has no interest. There was no possibility of defense. . . . The garrison numbered only fifty or sixty men. The naval force in the harbor consisted of the frigate already mentioned, of thirty-eight guns, and five smaller American vessels, of from twelve to twenty-six. . . . The Americans on the island made an offer to the governor to defend it, and a large body of American sailors retired to the interior and made a show of resistance; but hunger and Vaughan's troops soon compelled them also to surrender at discretion. St. Martin and Saba presently yielded to a detachment of the British forces. Learning that a rich convoy of twenty-three merchant vessels, under the protection of a sixty-gun Dutch ship, had sailed homeward from the island about thirty-six hours before his arrival, Rodney sent after it another detachment, and the whole convoy was captured after a brief engagement, in which the Dutch rear-admiral was killed—the first Netherlander slain in the war. With stratagem perhaps not illegal but certainly not glorious, the Dutch flag was kept flying over the town and fort, in order that Dutch, French, Spanish, and American vessels, ignorant of the capture and perhaps of the war, might be decoyed into the roadstead and seized as a part of the spoils.

But if the capture of St. Eustatius was not glorious, undoubtedly it was lucrative. Rodney himself was surprised at the magnitude of the spoil. "The riches of St. Eustatius," he wrote to his wife, "are beyond all comprehension; there were one hundred and thirty sail of ships in the road," besides the war-vessels. The convoy which had been overtaken by his subordinates was valued at more than half a million pounds sterling. "All the magazines and store-houses are filled, and even the beach covered with tobacco and sugar." A convoy from Guadeloupe was brought in. There was scarcely a night without an additional American capture. March 26 the admiral reports, "Upwards of fifty American vessels, loaded with tobacco, have been taken since the capture of this island;" and the letters found on board proved that their whole outfits, everything save hulls and masts, had been obtained through St. Eustatius. The island, said Lord George Germain, was a vast magazine of military stores of all kinds. Several thousand tons of cordage had been found, though Rodney complained that he had been unable to procure any for his needs, and had been told that there was none to be had. Altogether, the value of the capture was estimated by sober authorities at more than three million pounds sterling. Besides the other inhabitants of all nations, more than two thousand American merchants and seamen were secured. It was a pardonable exaggeration if the admiral, in the flush of victory, wrote to his wife that "There never was a more important stroke made against any state whatever."

How profound an impression the disaster made upon public opinion in Holland may be seen from what John Adams, an eyewitness, reports to Secretary Livingston: "You can have no idea, sir, no man who was not upon the spot can have any idea, of the gloom and terror that was spread by this event." . . . In England, on the other hand, there was great exultation. The guns of the Tower were fired, and the government stocks rose one and a half percent. George Selwyn noted the joy which prevailed at White's. "Your express," wrote Lady Rodney, "arrived on the morning of the 13th (March). My house has been like a fair from that time till this. Every friend, every acquaintance came. I went to the drawing-room on Thursday following. It was more crowded than on a birthday; and the spirits which every one was in was enlivening to a degree, and the attention and notice I received from their Majesties were sufficient to turn my poor brain. . . . This glorious news has been a thunderbolt to the opposition, very few of whom appeared in the House of Commons. Negotiations towards peace had been talked of for some time before its arrival, and it cannot fail to produce a favourable effect upon them." Rodney was raised to the peerage, and a pension of two thousand pounds per annum was bestowed upon him.

. . . Of the temper in which he approached his task Rodney has left no doubt. "A nest of vipers," he called the island, "a nest of villains; they deserve scourging, and they shall be scourged." "The island has long been an asylum for men guilty of every crime, and a receptacle for the outcast of every nation; men who will make no scruple to propagate every falsehood their debased minds can invent." "We thought that this nest of smugglers, adventurers, betrayers of their country, and rebels to their king, had no right to expect a capitulation, or to be treated as a respectable people, their atrocious deeds deserve none; and they ought to have known that the just vengeance of an injured empire, though slow, is sure." He hoped to leave the island, "instead of the greatest emporium upon earth, a mere desert, and only known by report." His exasperation was greatest against the British merchants of the island, and especially against those who, for the better prosecution of the illicit trade, had made themselves Dutch burghers.[6] Indeed, many passages in his correspondence show that he had formed a low opinion of the rectitude and patriotism of most of the West Indian subjects of the English crown—a turn of mind which, ill-concealed, was destined to react unfavorably on the success of the British naval operations in the months succeeding. . . .

Begun in the spirit of boundless exasperation, the measures of the British admiral were summary and sweeping. Briefly, it was decreed that all the inhabitants of St. Eustatius were to be held as prisoners of war, and all the property found there was to be confiscated to the king—as Burke phrased it, "a general confiscation of all the property found upon the island, public and private, Dutch and British, without discrimination, without regard to friend or foe, to the subjects of neutral powers, or to the subjects of our own state; the wealth of the opulent, the goods of the merchant, the utensils of the artisan, the necessaries of the poor, were seized on, and a sentence of general beggary pronounced in one moment upon a whole people." . . . Prisoners of war were at the admiral's mercy. Samuel Curzon, who had been the local agent of Congress since the beginning of the war, and Isaac Gouverneur, Jr., who of late had been his partner, were sent as prisoners of state to England, where they were committed for high treason, but released by the Rockingham ministry after a rigorous confinement of thirteen months. The French merchants were treated somewhat better than the others, partly, it may be supposed, because it was impossible wholly to escape remembrance of the considerate behavior of the French at the capture of Grenada, partly because of the warm remonstrances and threats of the Marquis de Bouille, governor of Martinique, and of Durat of Grenada. They were to be sent away in cartel vessels to Martinique and to Guadeloupe, taking with them their household furniture, plate, and linen, and their numerous domestic slaves. The governor, the Dutch, American, Bermudian, and British merchants were also to be allowed or compelled to retire, taking with them their household goods. Only the sugar-planters were to be treated with positive favor.[7]

* * *

The hardest measure of all was meted out to the Jews. Not only were they deprived of their property and laid under sentence of banishment, but they were given but a day's notice for their departure, and were told that they were to go without their wives and children. They assembled the next day, to the number of 101. Forthwith they were confined in the weighhouse and strictly guarded. They were stripped, and the linings of their clothes ripped up in search of money. Eight thousand pounds sterling were obtained in this way. . . .

It was inevitable that such wholesale devastation should excite the indignation of Europe, especially since most of Europe was at war with England or sympathized with her enemies. . . . It was also made the subject of a warm attack in the House of Commons, an attack illuminated by the genius of Edmund Burke. Upon motions for an inquiry into the conduct of the chief commanders, the whole affair was debated in May, and again in December, when Rodney and Vaughan, who were members of the House, were able to be present. Burke had no difficulty in showing that a wholesale confiscation of private property found in a captured place was contrary to the law of nations. He defied his opponents to mention one other instance, in the warfare of the fifty years preceding, in which such a confiscation had taken place. He showed that, on the contrary, from the moment of surrender the conquered inhabitants were entitled to the royal protection; inveighed against the unrighteousness of punishing all for the illicit commerce maintained by some; and declared, apparently with much truth, that public injury comparable with that caused by the illicit trade had been inflicted by Rodney's gigantic auction.[8] At that auction the whole property had been sold at far less than its value, and the ultimate result had been that, in spite of the admiral's precautions, the Americans, French, and Spaniards had been supplied by the British government at a much cheaper rate than they otherwise could have been. Passing to the case of the British subjects, he pointed to the positive acts of Parliament under which English merchants traded to the island, and ridiculed the contention that if wronged they could have redress through the courts, when all their books and papers had been seized.[9] . . .

More serious from a professional point of view was the accusation that the admiral, intoxicated with the pecuniary brilliancy of his prize, had lingered in the road of St. Eustatius, superintending with eager care the disposal of the spoil, and thus squandered away the opportunity of important naval successes which had been afforded him by the temporary naval weakness of the allies in the Caribbean. "Admiral Rodney," says Horace Walpole tartly, "has a little overgilt his own statue." Certain it is, that he remained at the island three months and a day, and that meanwhile De Grasse, watched only by Hood's squadron, had slipped around the shoulder of Martinique and joined the other French ships in the roadstead of Fort Royal. Yorktown itself might never have happened if this juncture of the French had not been effected, and in all probability it would not have been effected if Rodney, with his whole fleet, had been where Hood wished him to be, to windward of Martinique.

* * *

NOTES

1. See the pamphlet by B. F. Prescott entitled *The Stars and Stripes: The Flag of the United States of America; When, Where and by Whom was it first Saluted?* (Concord, 1876); also an article by W. E. Griffis, "Where our Flag was first Saluted," in the *New England Magazine, n.s.,* VIII, p. 576 (1893).

2. The chief source of information on De Graaff's conduct generally, is a voluminous Dutch "blue book" of 1779 entitled *Missive van Repraesentant en Bewindhebberen der Westindische Compagnie.*

3. The correspondence regarding it (1837) is in Mr. Prescott's aforementioned pamphlet; the portrait was copied in Surinam from a painting owned there by De Graaff's grandson.

4. In 1778 Great Britain had, of ships of sixty guns and more (then the essential instruments of naval warfare) 122, France 63, Spain 62, the Netherlands 11. See H. T. Colenbrander, *De Patriottentijd. Editor's note:* Colenbrander estimated that the Dutch had doubled their trade to the new world by 1780.

5. *Letters from Sir George Brydges, now Lord, Rodney to his Majesty's Ministers, etc., Relative to the Capture of St. Eustatius and its Dependencies* (1789). As most of the letters given in this book (of which there was an earlier and less complete edition (1787), privately printed and very rare and not in Sabin) are reprinted in Mundy's *The Life and Correspondence of the Late Admiral Lord Rodney* (London, 1830), and as the latter is much more accessible, I shall refer to the former only for letters which are not to be found in Mundy, or for passages which Mundy, who seems to have taken considerable liberties with his texts, gives in a different form.

6. An amusing illustration of the possibilities of British trade may be derived from the story that Hood, who had missed twelve large merchantmen from his convoy as he neared the West Indies, had found them in the road of St. Eustatius when the island was captured, busily engaged in transferring their cargoes to American vessels.

7. All the French left the island March 24, the Americans a few days later. They had been detained lest they should return to America and give warning.

8. Solicitor-General Yorke, in 1759, declared that the inhabitants of Guadeloupe, after conquest, were British subjects, with or without the taking of oaths of allegiance.

9. Attorney-General Northey, in 1704, gave it as his opinion that it was no offense for a British subject on a neutral island to trade with the enemy during war-time, provided it was not in materials of war.

RAYFORD W. LOGAN

SAINT DOMINGUE: ENTREPÔT FOR REVOLUTIONARIES

There was a certain truth to Admiral Rodney's argument for the reduction of St. Eustatius that "had it not been for this infamous island, the American rebellion could not possibly have subsisted." This conclusion, however, should not becloud the fact that there was another center through which the sustenance for revolution was channeled—Haiti, which in the eighteenth century was known as St. Domingue and which was part of the massive island of Hispaniola controlled by the Spanish.

For French leadership the trade between the thirteen colonies and St. Domingue was not an end in itself, although it was established policy on the eve of the American Revolution to secure needed staples from the American mainland. The Declaration of Independence, however, set into motion a policy of French "secret" aid to the Americans which swiftly developed St. Domingue into one of the most active of entrepôts in the West Indies. The elimination of St. Eustatius would only serve to increase the maritime fame of such ports as Cap Français, Môle St. Nicholas, and Port au Prince. When captains of merchant ships and privateers said "the Cape," they spoke of Cap Français which they knew as intimately as the harbors of Charleston, Philadelphia, or Boston.

Before the Treaty of 1778 which formalized American trade to, and through, St. Domingue, a romantic flavor was added as Caron de Beaumarchais (together with Franklin and Silas Deane), with the flourish of a popular libretto, established the trading house of Rodrigue Hortalez. The motives of Beaumarchais were mixed, a combination of desire for profit, a

From *The Diplomatic Relations of the United States with Haiti, 1776–1891.*
University of North Carolina Press, 1941.

poetic response to the fight for liberty, the ecstasy of romance with the dark-skinned Pauline from the West Indies, and French patriotism mixed with ambition. Truly Beaumarchais reads like a novel. As Rayford Logan remarks: "the inimitable author of Le Mariage de Figaro *and* Le Barbier de Séville *had not exhausted in those two delightful comedies his genius for intrigue and skullduggery."*

The alliance of 1778 turned the American war for independence into a European war, and especially a war of conquest, or attempted conquest, in the West Indies. St. Domingue, together with Martinique, became the great funnel for European and French goods. And through these French possessions in the West Indies traveled many of the American and European leaders—or like Lafayette, fooled the British into thinking that St. Domingue was the ultimate destination. And it was from Cap Français, of course, that Admiral de Grasse sailed with his fleet for his rendezvous with destiny called Yorktown.

Whatever may have been the role of the French West Indies in determining French policy from 1775 to 1778, the guarantee of those possessions by the United States "forever from the present time and against all other powers" constitutes probably the most entangling permanent commitment in the history of the United States. On the face of this provision in Article XI of the Treaty of Alliance of February 6, 1778, the United States promised to support France by military measures in defending the French West Indies from attack. It is, of course, possible to argue that this American guarantee reveals a real fear on France's part of a British attack on her Caribbean colonies. Fortunately for the United States the wars of the French Revolution were to permit her to liberate herself from an entanglement that might have changed her history.[1]

Another possible reason for French aid and the alliance was the desire to promote commerce between the United States and France, including the French West Indies. In the opinion of one writer at least, the desire to increase France's commerce with the United States was the main reason for French policy. This interpretation, even with the support of new documents, seems strained. It is true that Vergennes adumbrated the importance of commerce between the United States and Saint Domingue as early as September 20, 1776. In a letter of that date to D'Ennery he referred to Spain's permission for France to obtain supplies for her West Indian colonies from certain of Spain's possessions, including Louisiana. Since these would hardly suffice, however, help from the Americans "would be more direct and more abundant." He therefore favored a relaxation of the former restrictive measures. "Our best friend," he concluded, "is the one who helps us to live." Again, on December 20 of the same year he expressed to D'Ennery the hope that many American ships would carry to Saint Domingue during the winter supplies, timber and tobacco. He was even optimistic enough to foresee the possibility that D'Ennery might obtain from the Americans a surplus that he could send to France.[2]

How much American commerce went to Saint Domingue during the war is difficult to determine. At all events, Stephen Girard, "the first private banker in the United States," laid the foundation for his later enormous fortune by trading with Saint Domingue during the American Revolution and the years afterward.[3] The opening of the colonial ports to foreign vessels in 1778 shows the dependence of those possessions upon foreign trade when France was engaged in war. Finally, Louis-Guillaume Otto, a competent French diplomat who was at one time chargé d'affaires in the United States, declared in 1797: "In sacrificing so many men and millions [of francs] to sustain the United States, the Royal Government had in view making the United States the complement to our western colonies by finding in the United States at all times provisions for our West Indies or for our warships." In other words, an independent United States would, in war as well as in peace, furnish Saint Domingue and the other French Caribbean possessions with necessary supplies that British colonies might be prevented from providing. But this argument was advanced at a time when some French statesmen were advocating in the face of considerable opposition a friendly policy toward the United States.

That the desire for commerce between the United States and the French West Indies was only a secondary consideration is evidenced by the terms of the treaty of commerce which was signed on February 6, 1778. The most-favored-nation treatment which it granted to Americans was confined to the French ports in Europe. France did promise to keep open the existing free ports in the Caribbean, but she did not open any new ones there. In only one respect did the treaty seek to promote trade between the United States and the French West Indies. The original treaty exempted molasses taken by Americans from those islands from the payment of duty in the United States in return for a promise not to impose an export tax on goods taken by Frenchmen from the United States to those possessions. When temperance advocates and southern interests, which saw in these provisions an increase in trade for the northern states, prevented the adoption of these clauses by the Continental Congress, France did not insist upon their being retained.[4] Later, commerce between Saint Domingue and the United States did assume a role of major importance, but it seems not to have been a primary reason for the French desire in the days of the American Revolution to aid in the establishment of an independent United States.

In evaluating the motives behind the French policy, we must also consider the opportunity for profits foreseen by some enterprising French friends of the United States. This examination will permit us at the same time to assay the importance of Saint Domingue in the scheme of secret aid and to indicate the personal interest of some American officials in transactions conducted through the colony.

As early as September 1775, D'Ennery reported that Americans had bought a lot of powder in Saint Domingue during that year. "You understand," he wrote perhaps facetiously to Vergennes, "how very difficult it is, even with the best intentions in the world, to prevent a merchant here from selling his powder to one who is obscurely the secret agent of some merchant from New England." He further reported that the Dutch had purchased a lot of powder in Saint Domingue and had carried it to the Dutch island of St. Eustatius for resale to the Americans. The role of that island in providing powder that enabled the Americans to keep fighting and to win at Saratoga has been convincingly portrayed, but the powder that went to the United States from Saint Domingue either directly or by way of St. Eustatius cannot be entirely discounted.[5]

The Continental Congress did not fail to take advantage of the opportunities for buying in the Caribbean the supplies that the Americans sorely needed. On October 13, 1775, the Committee of the Whole resolved that it be recommended to the various revolutionary assemblies that they export certain products at their own risk to the foreign West Indies in return for "arms, ammunition, sulphur and salt petre."

But it was the fertile mind and the penurious circumstances of Caron de Beaumarchais that evolved the scheme by which France sent through Saint Domingue considerable aid to the Americans. Beaumarchais had already had a romantic interest in Saint Domingue as a result of his love affair with the beautiful "dark-skinned" Pauline de Breton from that colony. He had also had a financial interest in the colony as a result of investments that he had made there.[6] He may have had Saint Domingue in mind when he wrote his famous memoir, "Peace or War," in 1776 that helped to crystallize the ideas already in the mind of Vergennes.[7] At about the same time Beaumarchais submitted a confidential memorandum to the king in which he proposed the formation of a commercial house, Roderigue Hortalez and Company, to facilitate the secret French aid. He pointed out that by using French vessels they could be absolutely sure of the transportation of munitions to Cap Français which Hortalez had chosen to be his first port of deposit in America. In the spring of 1776 Arthur Lee, on the basis of information given him by Beaumarchais, wrote from London to the Secret Committee of Congress that

France was "ready to send five millions worth of arms and ammunition to Cap Français to be thence sent to the colonies."[8]

Vergennes in his *Réflexions* of 1776, suggested: "The colonists would send to our ports their ships laden with goods and take in return arms and ammunition, paying the difference not in currency but in goods delivered to either Saint Domingue or to one of our European ports." It is thus evident not only that aid would be sent to the Americans through Saint Domingue but that the Americans would be expected to aid the French colony.

Just how much aid went to the Americans by way of Saint Domingue could be established only after exhaustive research. The British curtailed trade relations early in 1776 by stationing two frigates off Môle St. Nicholas. In June, however, the British were again protesting against the sale of powder in Saint Domingue to the Americans. Vergennes wrote D'Ennery four months later that the contraband trade between the colony and the United States was probably not so great as alleged to be. Nevertheless, in order to convince Great Britain of France's desire to remain on friendly terms with her, he wanted the contraband trade completely stopped.

Behind this cloak of friendship for Great Britain Vergennes and Beaumarchais were perfecting their plan of secret aid to the Americans. It was not until the end of the year, however, that apparently the first ship of Hortalez and Company set sail for the United States via Saint Domingue. In December of that year Beaumarchais informed Vergennes that he had ready the *Amphitrite* to carry a regiment of Irish soldiers and supplies to the United States. All the ship's papers were in order to show that the entire consignment was for D'Ennery. (France, of course, had the right to send reënforcements and supplies to her own colony). In order to supervise the operations of his company in Saint Domingue Beaumarchais kept one of his agents, Carabas, there for a number of years. On July 1, 1777, Beaumarchais notified Vergennes that the cargo of the *Amélie* had already reached Saint Domingue and had left for the United States on several American ships. On December 20 of that year Beaumarchais wrote to Francy, his agent in the United States, that he was sending to Saint Domingue a vessel with uniforms for American soldiers and more than one hundred cannon. The United States was to send ships to lie off Cap Français. After giving a preliminary signal, they were to hoist the Dutch flag to the main mast and then fire five shots. The French ship was then to go out and permit itself to be captured and carried into an American port where, after trial, it was to be released. But, in the meanwhile, the cargo would have been turned over to the Americans. Evidently, the inimitable author of *Le Mariage de Figaro* and of *Le Barbier de Séville* had not exhausted in those two delightful comedies his genius for intrigue and skullduggery.[9]

The Americans, in the meanwhile, were equally active. Their first pur-

chasing agent in the Caribbean, William Bingham, went out to Martinique in
the middle of 1776 and played an important part in forwarding supplies to
the United States. Richard Morris of the Secret Committee of Congress
wrote Silas Deane, the first American agent in Paris, on August 11, 1776,
that Richard Harrison was being sent in a similar capacity to Cap Français,
but evidence is lacking that he fulfilled his mission. At the same time Morris
suggested to Deane that they engage in a little private business for themselves through Saint Domingue. A month later Morris wrote him that Stephen Ceronio and John Dupuy were the American purchasing agents at Cap
Français and Môle St. Nicholas respectively. He instructed Deane to continue sending supplies by way of Martinique and Saint Domingue. Three
months later Nicholas Rogers, an American agent at Port-au-Prince, informed
Deane that there were eleven American ships at the Cap and that five or six
had just left the Môle for the United States. At the end of June 1777, Morris
announced to Deane the safe arrival at Charleston via Saint Domingue, of
the ship *La Roche* in which he and Deane had an interest of one hundred
thousand livres. On September 5 Deane advised a Captain Landais to go to
the United States by way of the colony. If he took any artillery officers
with him, they should be disguised as sailors or passengers for Saint Domingue. A few days later Deane wrote the Committee on Foreign Affairs of
the Continental Congress that he hoped that the *Thérèse* which he had sent
by that route had arrived.[10]

One must be very cautious in any statement as to the value of the aid that
the United States received through Saint Domingue. Even when ships landed
their cargo in the island, it did not necessarily reach its ultimate destination.
For example, Franklin in 1779 wrote to the Continental Congress that the
supplies from two large ships were still in Saint Domingue although they had
been landed there many months before. It is nevertheless clear that the aid
both prior to the French alliance and after it was considerable.[11]

Saint Domingue was also utilized by some of the foreign volunteers as a
means of assuring safe passage to the United States. One of the very first of
these, a Prussian by the name of Voidke who later participated in the siege
of Quebec with the rank of brigadier general, passed through the colony in
the fall of 1775 with a passport from Vergennes authorizing him to join the
Americans. General du Portail who served as chief of engineers at Valley
Forge in the winter of 1777 to 1778 and who, according to his biographer,
constructed there the defenses that saved Washington's army, had gone to
Philadelphia by way of Saint Domingue.[12] Lafayette, De Kalb, and their
comrades on *La Victoire* solemnly but falsely swore to the port authorities
of Bordeaux in March 1777, that they were going to Saint Domingue.

Prior to the French alliance Saint Domingue was not the scene of any important military or naval operations. On May 9, 1777, the Continental Con-

gress did appoint a committee to arrange with a Frenchman, Bajeu Laporte, the terms of a contract for raising a regiment of French soldiers in Saint Domingue and Martinique, but the records fail to reveal whether the contract was executed. The Continental brig, *Lexington,* did make a cruise to the Caribbean in the spring of 1776, but it was captured on its way back from Cap Français. Most of the hundreds of privateers which the Americans commissioned confined their activities, as far as the Caribbean was concerned, to the eastern end.

Even after France entered the war, most of the naval engagements took place in the eastern end of the Caribbean. But when the French wished to join the Americans in naval or military operations on the North American mainland, Saint Domingue naturally became the base of operations. It was from there that Admiral D'Estaing sailed in 1779 to attack the British at Savannah.[13] Some six hundred colored and Negro troops from Saint Domingue participated in the attack. According to a reliable report, they displayed conspicuous courage in covering the retreat of the French and American forces after a brave but poorly organized attack that had been revealed in advance to the British. Although the attack failed and the French fleet had to return to the West Indies, news of the expedition, in the opinion of Alfred Mahan, made the British abandon Narragansett Bay which Rodney called "the best and noblest harbour in America."[14] It may well be that the experience of fighting for the independence of others awakened a yearning for their own liberty in the minds of the more intelligent Negroes and mulattoes like Christophe and Martial Besse.[15]

It was from Cap Français that the French fleet under Admiral de Grasse sailed on August 5, 1781, and by its victory in Lynnhaven Bay brought the actual fighting, as far as the Americans were concerned, to a close with the surrender of Cornwallis at Yorktown. At Cap Français was assembled also a large part of the French fleet that Rodney defeated in the decisive Battle of the Saints in April of 1782. Rodney kept a close watch on the Windward Passage (which separates Cuba from Hispaniola) to the end of the war. On the other hand, French naval assistance to the United States was limited by the necessity of guarding the merchant fleet from Saint Domingue from the danger of a British attack, the possibility of which caused "consternation" among French merchants.

Although Saint Domingue was not mentioned in the treaty of peace between France and Great Britain, it had been frequently discussed in the negotiations. One of the proposals looked to the exchange of Gibraltar by the British for certain French and Spanish possessions. But some British planters feared that France, in return for helping Spain in her efforts to recover Gibraltar, might be given Santo Domingo. In that event, they contended, France with her already vast sugar estates in Saint Domingue would be able to control the world sugar market. While this fear was not the only reason for Britain's refusal to relinquish Gibraltar, it indicates a vital interest in Saint Domingue that will help to clarify British policy during the quarter of a century in which the diplomatic history of the United States was most closely connected with events in Saint Domingue.

The war was hardly over before Americans began to turn their eyes toward Saint Domingue. There was probably no real foundation for the fear of certain French statesmen in 1783 and later that the winning of independence by the United States would lead her naturally to attempt a conquest of the French West Indies. But the repetition of this fear might lead one to conclude that the French had developed a psychosis with respect to their cherished possessions in the Caribbean. At all events they were entirely correct in their fears that the United States would demand additional commercial facilities there, for during the "critical period" of early American independence one of the gravest problems was commerce. At the conclusion of the war Franklin had induced Lafayette to submit a memoir to Vergennes in which he urged that, in order to develop commerce between France and the United States, France should remove some of her restrictions on American trade with the West Indies.

French policy was naturally divided. On the one hand, the French government revoked in 1783 an ordinance of 1778 that had freely admitted foreign vessels into the colonial ports. But the repeatedly expressed fear of an American invasion and the realization that, while France had helped to liberate the United States from Great Britain, American commercial relations were continuing as much as possible in their former British channels, led to important commercial concessions in the French West Indies. The first of these were contained in the royal ordinance of August 30, 1784. It opened all the French West Indian ports to foreign ships under sixty tons carrying foreign products that included some of the principal American exports, except flour, provided that they did not compete with goods of French origin. The limitation to sixty tons greatly aided the American vessels since European vessels of such small size could hardly compete with the American ships which had a much shorter distance to travel. The decree added Cap Français and Cayes-St. Louis to the Môle as free ports in Saint Domingue, but allowed the exportation of only molasses and rum. Even before the promulgation of the decree the merchants of Bordeaux had protested against it, and a flood of new protests condemned it after it had been published. As a consequence, a new decree of October 31, 1784 restricted the colonial trade to ports capable of receiving vessels of one hundred fifty tons.[16]

But according to Otto who was about to leave for the United States as chargé d'affaires, even these liberal concessions would not satisfy the Americans. Nothing short of complete liberty of trade with the French West Indies, he declared in a long memoir of May 17, 1785, would be acceptable to the Americans. He contended that France would not benefit in a corresponding measure because the Americans preferred British goods and because the weakness of the American government would prevent the execution of a treaty between France and the United States. On the other hand, certain modifications in the colonial commercial regulations might "cement more and more our relations with the United States." Moreover, he concluded, there would probably be so much smuggling from the United States into the French West Indies that it might be politic to permit the articles to come in legally.[17]

Otto's prophecy that the concessions granted by the decree of August 30, 1784, would not satisfy the Americans proved to be correct. Their demands continued to be so insistent that, in spite of an important anonymous publication that renewed in 1787 the denunciation of the decree, the French government in its instructions of October 10, 1787, to Moustier, the new minister to the United States, examined the possible necessity for granting new commercial concessions in the French West Indies. The instructions pointed out that the Americans would probably complain of the few favors that they enjoyed in the French possessions and that Great Britain would use their complaints in order to "diminish the sentiments that should attach the United States to France." Moustier soon became convinced of the determination of the Americans to enjoy complete liberty of trade in the French colonies in the Caribbean. Even Washington, who opposed the importation of rum from the French West Indies because of its baneful effects, urgently advocated further opportunities for commerce there. On March 12, 1788, Moustier reported that the Americans were carrying on an extensive smuggling trade with the French West Indies.[18]

The reports of Moustier evidently more than offset the cries of alarm and demands for a limitation of American trade with the French colonies that were being sent by the French consular agent, Ducher. It may have been fear of American violence coupled with the desire to woo the Americans from their British predilections that swung the balance in favor of additional concessions. By the decrees of December 29, 1787, and December 7, 1788, France admitted American whale oil to the West Indies while at the same time she forbade the importation of that product from any other foreign country. In the latter year two-thirds of the produce of the American codfisheries found free sale in the French West Indies, and fifty thousand barrels of sugar went to the United States from Saint Domingue.[19]

But even then the Americans were dissatisfied. On July 2, 1789, therefore, Moustier submitted a memoir to the French foreign secretary, Montmorin, in which he recommended first, the increase of the French triangular trade by granting permission to French ships to carry flour, salt pork, butter, and cheese from the United States to the French West Indies; second, the manufacture of molasses into rum in the islands for sale in the United States; third, permission for French ships to carry directly from the French West Indies sugar and coffee to the United States in exchange for rice and naval stores since the winds forced the French ships to take that route back to France and since two-thirds of the sugar and coffee consumed in the United States came from the French West Indies. Under no circumstances, however, should the Americans be allowed to carry flour to the French West Indies or to reexport the sugar and coffee from the islands. On the contrary, they should be kept within the clauses of the decree of August 30, 1784, which "already give them too many advantages." Above all, whatever concessions were made to the Americans, they should not be embodied into a convention. "It is necessary that with regard to the West Indies," Moustier continued, "the Americans persuade themselves that they have nothing to demand, and that they must expect everything from the benevolence rather than from any obligation of His Majesty."[20]

In January 1790 Gouverneur Morris who, after the departure of Jefferson, was the most influential American in Paris, told Montmorin that "nothing could tend so much to make the United States desirious of an alliance with Britain, as to exclude them from a free trade with the French colonies."[21] These developments may well justify the conclusion of a specialist of the period that "the background of Genêt's failure, of the Jay Treaty, and of the Quasi War is to be found in the failure of French policy to develop the natural sympathies of the Americans by intensifying the bonds of commerce." If this conclusion is correct, Saint Domingue, which was much more important than either Martinique or Guadeloupe, loomed conspicuously in the background.[22]

NOTES

1. *Editor's note:* For a recent compilation of America's international arrangements, see Charles I. Bevans, ed., *Treaties and other International Agreements of the United States of America, 1776-1949* (Washington, 1968-). 10 volumes published through 1972.

2. George F. Zook, "Proposals for a New Commercial Treaty between France and the United States, 1778-1793," *South Atlantic Quarterly*, VIII (1909).

3. John B. McMaster, *The Life and Times of Stephen Girard, Mariner and Merchant* (Philadelphia, 1918). 2 volumes.

4. Francis Wharton, ed., *The Revolutionary Diplomatic Correspondence of the United States*, I (Washington, 1889), pp. 344-46. 6 volumes.

5. Orlando W. Stephenson, "The Supply of Gunpowder in 1776," *American Historical Review*, XXX (1925), pp. 271-97. See also J. Franklin Jameson, "St.

Eustatius in the American Revolution," *American Historical Review,* VIII (1903), pp. 683–708.

6. Paul Frischauer, *Beaumarchais, Adventurer in the Century of Women* (New York, 1935).

7. The priority of the memoir over the *Reflexions* of Vergennes has only recently been established. See John J. Meng, "A Footnote to Secret Aid in the American Revolution," *American Historical Review,* XLIII (1938), pp. 791–95.

8. Quoted by Elizabeth S. Kite, *Beaumarchais and the War of American Independence,* II (Boston, 1918), p. 68. 2 volumes.

9. Louis de Loménie, *Beaumarchais et son temps,* II (Paris, 1856), pp. 139–ff. 2 volumes. *Editor's note:* The English edition was published in London in 1856 (4 volumes), and the American edition in 1857 by Harper's in one volume.

10. The Deane Papers will be found in volume 19 of the *New York Historical Society Collections* (New York, 1886); and volume 23 of the *Connecticut Historical Society Collections* (Hartford, 1930). Charles O. Paullin, ed., *Out-Letters of the Continental Marine Committee and Board of Admiralty, 1776–1780* (New York, 1914). 2 volumes. *Editor's note.*

11. *Editor's note:* Aside from the aforementioned *Beaumarchais* by de Loménie, some material on French aid will be found in Jules Marsan, *Beaumarchais et les affaires d'Amérique* (Paris, 1919).

12. Elizabeth Kite, *Brigadier General Louis Lebègue Duportail, Commandant of Engineers in the Continental Army, 1777–1783* (Baltimore, 1933).

13. See H. B. Hough, *The Siege of Savannah* (Albany, 1866). *Editor's note:* See also Alfred T. Mahan, *The Major Operations of the Navies in the War of American Independence* (Boston, 1913). Reprinted by Greenwood Press in 1969.

14. *Editor's note:* Aside from the aforementioned work of Mahan, see Gardner W. Allen, *A Naval History of the American Revolution* (Boston, 1913).

15. The number has been estimated at from six hundred to fifteen hundred. See Theophilus G. Steward, *How the Black St. Domingo Legion Saved the Patriot Army in the Siege of Savannah, 1779* (Washington, 1899).

16. See Frederick L. Nussbaum, "French Colonial Arrêt of 1784," *South Atlantic Quarterly,* XXVII (1928), pp. 62–78. *Editor's note:* It is interesting to note that when the *Jay Treaty* was drawn up in 1794, and the British stipulated a maximum of 70 tons, not even Washington's influence could prevent the Congress from deleting this section of the treaty.

17. The subterfuges to which Stephen Girard resorted in order to carry on prohibited trade with Saint Domingue abundantly justify Otto's conclusion.

18. Henry E. Bourne, ed., "Correspondence of the Compte de Moustier with the Comte de Montmorin, 1787–1789," *American Historical Review,* VIII (1903).

19. Particularly valuable for this period is James Duncan Phillips, "Salem Ocean-Borne Commerce from the Close of the Revolution to the Establishment of the Constitution, 1783–1789," *Essex Institute Historical Collections,* LXXV (April, July 1939).

20. *Editor's note:* At this time the United States was involved in a considerable diplomacy with England concerning their "natural" right to trade freely in the British West Indies, but met the same failure since mercantilist sentiment remained a strong influence in both France and England. For this episode see Charles W. Toth, "Anglo-American Diplomacy and the British West Indies, 1783–1789," *The Americas,* XXXI (1975).

21. Anne C. Morris, ed., *The Diary and Letters of Gouverneur Morris,* I (New York, 1888), p. 275. 2 volumes.

22. See Frederick L. Nussbaum, "French Colonial Arrêt of 1784," *South Atlantic Quarterly,* XXVII (1928), pp. 62–78.

JAMES M. CALLAHAN

CUBA: OUTPOST FOR EMPIRE

*The capture of Cuba (1762) by the English during the Seven Years' War
was to have a lasting effect upon the Spanish mind. The Spaniards would
not easily forget that steeple bells from Charleston to Boston heralded the
victory, and that for the thirteen colonies "the conquest of Canada had exalted the American heart, and now they rejoiced at the conquest of Cuba."
Thus Spanish policy during the rest of the eighteenth century was to be one
of cautious rebuilding, and of avoiding any situation which would cause her to
lose her "mercantile gems" in the West Indies. Therefore when France made
her alliance with America in 1778, it was not surprising that Arthur Lee
would be confronted by ambiguous conduct in Madrid; and that John Jay
would spend almost four fruitless years (1779–82) attempting to gain official recognition as minister to Spain, finally to leave in disgust for Paris as
a member of the negotiating team for peace.*

Spain, in spite of the Family Compact, *hesitated to join France at first.
And when she did, by declaring war on England in 1779, it was made quite
clear that there was to be no formal alliance with the United States. Such
an alliance was not even dangled before the Continental Congress, although
aid was promised for assurances of American help in restoring Spanish he-
gemony on the mainland—especially to secure East Florida. And American
leadership had to provide at least vague assurances that it would be generations before the American people would have any specific interest in the
region of the Mississippi.*

Cuba was to be opened to American ships during the latter stages of the

---

From *Cuba and International Relations, A Study in American Diplomacy.*
Johns Hopkins University Press, 1899.

war, but for a price—helping to restore Spanish control and power in the New World. Thus Cuba became not an entrepôt for revolution, but rather a staging area for the export of Spanish power from the Floridas to the Mississippi. Although Cubans were to see numerous American masts after 1780, Havana would never become a Cap Français of the West Indies serving so consistently the cause of the American Revolution.

* * *

In the treaty of 1763, Lord Bute would have returned Cuba without a word, but his colleagues decided to ask for Florida or Puerto Rico in return for it. Florida was of little use to England; Cuba would probably have been much more useful to her, especially during the American Revolution. . . . In the Commons, on December 9, Pitt suffering with pain, so that he had to sit while speaking, made a speech nearly four hours in length against the treaty. He said Florida was no compensation for Havana, which he himself had planned to take in 1760. He thought that too much was allowed to Spain and France in the West Indies, and said: "From the moment that Havana was taken, all the Spanish riches and treasures in America lay at our mercy. Spain had purchased the security of all these, and the restoration of Cuba also, with the cession of Florida only. It was no equivalent."

But for the Seven Years' War, the American Revolution would not have occurred when it did. It has been said that George III forced peace upon his unwilling subjects in 1763, and that this was one reason why England was unable to conquer America in the Revolution. The surrender of Cuba to Spain in 1763 probably had a great influence on the course of events in American history. If England had held it during the American Revolution it would doubtless have delayed the success of the American colonies. It was there that many of the fleets which harmed England found a harbor. If England had held Cuba after 1783, the United States boundary might have been limited to the Mississippi.

With the close of the Seven Years' War England resolved to enforce the trade restrictions. . . . The Molasses Act had never been duly executed. In a letter of November 10, 1764, Bernard, the royal governor of Massachusetts, said that it had long been admitted that the American trade with Spanish West Indies ought to be encouraged by all means. He thought that the duty should be lowered; but in 1764 England resolved to enforce the high duties, and to stop the smuggling of goods from the French and Spanish colonies in the West Indies. . . . The trade between the British and the Spanish colonies, which, though it had not been strictly according to law, had been connived at, was now almost suddenly destroyed. Spain cooperated with England to prevent the trade. England laid heavy duties on all articles imported from the West Indies to her American colonies. . . . When the imperious breath of Parliament and king was closing up the commerce of American towns, the pulse of the people ceased to beat calmly. Not only had they felled the mighty monarchs of the forest; not only had they successfully occupied the land and carried civilization from the valleys by the sea to the foot of the mountain, but, as Burke said, there was no climate that was not witness to their toil, and no sea but what was vexed by their fisheries "among the tumbling mountains of ice . . . and along the coasts of Brazil." The width of the Atlantic was a great factor in leading the colonies to follow their own destiny, and to blossom into self-governing communities that should become a shining example for the Spanish colonies to the southward.

One of the first steps of the English colonies, when they decided to make themselves independent of the mother country, was to apply for aid to France and Spain, the recent enemies of England. During the Seven Years' War the expeditions against the French and Spanish islands were supplied from England's American colonies; but these colonies were now ready to furnish supplies for expeditions to seize the English islands. In a letter of Franklin Deane, and Lee, to Vergennes, in January 1777, they applied for manned ships to protect American coasts, and suggested that France might furnish troops. They stated that if England made it a cause of war, the united forces of France, Spain, and America could take from her most of her possessions in the West Indies, and most of her commerce.

The French soon decided to ally themselves with the Americans, but the attitude of Spain remained uncertain. Some Spaniards, who were friendly to the American cause, furnished money which was vested in war supplies; but the Spanish government was uncertain whether it would be convenient for it to form an American alliance. Arthur Lee was impressed with the ambiguity of the conduct of Spain. It was clear that she did not intend to embark upon any war which did not contribute amply to her own benefit.

* * *

Spain, carefully watching the course of events, declared war against England in the summer of 1779, and decided to cooperate with France and the American colonies, though she did not enter into any formal alliance with the United States. Her first step was to regain her former possessions by means of American aid. In 1777 Cuba had been given independent colonial administration under a captain-general, who now took command of the Spanish forces in that vicinity and conducted the plans of campaign; he asked the American Congress to lay siege to St. Augustine, in order to divert the English while Spanish troops attacked Pensacola. He also invited Congress to undertake the conquest of the territory northeast of Louisiana, and asked what kind of productions the United States could furnish for the assistance of Havana and Cuba. While the English held New York, Washington did not consider it wise to weaken his army by sending troops to aid Spain; but Congress decided to send 4,000 men and three frigates to Charleston, and to give power to the commander of the southern army to act in concert with the Governor of Havana in regard to plans for taking East Florida. The Charleston troops were expected to create the diversion which the Governor of Cuba desired.

Jay was sent as minister to Spain in September 1779; and he arrived at Cadiz the following December, and sent his credentials to the Spanish government. He vainly sought recognition in an official capacity until May 1782, when he left in disgust for Paris.[1] But he had several communications which gave him the impression of the policy of Spain. He saw from the first that Spain would have fears of the rapid extension of the new American nation toward the West. In sending Mr. Carmichael to sound the Spanish government, Jay instructed him that while he should do justice to Virginia and to the western achievements against the savages, he should, nevertheless, try to leave the impression that it would require ages to settle those extensive regions. Mr. Jay was especially anxious to know whether Spain was likely to carry on any serious operations for possessing herself of the Floridas and the banks of the Mississippi. It seemed to him that the islands of the West Indies would be the principal objects of contention.

In May 1780, while a treaty with America was in contemplation, Count Florida Blanca, in a conference with Jay, said that Congress having once relinquished pretensions to the navigation of the Mississippi, should not now insist upon it. He desired to exclude the Americans from the Mississippi, and, if possible, to keep the English from the Gulf of Mexico. When Jay stated that some of the American states were bounded by the Mississippi, Blanca said that he did not think the king of Spain would be willing to admit it.

The American colonies did not receive the assistance which they had expected from Spain. It appears that some little aid had been sent "from Spain, Havana and Louisiana" in 1779; but in the spring of 1780, Blanca informed Jay that the Spanish expenses had been so heavy that they could not give hope of rendering as much aid as they might have been able to do the year before. Spain was watching her own interests. In America there were many reasons for distrust of her. Delays and slights had a bad effect on the mutual harmony and confidence which should have existed. There were many causes for complaint. When Pensacola was captured by Spain it served to strengthen the British garrison of New York and Charleston by the addition of the troops from the former place. The Havana trade was advantageous to Spain, but she seriously interrupted it by the detention of American vessels for months at a time, to aid in her expeditions. She made use of these American trading vessels without rendering proper compensation, and often sent them away without a convoy to prevent their capture by the enemy. The trade with Havana was in this way much discouraged.

To the provisional articles of peace signed by Oswald and the American commissioners, November 30, 1782, was attached a separate secret article which agreed that, in case England at the close of the war should obtain possession of Florida, the line of boundary between it and the United States should be a line from the mouth of the Yazoo River where it unites with the Mississippi due east to the Appalachicola.

A short time after this secret article was added, the condition of England enabled Spain to get Florida. Lafayette saw that this might in the future lead to boundary disputes with the United States. He told Livingston that Spain would always be extravagant in her territorial notions, and that she would insist on holding all the territory on the left bank of the Mississippi, not because she wished to occupy it, but because she feared neighbors who had the spirit of liberty.[2]

Spain hoped to induce the American government to guarantee her future possession of all the territory that she held in America at the close of the war. Such a guarantee would have made it the duty of the United States to fight for Spain. Jay, at a later date, in order to induce the Spanish minister to negotiate for a treaty, had also offered a guarantee of territory, but in a letter to Livingston in April 1783, he declared that the United States, when she proposed the guarantee, did not intend to fight for Spain. He said: "That, we should so guarantee the Spanish possessions as to fight for them was as far distant from my design as it could be from that of Congress. A common guarantee means nothing more than a quit-claim, to which we certainly could have no objection."

At the close of the war the consideration of possible future alliances was a subject of concern. In April 1783, Jay was afraid that Spain and England might form an alliance looking to the security of their possessions in America. A short time before, when it was feared that England would make reprisals on Cuba, Spain had sent reinforcements to Havana. Tory refugees in New York, during the Revolution, while favoring a submission to England instead of a treaty, said: "Will not the perfidy of France and Spain justify Great Britain in entering into an alliance with Russia, Prussia and other powers, against France and Spain, the common disturbers of public tranquility, to take and divide among them all their islands in the West Indies?"

Notwithstanding the friendly advances of David Hartley, the policy of England after 1783 was to prevent trade between the United States and the British West Indies in order to encourage the trade with Nova Scotia, Canada, and St. John's Island. Spain was disposed to be more liberal. About 1783 Havana and Santiago were open to free commerce with foreign nations, except as to the slave trade. Havana as the center of this trade grew rapidly. In 1790 the restrictions on it were removed. Internal development as well as commerce was encouraged.

In 1783 Spain governed all the territory from Oregon to Cape Horn. When France had once claimed all the Mississippi system and the region from Mobile to the Rio Grande, Spain had objected and had claimed that the Gulf of Mexico was a closed sea. She now owned all the shores of the Gulf of Mexico. With Cuba as a center of a vast empire, she still hoped to add more territory to Florida and Louisiana, her dominions on the continent.

NOTES

1. *Editor's note:* Jay left for Paris to join Benjamin Franklin and John Adams to negotiate a treaty of peace with England. The *Treaty of Paris* was signed by them on September 3, 1783.
2. *Editor's note:* When the *Pinckney Treaty* was drawn up in the 1790s Jefferson remarked that it would not be in the interest of the American people to cross the Mississippi for generations to come. But the treaty, which gave the United States the right to navigate the Mississippi, simply expressed a westward movement which started before the Revolution, and which was quite manifest to the peoples of Europe.

ARTURO MORALES-CARRIÓN

PUERTO RICO: THE BREAKDOWN OF SPANISH EXCLUSIVISM

During the eighteenth century Puerto Rico was to be found in a state of considerable isolation due to two factors: (1) its role as a military fortress on the eastern perimeter of the Spanish empire which, far from being exposed to the non-Hispanic world around it, continued to be a "tightly huddled community surrounded by its rings of walls," and (2) the policy of royal exclusivism which resulted partly from the mercantilist practice of the age, and partly from the persistent Anglo-Spanish rivalry. Therefore Spain could not escape the winds of war, either in Europe or the Caribbean, and during the eighteenth century Cuba was captured and temporarily held by the British, while Puerto Rico received an occasional buffeting.

Although Spain could not by herself withstand the onslaughts of the British as she attempted to expand her empire in the West Indies, she had two allies which eventually protected both Cuba and Puerto Rico—France, and the English sugar planters who opposed further British control of more islands in fear of the competition which would result from the opening of new fields in the West Indies.

With respect to Puerto Rico, not all of its population was found "huddled" behind the heavy fortress walls. Privateering in wartime, and smuggling at all times, linked many Puerto Ricans with the non-Hispanic community, and as the eighteenth century progressed Spanish officials appeared more concerned in controlling illicit trade than abolishing it. What Puerto Rico needed, of course, was a legal and systematic commercial life to bring it closer to both the Hispanic and the non-Hispanic Caribbean. This demanded a considerable

From *Puerto Rico and the Non-Hispanic Caribbean: A Study in the Decline of Spanish Exclusivism.* University of Puerto Rico Press, 1952.

revamping of the imperial system, especially to break down the old Spanish policy of exclusivism.

It is interesting that in its attempt to curb illicit trade, the Spanish Crown issued a royal Cedula *within months after the signing of the Declaration of Independence—a declaration which was to open up a new era for smuggling in the West Indies just at the moment when Spain tried to end it as a basis for the economy of Puerto Rico. Even the church was called in, as the* Cedula *called upon all the bishops in the Americas to warn against this sin. Needless to say, contraband trade flourished in Puerto Rico as at no other time in its history. And the exclusivism which the Crown tried to achieve, as an expression of the mercantilist practice of the age, also faltered. The American Revolution forced open the doors of Puerto Rico to France and America, and at precisely that moment Spanish thinking was further unsettled by the popularity of the Abbé Raynal who was to advocate free trade as an economic solution for the problems of all of Europe's empires.*

So as the Spaniard began to rediscover what the Abbé Raynal called "one of the best of the islands of the New World," he also had to face the winds of revolution which were to engulf the Atlantic community during the last quarter of the eighteenth century. At the end, although the Spanish islands in the West Indies did not separate from the mother country, "the long experiment in artificial isolation was at least over."

With the dawn of the eighteenth century, the social and economic development of Puerto Rico was increasingly affected by the crucial role which the non-Hispanic Antilles played in the struggle for trade and power among the western states. The British West Indies was considered the most valuable part of the empire and the pivot of its American commerce, while the French were soon to have in Haiti one of the richest sugar colonies in the world.[1] The exposed position of Puerto Rico could be turned to good advantage as a base for intercepting this rich foreign trade, while the proximity of St. Thomas and Jamaica as distributing centers for slaves and European merchandise contributed to the flourishing of smuggling as an established social habit in which practically all classes participated. If privateering added to the fuel of war, smuggling was the link with the outside world, the mechanism of trade through which the products of the land were exchanged for goods the colonists could not purchase in the walled city; the means, in short, for natural economic forces to assert themselves.

In analyzing the history of inter-insular contacts as they affected Puerto

Rico, it is well to bear in mind that the old social dichotomy persisted and was further intensified by the pressure of the armed struggle in the Caribbean. San Juan continued to be a tightly huddled community, surrounded by its rings of walls and imposing fortresses, expressing in their planning and architecture royal defiance of aggressors from afar. The rest of the island was left pretty much to itself, with little encouragement given to its productive occupations and living theoretically within the narrow system prescribed by royal exclusivism. There was still the sharp cleavage between town and country, between the military *presidio,* whose sustenance was derived from the Mexican remittances, and the pioneer society of the seaboard and the interior, which traded freely with the interloper. This lack of integration in the society and the economy was a constant factor throughout the century and, as shall be later seen, deeply influenced official thinking in the progressive era of Charles III, when an effort was made to curb smuggling and open up legitimate channels for the insular trade.

The Anglo-Spanish rivalry in the Caribbean left a vivid imprint on the history of Puerto Rico, as the two imperial powers engaged time and again in intermittent warfare.[2] The anarchy that reigned in the Caribbean, and particularly in the central West Indian area, drifted both England and Spain towards a formal armed conflict in 1739, in spite of the moderate elements in the two governments who were anxious to preserve the peace in Europe and reach some settlement concerning the trade war in America.[3] The aggressiveness of the English interloper had been matched by the ruthless campaign of the colonial *guarda costas.* The control of illicit trade rather than its abolition had been the goal of officials like Abadia. The crafty governor well knew that the Spanish claim to a trade monopoly over Puerto Rico could not be upheld in the light of conditions in the area. His vigorous persecution of English traders was no doubt inspired by the need to protect his own lucrative commerce with the French, the Dutch, and the Danes.

* * *

Spanish fears concerning the fate of Puerto Rico proved to be unjustified by events. The annexationist attitude, exemplified in the earlier part of the century by the proposals of Parke and Hart, was not strong enough to command support in England or in the islands. In 1745 Rear Admiral George Townsend was empowered to attack Puerto Rico if the Leeward Islands were invaded by the French. But the West Indian planters were hostile to the idea of conquering a colony which could become a dangerous competitor as a sugar-producing area.

The War of Jenkins' Ear in this border area of the two clashing empires of England and Spain was one more episode in the long-standing struggle between the colonials. As far as Puerto Rico was concerned, conditions were somewhat different from the somber picture painted by Fray Francisco at the end of the seventeenth century. The venality of royal officials had certainly not changed, but privateering had opened up a new and rewarding field of activity to the natives, and the island was constantly enriched by the booty they brought back from their hunting expeditions. The steady stream of fugitive slaves was adding continually to the population, much to the chagrin of the foreign colonists. The Puerto Rican settler, under the leadership of aggressive and unscrupulous governors, was making the most of his contacts with the outside world and showing an enterprising spirit of his own as a sailor and corsair. The old Spanish policy of exclusivism had failed to isolate the colony. The coasts were wide open to the foreign interloper and illicit trade was the order of the day, though the foreign smuggler, if perchance English, was bound to suffer more than any one else from the relentless persecution of the native privateers.

Smuggling was the prime enemy of Bourbon colonial policies in Puerto Rico. In the second half of the Eighteenth Century, a war was waged against the stubborn foe as the reawakening of Spanish power under Charles III revamped the bureaucratic tradition so entrenched in the imperial system of government. The fight against the dislocation of trade was a major consideration of the new reformist attitude, particularly with regard to the sensitive Antillean area where the island settlements were exposed to contacts with one of the richest commercial regions anywhere in the world. And yet, as shall presently be seen, it was largely a losing battle.

The trade conflict described has revealed the interrelationship between privateering and illicit commerce. The former had embroiled Spain in serious complications with the English, but had failed in its primary purpose of curbing the foreign interloper. Even though Matias de Abadia, the most representative figure of the era, was at long last divested of his power, the more responsible officials that succeeded him were unable to cope with the ingrained social habit of trading with outsiders. Contraband during the late fifties was extreme, with the English and the Danes boldly calling at the island's ports in spite of the renewed activities of the *guarda costas.*

* * *

The disastrous war which came to an end in 1762 spurred the Spanish government under Charles III to new efforts in the reorganization of imperial rule in the West Indies. A report, presented to the king in 1761, had stressed the role of contraband trade in the overseas empire. The English were denounced as the worst offenders, and their illicit commerce valued at 6,000,000 pesos each year. The king naturally resolved to end their clandestine transactions which he considered as one of the worst dangers to the security and progress of his far-flung domains.[4]

The need was felt for accurate reports on the extent of this evil and its relations to the social and economic development of the West Indies. To that effect, Marshal Alejandro O'Reylly, an Irishman in the service of Charles III, was entrusted with the responsibility of visiting the Antilles and rendering a report on their state of defense, resources, and needs. In regard to Puerto Rico, O'Reylly performed his task with exemplary thoroughness and utmost loyalty. The discovery of the crucial role of smuggling in the island's history is the basic revelation and guiding thread of his *Memoria*. To that remarkable document the attention must now be turned as a landmark in the analysis of the impact of foreign contacts on eighteenth century Puerto Rico.[5]

In its determination to curb the foreign smuggler, the Crown called upon the Church to aid in the fight by using its spiritual powers. A royal cedula, dated September 15, 1776, exhorted all bishops in America to enlighten the faithful with regard to the sin of smuggling. . . . In a separate cedula the governors were also urged to make the most of the authority conferred upon them in order to prevent illicit trade within their jurisdiction. The stern campaign reached its climax when on January 16, 1777, the Crown gave its approval to a drastic order of the governor of Puerto Rico which threatened with the death penalty all those who sold livestock to foreign colonies.

But no admonition, temporal or spiritual, could prevail upon the islanders' ingrained habit of trading with the interloper. Not even the most extreme measures could stop the furtive transactions through which the rapidly developing colony was able to subsist. The basic fact that Puerto Rico was in the center of a rich trading area which could supply the colonists with the goods they needed in exchange for their tropical produce could not be overcome by laws, decrees, and regulations still inspired in the theory of exclusivism and commercial monopoly. The measures taken by the Crown were obviously inadequate. Trade was somewhat revived with Spain and the island's revenues increased, but contraband, the underlying "sin," continued to flourish as an imperative of a social and economic reality, impervious to royal pronouncements.

The evidence was soon available to the authorities at Madrid. On August 25, 1782, the manuscript of a book was submitted to the count of Floridablanca, the enlightened minister of Charles III. The book had been written, at the request of the minister, by a learned Benedictine friar, Iñigo Abbad y Lasierra, who had visited Puerto Rico and traveled far and wide throughout the land. This *Historia Geográfica, Civil y Natural de San Juan Bautista de Puerto Rico* went much farther than O'Reylly in its analysis of the island's history and contemporary state, and served as a useful index to measure the real import of the reform legislation. From its wealth of observations on the social, administrative, and political conditions of Puerto Rico during that period, some revealing data may be obtained with respect to the island's contacts with foreigners and their impact on the social and economic growth of the colony.[6]

The scholarly friar scanned all available sources on the history of Puerto Rico, and well versed in the histories of the conquest and colonization of the Antilles and in the writings of Raynal and Robertson, injected into his work an enlightened and humanitarian spirit which marks him as the founder of modern Puerto Rican historiography. An indefatigable traveler, he went into the rural interior and made careful notations on its population, customs, resources, and products. He portrayed the transculturation that went on in the society, its adjustment to the tropical habitat, and its willingness to enter into a close trade partnership with the smuggler, in defiance of imperial regulations. As in O'Reylly's report, he emphasized the peculiar growth of the island's population and related it to the evolution of contraband. The deserters from the Spanish *flotas*, the soldiers whose term had expired, the emancipated Negroes, the runaways, in fact, a substantial bulk of the settlers arriving from Spain sooner or later took to smuggling and piracy as an easy way of making a living.

As the surge of Bourbon reformism began to recede, two facts stood out in the writings of those who had investigated conditions in Puerto Rico or given careful consideration to the island within the framework of the empire: Puerto Rico was the focus of a contraband trade which had flourished in spite of all the laws and provisions made to the contrary; it was also a colony of great potentialities, which still lacked adequate official encouragement to its trade and its agriculture. The role of Puerto Rico as a smuggling center was frankly stressed by the historian Antonio de Alcedo when in his famous *Diccionario* he wrote with reference to the capital that "It has been the focus of a contraband trade carried on by the English, French, and Dutch, with the Spaniards, in spite of all the laws and provisions made to the contrary."[7]

This Spanish appraisal of the island's worth and limited development found its way into one of the most popular histories of the period. In the earlier editions of his *Philosophical and Political History of the Settlements and Trade of the Europeans in the East and West Indies,* the Abbé Raynal had already called the attention of his readers to the value of Puerto Rico. "This island," he said, "the possession of which would have made the fortune of an active nation, is scarcely known in the world." He thereupon proceeded to draw a picture of indolence and neglect for which he naturally made Spain responsible.[8]

*   *   *

Raynal's work, as has been already noted, was well known to Abbad, who used it as one of his principal sources in the preparation of his book. But if the Spaniards read Raynal, the latter also kept himself in close touch with the views of the enlightened advisers of Charles III and his ministers. The 1788 edition of Raynal's *Philosophical and Political History* added considerable material on Puerto Rico. The addition was probably partly dictated by Raynal's interest in the island as a good case of Spanish mismanagement and negligence. He still had the highest opinion of the island's worth. "We may venture to affirm," he wrote, "that it is one of the best, if not entirely the best, of the islands of the New World, in proportion to its extent." Familiarity with Abbad's work led him to modify somewhat his former views on the languid state of the colony. He felt particularly that the agrarian reform provided by the cedula of 1778 gave rise to great expectations.[8] But he still argued that the solution was free trade with the French, the Dutch, the English, and the Danes. . . .

So in the second half of the eighteenth century the small island of Puerto Rico lay no longer neglected and forgotten. The Spaniards in a sense had rediscovered their tropical possession, and had become increasingly aware of the dynamic growth of its population and economy. But Bourbon reformism had not measured up to the task of making the colony an asset within the empire. The Bourbons had lost their fight against the foreign smuggler, and their modified mercantilism was soon engulfed and swept away by the revolutionary storm that blew from America into Europe and back again across the sea. In the upheaval that followed the island of Puerto Rico became once more a coveted prize of war, a strategic objective of the first importance, as the struggle for power raged in the Caribbean, opening up another chapter in its long history of lawlessness, piracy, and chaos.

There was no doubt that Puerto Rico continued to be a most troublesome neighbor to the British in the middle Antillean area, and a stumbling block to their commerce and interests. When in the course of the War of American Independence, Spain joined in the conflict against England in June 1779, the British considered the possibility of aggressive operations against the West Indian island.[9] British military intelligence had kept the admiralty informed of the strength of Spanish forces in the colony, and on December 7, 1779, a draft was prepared for Major General Vaughan describing a project for an attack on Puerto Rico. The weakened state of British forces, however, did not enable Vaughan to challenge the Spanish hold on the island. On January 25, 1781, he wrote from Barbados that offensive military operations were impossible in spite of the arrival of three regiments. As a matter of fact, the British position in the West Indies was precarious until Admiral Rodney's great victory over the French fleet (Battle of the Saintes) on April 12, 1782.[10]

If the fortunes of war spared Puerto Rico on this occasion, the island's fate as a Spanish colony was much less secure as the diplomats engaged in the preliminary negotiations leading to the peace. The English were intent on making up for their loss of a considerable part of the New World empire, while the Spaniards considered the reconquest of Gibraltar as one of the great objectives to be attained by their entrance in the war. These two goals of the respective diplomacy of the powers eventually linked the fate of Puerto Rico to that of Gibraltar and assigned to the Caribbean island a rather conspicuous role in the peace negotiations.

* * *

In spite of Spanish reluctance to consider the cession of Puerto Rico, the English persisted in the idea of an exchange. In June 1782, the subject was brought up again at the beginning of the peace negotiations between England and the American commissioners. In a conversation between Benjamin Franklin and Richard Oswald, the British representative, Spanish claims to Gibraltar were discussed as the principal obstacle to peace. Franklin suggested that the English could obtain in return trade privileges in the Indies to which Oswald retorted "that only an equivalent in territory, such as Puerto Rico, would ever satisfy the English nation in return for Gibraltar." The British still held to this view when T. M. Gerard de Rayneval reached London in September as French envoy to discuss the conditions of peace. Rayneval hastened to see Lord Shelburne, the British prime minister, and again the subject of Gibraltar became the stumbling block in the negotiations. In reporting to the king, Lord Shelburne remarked on September 13, that Rayneval

states himself as no ways authoriz'd to treat for Spain, but alledges that no Peace can take place without Gibraltar, that in his opinion, supposing it taken or not, The King of Spain would be dispos'd to cede Oran and its dependencies to Your Majesty, which he affects to consider as a better harbour than Port Mahon. I upheld the impossibility of ever ceding it so strongly, that I could form no guess about their disposition regarding Puerto Rico.[11]

In commenting on this report, George III urged caution to avoid a bad peace, and with regard to the Spanish disposition to cede Oran observed,

That Oran is a good port is quite new to Me, and I certainly doubt it, as it is offered as an equivalent for Gibraltar; Porto Rico is the object we must get for that fortress.

The keen British interest in Puerto Rico was once more reflected in the correspondence between Lord Shelburne and the king with regard to the former's conversations with Rayneval before the French envoy departed for Paris. On September 15 Lord Shelburne sent detailed information to George III "on what passed between Mr. Rayneval and me previous to his leaving this. . . ." With respect to the proposed exchange, Shelburne added,

I have held the point of Gibraltar so high that the alternative of Porto Rico may be catch'd at, I flatter myself whenever the time comes for it to be hinted by way of compensation or Exchange on the part of Your Majesty.

The tactful diplomatic maneuver won the full approval of the king, who replied to Shelburne on September 16 that "The holding Gibraltar very high is quite judicious and if not taken I should hope Porto Rico may be got for it."

As the negotiations reached the final stage, two movements of opinion were discernible with respect to the thorny question of the ultimate fate of Gibraltar and Puerto Rico. The British Cabinet, although prepared to consider other alternatives, still clung to the hope of acquiring the Spanish island and put it at the top of the list of its preferred choices. Floridablanca, as late as November 21, despairing of obtaining Gibraltar by any other means, was reluctantly willing to consider the possibility of ceding Puerto Rico. The lineup against this proposed exchange included the opposition in the British Parliament led by Fox and Burke; the French diplomats who feared the strengthening of British power in the Antilles; and Aranda, whose obstinate refusal to consider the cession of any of the Spanish islands for Gibraltar was based on an accurate appraisal of the damage that would have resulted to Spanish interests in the Caribbean. It was Aranda who cut the Gordian knot. . . . In submitting to Charles III and Floridablanca a "fait accompli," he made possible the rendering of a general peace and, with respect to Puerto Rico, contributed perhaps more than anyone else to save the island from a drastic deviation in its history.[12]

The last phase of Spanish exclusivism in Puerto Rico saw the rise amidst the havoc of the revolutionary era, of increasing trade dependence on the United States. The close ties with the French nation, on the other hand, brought an influx of French settlers into the island. Thus the old exclusivist concepts with regard to commerce and colonization were gradually and reluctantly abandoned as Spain entered the most critical period in her modern history.

The relations between the Puerto Rican colonists and the Anglo-American colonials originated in the dangerous business of privateering or in clandestine transactions conducted at the expense of the mercantile system of the powers. Even before independence, the thirteen colonies had developed a flourishing trade with the Spanish Indies, and merchants from New York, New England, and Pennsylvania were enriched by supplying fish, flour, and staples. With the beginning of semilegal trade in flour, under the concessions granted to Aguirre, Ariztegui and Company in 1766, vessels from Philadelphia called on the island's chief port and in connivance with the company's factor engaged in smuggling activities.[13]

The War of American Independence contributed to a further development of these early contacts. On September 20, 1776, the king of Spain ordered that in urgent cases ships flying the rebels' flag be admitted in Spanish ports in the Indies and treated with the same hospitality as French and English vessels. American privateers in Puerto Rican waters soon took advantage of these privileges in their raids against British commerce.[14] . . .

After independence was achieved, efforts were made by the young republic to obtain trading privileges with regard to the Spanish islands. On April 20, 1784, Don Francisco Rendón, Spanish agent in Philadelphia, wrote to José de Gálvez, minister of the Indies, that Robert Morris, American superintendent of finance, had sent him a communication on that date on the reciprocal advantages that would accrue to the two countries if a limited permit were granted to enable the United States to trade with the Spanish islands and possessions in America. This permit could be restricted to the provisioning of the armies and navies, or extended to include the supply of foodstuffs to the inhabitants if the King of Spain had no objection, under the express condition that the privilege be given to a company comprising a limited number of merchants in order to prevent smuggling. Rendón, however, was opposed to the idea on the basis that the trading concessions granted to Americans in Cuba, during the revolutionary struggle, had led to "innumerable confiscations of clothing taken by ships of these States." The Spanish agent further added that the price of manufacturing goods in the new republic was much lower than that in any of the king's possessions. He feared that if privileges were granted, Spanish trade would suffer great harm, as the American merchants could easily undersell their Spanish competitors. Rendón was also skeptical regarding the American promise to prevent smuggling and urged that the trade between the United States and the Indies be in the hands of a Spanish company with agents in Charleston, Baltimore, Philadelphia, New York, and Boston.

Spanish reluctance to consider the American petition affected the development of licit trading relations with the island. After 1784, trade died away and the next four years were, according to the historian Roy F. Nichols, "a barren interlude." The Spanish edict of 1789 allowing for the introduction of vessels bringing Negro slaves revived commerce with the West Indies, and by 1790 it was apparent that a trade of some small proportion had developed again. This trade was further encouraged by the wars in which Spain was engaged after 1790. The emergence of enemy privateering crippled Spanish commerce with the Indies and forced the governors and the home government to admit the necessity of importing foodstuffs from the United States. Thus, by the end of the century, the pressure of war contributed to the strengthening of inter-American relations in the commercial field.[15]

As Spain and her overseas empire entered a most crucial period in their history, it was obvious that even in the field of theory the system of exclusivism was no longer able to hold its own. Where trade was concerned temporary concessions to foreigners were becoming a habit and particularly with regard to American flour there was no longer any pretense of adhering to the spirit of the laws. The immigrations of French settlers had also breached the exclusivist wall, and proved its worth in fostering economic productivity and cultural diffusion. When the crisis came, these experiences in trade and colonization were fully utilized by the native oligarchy in pressing its claims for a more liberal form of government, although its traditional monarchical attachment prevented the outburst of strong separatist feelings.

The long experiment in artificial isolation was at last over. The exclusivist system had proved to be a narrow, unworkable policy, quite remote in its outlook and implications from the peculiar social realities of Puerto Rico. It failed to realize the exposed location of the island in a sensitive area of international rivalries, as well as its geographical proximity to the flourishing trade of the maritime empires. By straight-jacketing colonial commerce, it had forced the inhabitants to engage in clandestine practices and had stimulated their contacts with the foreign establishments. Thus there grew a strong economic attachment to the rest of the West Indies, and in later years to the United States, far more enduring than the hatreds and feelings of repulsion which the colonials had inherited from the struggles of their respective mother countries in Europe.

NOTES

1. Richard Pares, *War and Trade in the West Indies* (Oxford, 1936). For the value given to the island colonies of Great Britain, see also G. L. Beer, *British Colonial Policy, 1754-1765* (New York, 1933).
2. *Editor's note:* Curtis Nettels, "England and the Spanish American Trade, 1680-1715," *The Journal of Modern History,* III (1931).
3. For the diplomatic background of the war see, H. W. Temperley, "The Causes of the War of Jenkins' Ear, 1739," *Royal Historical Society Transactions,* 3rd series, III (1909), pp. 197-236.
4. For the significance of British trade during this period, see, Allan Christelow,

"Contraband Trade between Jamaica and the Spanish Main, and the Free Port Act of 1766," *Hispanic American Historical Review*, XXII (1942), pp. 309–43.

5. "Memoria de D. Alejandro O'Reylly sobre la isla de Puerto Rico," in Tapia, *Biblioteca*, pp. 516–45.

6. The original manuscript is found in the Rich Collection, New York Public Library. For a study of Abbad's ideas, see: Isabel Gutiérrez del Arroyo, "Fray Iñigo Abbad y Lasierra y su Historia de Puerto Rico," in *Estudios de Historiografía Americana* (El Colegio de México, 1948), pp. 13–105.

7. Antonio de Alcedo, *The Geographical and Historical Dictionary of America and the West Indies*, G. A. Thompson, ed., IV (London, 1812–15), p. 229. 5 volumes. The Spanish edition appeared from 1786 to 1789.

8. Abbé Raynal, *A Philosophical and Political History of the Settlements and Trade of the Europeans in the East and West Indies*, III (Dublin, 1779), p. 185. 4 volumes. Third revised edition of the Justamond translation.

9. See Vera Lee Brown, "Anglo-Spanish Relations in America in the Closing Years of the Colonial Era," *Hispanic American Historical Review*, V (1922).

10. For the influence of this victory over the peace negotiations, see Samuel F. Bemis, *The Diplomacy of the American Revolution* (New York, 1935).

11. Sir John Fortescue, ed., *The Correspondence of King George the Third*, V (London, 1927–28), p. 124. 6 volumes.

12. Aranda had replied to a French inquiry as to whether Puerto Rico or Trinidad could be considered as exchanges by expressing the opinion that the increase of English power in the Antilles was a greater threat to Spain than English possession of the Rock. "The case of Gibraltar," he wrote, "is bad and grave, but it has not so many bad consequences as the placing of ourselves in such an unfortunate position in that part of the world." See Stetson Conn, *Gibraltar in British Diplomacy in the Eighteenth Century* (New Haven, 1942).

13. Harry Bernstein, *Origins of Inter-American Interests, 1700–1812* (Philadelphia, 1945).

14. Herminio Portell Vilá, *Historia de Cuba en sus Relaciones con los Estados Unidos y España*, I (Havana, 1938), p. 77. 3 volumes.

15. Roy F. Nichols, "Trade Relations and the Establishment of the United States Consulates in Spanish America, 1779–1809." *Hispanic American Historical Review*, XIII (1933), pp. 289–313.

FLORENCE LEWISOHN

ST. CROIX:
YEARS OF SURVIVAL

The history of the West Indies is the history of many flags, and the Virgin Islands have flown seven. During the American Revolution St. Thomas, St. John, and St. Croix were already Danish. St. Thomas was destined to become the great entrepôt in the nineteenth century, much as the Dutch island of St. Eustatius had been in the eighteenth century. But at the time of the disruption of the British empire resulting from the revolt of the thirteen colonies, St. Croix was the more important of the Virgin Islands since its topography allowed it to be a valued sugar-island. It was thus a Danish gem of the West Indies, and as such Danish policy was one of caution lest St. Croix share the fate of such islands as St. Eustatius.

A "prosperous island, dreaming in the sun," St. Croix could not remain unaffected by the activities of the contentious empires around it, for its dreams were the dreams of profit from sugar, rum, and shipping. But a strict neutrality (more or less) was the order of the age for Denmark. There were occasional slips, but Copenhagen jumped when the British lion growled. And the lion almost roared as St. Croix achieved the distinction of being the first to salute the new flag of America. But since it was all unofficial (and the vessel raised the flag while departing Fredericksted), historians have awarded this distinction to St. Eustatius whose governor boldly gave a nineteen gun salute to the arriving Andrew Doria.

Copenhagen ordered Governor Claussen to export all goods to Denmark, but smuggling was a way of life in the West Indies in time of peace as well as in war—and they were good at it. So good that Governor Claussen had to allow the indignity of a resident British official to oversee the neutrality laws.

From *St. Croix Under Seven Flags.* The Dukane Press, 1970.

In the meantime, as Florence Lewisohn writes, "the fleets of half of Europe were dodging or engaging each other around the islands." And this was especially true after Yorktown, at which point the story usually ends for Americans reading the history of their Revolution. But the Danish islands had to survive two more years of perilous neutrality until the Treaty of Paris was signed in September of 1783.

St. Croix on the eve of the revolt of the northern British colonies was a secure, still prosperous little island, dreaming in the sun about profits from sugar and rum, shipping and slaves; content to keep apart from the everlasting quarrels of the French, English, Spanish, and Dutch. These never-ending conflicts had an untidy way of spilling out from Europe to the West Indies.

The popular governor-general, Peter Claussen, had gone back to Copenhagen for two years, and in the interval the islands were governed by an *ad interim* head, Major-General U. W. Roepstorff, but Claussen returned in 1773 at the time of major changes in the colonial council system and then remained during all the war years.

Governor Claussen found a busy island with some 150 sugar plantations, all operating with animal mills and nearly half of them with windmills already built. The slaves numbered 22,344 as against 2,136 white persons and 155 free colored persons. Sugar prices were low that year of 1773, but soon to pick up and production advanced to some 18 million pounds; this figure was for all three islands, but sugar production was negligible on the other two. St. Croix was producing more cotton than ever and still had some good tobacco and ginger and even coffee crops.[1]

The Boston Tea Party took place the year Claussen returned, and from the viewpoint of the West Indians it might just as well have been a rum party, for all of New England imported molasses from the islands to distill into rum. Boston took the lead in the number of distilleries but Rhode Island, New York, and others of the thirteen colonies were not far behind. Duties on sugar and molasses brought up from the foreign islands were not only high, but were channeled into the British home treasury when they could be collected, but the colonists were adept at avoiding this.

By the time the first shots from Lexington-Concord were "heard 'round the world," the islands were beginning to reflect many events happening elsewhere. In February of 1775, all English captains sailing the American coast were ordered to capture all ships carrying forbidden wares and stores to the northern colonies. A copy of this order reached Governor-General

Claussen the next month and he dutifully published it in the islands. At least it gave proper warning of British intentions.

Soon the English representative in Copenhagen was protesting that war materials were clearing the harbors of all three of the Danish islands. He asked what was to be done about it. The Danish officials took the position that this was off-shore trading, which, indeed, much of it was. The king, however, did ask the islanders not to help out the northerners and he forbade the exporting of European war materials out to his own islands. The islanders could still legally buy incoming lumber, cattle, fish, and tobacco from the north. It was lucrative now to pay for these in war goods, procured with few questions asked. The supplies from North America came down with a 5 percent duty which was little to pay when the return contraband brought such good prices.

Ben Franklin had backed the Continental Congress in a Resolution which permitted all vessels carrying war materials into the colonies to take out American products of equal value; thus the incentive for carrying arms up to the rebels from trans-shipment points in the Caribbean.

The shipping rules were easy to bend to suit the changing situation. There was one later period during which war materials such as muskets, sailcloth, and gunpowder were legal from the Danish islands to the northern colonies, but they could enter or leave Danish harbors only on vessels not flying the new American flag, an evident attempt by the Danish to enjoy the munitions market but to stay neutral.

There was little doubt where the sympathies of most of the Cruzans lay and the British knew it, but the king of Denmark was determined to keep his country out of war. The islanders preferred the profits of neutrality to actual fighting, so they walked a tight rope of legal compliances and illegal trading.

There were more English than Danish settlers, and as planters and men of business tired of the tangle of trade restrictions laid down by Denmark, England, and the American rebels, they were willing to take chances on evading Danish regulations. This sometimes threatened the position of neutrality during the Revolution. Nobody thought the Yankees had much chance of winning so trading with them didn't seem too disloyal. This attitude prevailed, too, on the British islands where residents had for years been protesting along with their northern cousins over the Molasses, Sugar, and Stamp Acts. These islanders would have much preferred war against France or Spain, both of whom stood ready to pounce at England again, or to help the northern rebels resist her.

The Cruzans, from the highest officials on down, had to survive this war and it meant some trading outside the rules, come what might. What did come next was one of the unique, forgotten "firsts" in American history.

The first salute to the new flag of the thirteen colonies by any foreign nation took place at Fredericksted. It caused no end of repercussions.

It happened on October 25, 1776, when an unidentified schooner belonging to the rebel Americans slid quietly out of the Fredericksted roadstead after loading a small cargo of gunpowder. At a good distance off-shore, the schooner hoisted the new American colors and as they went up the ship saluted the fort with a volley as much as to say "Thank you." Then the astonishing thing happened. A rash officer in the fort ordered the salute returned. St. Croix's version of the "shot heard 'round the world" resounded from the hills. The reverberations from this exchange were begun by an onlooker, a Mr. Kelly, who two days later put his indignation on paper to British Vice-Admiral Young in Antigua, saying "my astonishment was great to find such a commerce countenanced by government here. The vessel went out under American colours, saluted the fort, and had the compliment returned the same as if she had been an English or Danish ship." Countenanced by whom became the touchy question.

Whether Mr. Kelly was only a visitor to the island or a resident planter is not recorded, but it seems apparent he was one Irishman still loyal to the British. From the British viewpoint, the incident was outrageous, a breach of neutrality, not to say an insult to her own flag. Sharp letters flew in the other direction this time from the naval chief of the British Leewards to Governor-General Claussen. No mention appears this time suggesting court martial of the unnamed man in the Fredericksted Fort rash enough to salute a rebel ship and its would-be new nation. The incident was naturally embarrassing to any number of Danish officials in Copenhagen who had to answer to further English protests. They could only follow Claussen's stand that the informant dispatched misinformation. It was a long haul for protests to go back and forth from Antigua to London to Copenhagen to St. Croix, and this allowed time for tempers to calm down. Still, two years later, Lord George Germain, the English secretary of state for the American Department had not finished writing letters about the insulting situation.

The new rebel flag was also linked to St. Croix in another round-about way. George Washington's speeches had captured the imagination of the expatriate islander, Abram Markoe, now established as a prominent merchant in Philadelphia. Fired with enthusiasm for the fray to come, Markoe organized what is now the oldest cavalry troop in the United States. In those days such things were done privately by men of means, and to Captain Markoe's Philadelphia troop of Light Horse came twenty-eight gentlemen of "social prominence and high respectability." None of this would be significant today if Captain Markoe had not needed an ensign, a flag to proclaim just what the Troop and the twenty-eight gentlemen stood for. He commissioned one which is thought to be the forerunner of the Stars and Stripes, inspiring the choice of design for the first flag of the new United States.

Neutrality was more of a problem than ever on the island. The English residents and the Danish citizens whose clandestine war trade was becoming more obvious to Copenhagen were ordered to send all goods straight home to Denmark, but the order was inadequate to cut off the smuggling. The island government set up a customs station at Salt River in this period, where shipmasters who knew the reef well often had done contraband loading.

The nearby Hollanders on their island of St. Eustatius were in the same trouble as the Danes. The English deeply resented the increasing flow of contraband out of this tiny neutral port and a better-known flag saluting incident took place there about a month after the presumptuous salute from the Fredericksted Fort honoring the rebel American ship. The Dutch islanders lost out in their claim to have given the first such recognition to the new Republic, although to this day the Danish incident is rarely mentioned while the Dutch one gets the attention of the war historians.

The shippers and merchants of St. Eustatius operated so openly that it could scarcely be called smuggling. Some of their best customers were English islanders busy trans-shipping goods up to the northern rebels. More than a mile of the waterfront was lined with big warehouses, rented out at over 1,200,000 pounds sterling a year. For the Danish islanders it was now safer to send goods to St. Eustatius than to risk the American ships coming into their own neutral ports.

This one-way traffic was intolerable to the English but it wasn't until nearly three years later that their Admiral Rodney decided it was imperative to clean out the "nest of vipers." One version calls them a "nest of villains" but there was no doubt of Rodney's feelings when he said "They deserve scourging and they shall be scourged." Most of all, Rodney detested the English merchants from nearby St. Christophers, now known by all as St. Kitts island. These neighbors had set up shop in the enormous warehouses along the harbor front in pursuit of quick Pieces of Eight. They had only a seven-mile sail to commute to work from English to Dutch soil. St. Kittsians in particular had been very "disaffected" by the war and their sympathies lay completely with the Yankees.

It was not long after the Danes and the Dutch islanders had recognized the new American flag that the British accused the Danes of harboring actual agents of the thirteen colonies on their islands. Worse, they were charged with permitting the rebels to bring their captured prize ships into the islands for resale. Soon Governor-General Claussen was again writing letters of pacification; this time to Governor Burt of the British Leewards at Tortola and Antigua. Burt, incidentally was in the awkward position of being related to St. Croix Heyligers whose family had long governed St. Eustatius.

Governor Claussen diplomatically denied everything. He invited the Eng-

lish to send an agent in to investigate. The British named a Mr. Richard
Forster of St. Croix to keep a steady eye out for infractions of the neutrality laws. The British also took direct and vindictive action. They sent His
Majesty's roving warships to rove the waters off St. Croix. Furthermore,
they set up an anchorage off Buck Island where smaller sloops and schooners
sent over from Tortola lay in wait for American rebel ships. The Danes
termed these Tortola ships privateers and the victims called them pirates.

In the midst of wartime a charming little pocketbook had been published
in Copenhagen to brief travelers about St. Croix. It gives a capsule picture
of life on the island as indicated by its title, *St. Croixian Pocket Companion
or A Brief Sketch of the Chief Things Necessary to be Known by The Dwell-
ers in, or Traders to The Island.* The *Pocket Companion* offered no advice
on how to stay neutral but despite all the salutes, gunpowder-running, prize
capturing, and letters of protest, the Danes squeezed by without losing their
privileged neutrality. The Dutch tumbled into the war with no forewarning
out in the islands when the British declared against them abruptly in 1780.

Nearly 3,200 ships had gone in and out of St. Eustatius during 13 months
of 1778 and 1779 alone. This astonishing amount of traffic was more than
the British could tolerate any longer since each shipload north reduced their
chances of putting down the rebellion.

The Dutch had been too long involved from the British viewpoint. Before
the Revolution even began, the Bostonians had two agents in Amsterdam
during the winter of 1774 buying up gunpowder to be trans-shipped through
the islands. The Dutch traders picked up 120 percent profit on this new
kind of Boston "tea" which came out in rice barrels and tea chests.

Now the presence of John Adams at the Hague, whittling away at involving the Dutch on the Yankee side, had also infuriated the British. Adams's
steady attrition paid off in 1780 when the Dutch recognized American independence. This was all too much and the British declared war, seizing on
a specific incident to do with an American ship given refuge in Holland itself.
The French had gone into the war nearly two years earlier, Louis XVI signing a treaty which pledged the rebel Americans to aid France in defense of
her West Indian islands if they were attacked by any foreign foe.

Suddenly the whole West Indies came aflame with war. It was no longer
a matter of smuggling contraband but one fleet against another, an island for
an island. While the land armies under George Washington and the British
generals were playing hide and seek along the mountains and rivers of the
continent (and keeping warm on West Indian rum) the fleets of half of Europe were dodging or engaging each other around the islands. As to the rum,
it should have been declared contraband. John Adams put it discreetly later
in his comment that "Molasses was an essential ingredient in American independence." There were times when the army quartermasters had little to

pass around the campfires but rum dispensed from Boston's forty-some distilleries. By the end of the Revolution the per-capita consumption of rum averaged two and a half gallons, although this figure included the women and children's share.

In St. Croix, where planters were doing their part in supplying rum, the *Royal Danish-American Gazette* was loyally publishing George Washington's war dispatches, letters, and other reports on its front page as fast as rebel boats could slip them in. The taking of St. Eustatius by Rodney early in 1781 left the Danish ports offering the only neutral spots left to all those homeless pirates, privateers, smugglers, and roving merchants barred from the Dutch island. The contraband trade rarely involved Danish ships but rather those of the Yankees and their friends the French and Dutch. "British" ships from Virginia and other southern states had become "Danish" when they cleared the islands. Some enterprising Virginians reportedly came down long enough to establish Danish citizenship and then went home to trade with St. Croix during this period.

Rodney himself later wrote that the "taking of St. Eustatius has been a severe blow to the French and Americans. I may venture to affirm that had it not been for this infamous island, the American Rebellion could not possibly have subsisted." Before he moved in on the island itself, he had been chasing and blockading Dutch ships in nearby waters. The minute he learned war was declared on the Dutch he seized ten vessels filled with sugar and coffee and cotton enroute from the French islands to St. Eustatius and St. Croix under the convoy of a Danish frigate.

Eventually Rodney served notice of his next intentions. In his *Letterbooks* kept during his stay on St. Eustatius is a copy of a warning to Governor-General Claussen in which he notes he has blockaded French Martinique and must seize ships of any nation attempting to enter its ports. He has, he said, given orders that "no Encouragement or Protection be afforded to the rebellious subject of the King, my Master, specifically that they not be supported with warlike stores or Material of any Kind, that may induce them to continue in the most unnatural contest that Colonies ever waged against a Parent state."

Mindful of that recently captured Danish frigate enroute from Martinique, Governor Claussen bowed to the not-so-veiled threat and wrote a soothing reply aimed at avoiding embroiling his government any further and at forestalling any thoughts of a Rodney swoop or blockade aimed at his islands.

Rodney set out in convoy for England bearing unsold prize ships and much spoils of war; leaving the rest behind on St. Eustatius. The convoy was overhauled by the French who managed to separate much of the booty from the admiral. Then his convoy was scattered by a hurricane and the fleet took substantial losses.

Rodney had left 'Statia itself insufficiently manned and vulnerable. A handful of French staged a daring raid ashore and captured the island along with a number of ships and some booty left behind from the recent auctions. The war goods and some of the ships had now changed hands two or three times, and all this caused one of the most involved tangles of more than sixty lawsuits for titles, possession, or reparations ever placed on record against the British admiralty.

Rodney reached London before this bad news came, but by the time he sailed in with his diminished fleet and booty Parliament was thoroughly upset, asking questions and viewing with alarm. The parliamentary inquiry delved into the confiscation of English property and the sale of it to His Majesty's enemies. Lord George Germain, secretary of state for the American Department, supported Rodney. It was asserted that the French and Americans had been supplied with stores from Rodney's sale at one-half the price they would have paid to the Dutch in the first place. As a result, it was implied Rodney's actions had greatly assisted the French and North Americans in their war effort. There was further implication that the admiral had lingered much too long consolidating his personal percentage of the gains on the Dutch island instead of prosecuting the naval war against the French and rebel Americans. In particular, he had let French Admiral de Grasse slip through the West Indies and on to North America with a large fleet which Rodney could have intercepted.

Yet, if Rodney had not lingered unduly on St. Eustatius, the French fleet under de Grasse would not have been offshore in Virginia to help put the finishing pincers on Lord Cornwallis when he became penned up at Yorktown. Rodney had indeed failed to intercept de Grasse coming in from Europe to Martinique and the French fleet was soon out of his grasp and headed for Virginia. This ended the Revolution in actual fact, although the signing of treaties would be a long while in coming.

The war was ended for the Yankees, but the encounters were only begun in the West Indies. The impact of the post-Revolution fighting in this area is rarely mentioned by the American history books, while a major war fought out between the British and French in the Caribbean during the next two years fills volumes of their own histories.

The Danes were done with their back-door participation in the Revolution but the first proposed Danish-American treaty of trade and friendship soon fell through. The islanders still had the problem of the English-French naval war swirling up and down the island chain while St. Croix merchants continued to pick up some of the trade scattered from the destruction of the St. Eustatius port. Nicholas Cruger now owned the 90 ton brig *Success* which he used in the Philadelphia trade, and with the firm of Nixon and Foster of Philadelphia was the joint owner of the brig *Mercury*. The Yard family of Philadelphia and St. Croix began to build up their trade again and some of the de Windts who had moved to New York also traded back and forth.

The Danish islanders had a local hero, too: their firm upright Governor-General Claussen who had guided the three islands so adeptly through all the mazes of diplomacy, war, neutrality, and trade. He stayed on as top official until his death in 1784 when he was buried with the fullest honors the grateful islanders could muster.

Soon after the Yankee war ended, some of the younger Markoes were back on St. Croix, down from Philadelphia to take up the family property and business. In these first post-Revolution years, Philadelphia was the commercial center of the new nation. Some of the islanders' successful northern trade, already expanding despite the foreign naval fighting still going on around them, developed through their strong business contacts with this city. A generation later, three more Markoes were to move back to the United States shortly before the Napoleonic Wars, as foresighted as their famous grandfather Abram had been.

Abram, meanwhile, had given his entire home property in Philadelphia to the new United States for the site of the first White House. When the location of the capital city was changed, this land was used instead for a Federal Post Office and Records building. At seventy-nine, the proud old French-Danish captain died and was buried in his adopted city. Perhaps his coffin was draped in the illustrious Markoe emblem and the Light Horse rode to muffled drums with all the military honors due its former captain.

Nicholas Cruger, now married to one of Abram's descendants, was to take a prominent part in the parade in which General Washington entered New York in November of 1783. Soon Cruger was presenting spoliation claims to the new United States government for depredations committed by the French against his ships during the Revolution. The government agreed to pay, but didn't; the exchequer was often in shaky shape until Cruger's former employee Alexander Hamilton took a hand in stabilizing the new country's finances. Thomas Jefferson corresponded with members of the Cruger family about these claims. One letter from Jefferson regrets that he cannot let the Crugers send a ship through the embargo to supply the family plantation on St. Croix, nor bring in produce from the island, nor collect debts for the Crugers. John Hancock, who had done a good business with the Crugers before the Revolution, set up a branch office in London with Cruger to handle American accounts which needed straightening out after the war ended.

St. Croix soon entered one of the few steady financial periods in its history, although the political situation was to change often. The number of sugar plantations increased rapidly and the price of sugar was good; new fortunes had been made during the war, and, as the visible outgrowth of wealth, the newer Greathouses were even more impressive than those already built.

NOTES

1. *Editor's note:* The Virgin Islands are composed of St. Croix, St. Thomas, and St. John, which today are under the seventh flag—the Stars and Stripes.

MICHAEL CRATON

TEN SERGEANTS AND TWO DRUMMERS: THE BAHAMAS AND THE DISRUPTION OF EMPIRE

Although the Bahamas are not exactly a part of that island chain known as the West Indies, they were a part, if not entirely intimate, of the British Empire stretching northwestward across the azure waters toward the thirteen colonies on the mainland. When the colonies revolted the impact produced a situation largely comic-opera, and this Gilbert-Sullivan atmosphere continued to prevail even after the Spanish arrived after Yorktown. During the interval the Bahamians shared in the prosperity (and tragedies) of the intense privateering of the time.

The expected American "invasion" came in March 1776, and, as the author relates, the whole affair had "the air of comedy." Governor Browne appeared at the door of Government House in his nightshirt only to find the Nassauvians entertaining the continental rebels. Dashing to the fort only to find ancient and rusted cannon blown off their mountings, he hastily ran back "to make himself a little decent." His appearance in full uniform the next morning did not prevent the Bahamas from having the dubious distinction of seeing the new American flag being planted for the first time upon foreign soil—all this while Admiral Esek Hopkins filled his ships with powder and cannon ball.

After the Bahamas reverted to England in 1783 the "invasion" of Loyalists from the American mainland appeared more disconcerting than anything previous, for it appeared that these people had sniffed enough of the spirit of independence to declare that they would "not (be) bound by any

---

From *A History of the Bahamas.* Collins, 1962

laws the Assembly passed." They also brought cotton and slaves and, as Daniel McKinnen described it in 1804, "injudicious planting" and "unremitting tillage" eventually proved fatal to all.

The governorship of Thomas Shirley, who succeeded his older brother in 1768, reminds us once more that, however interesting their history, the Bahamas were insignificant in the grand panorama of the eighteenth century. As in most periods of international peace, it was a time of domestic discord and discontent. But Governor Shirley's squabbles and problems were paltry when compared with the constitutional struggle rising to a climax on the nearby continent.

For these were the years of incipient revolt, which led downhill from the Stamp Act in 1765 to the Battle of Lexington ten years later. Thomas Shirley arrived in Nassau as the Townshend Duties were being levied in the thirteen colonies; he left in 1774 at the time of the first American Congress at Philadelphia. . . . Few echoes of these deathless events were heard in distant Nassau; only when the war broke out did the Bahamas take sides, and even then the chief question was not one of principle but of profit. And yet, despite this typically opportunist attitude, the war did result in great changes in Bahamian history. The period from 1767 to 1783 was the end of an era.

Early in 1767 when William Shirley had informed the members of the House of Assembly of the repeal of the Stamp Act, they drafted an address to the king in which they referred ingratiatingly to their "warmest sentiments of Gratitude for his paternal tenderness to his American Colonies so conspicuously shown in the Repeal."[1] Their loyalty was obviously not disinterested, however, for at the same time they petitioned for the improvement of Bahamian trade by the relaxing of the restrictions on free commerce with the French and the Spanish. They obviously had in mind the example of the Turks Islands which, as the board of trade well knew from their correspondence with the Shirleys and William Symmer, was flourishing as a base for the contraband trade between the northern colonies and the foreign settlements at Monte Christi and Cape Nicholas. Thomas Shirley backed up the arguments in favor of making Nassau a free port with a long letter in December 1768. But when nothing was done, the assembly held him to be responsible and began to cause trouble on the least pretext.

Over the question of the Turks Islands discord reached the point of rebellion. In April 1769, Shirley ordered Symmer the agent in the Turks Islands to observe all Bahamian laws. Symmer was reluctant, telling the commissioners of trade that "the settlers here are alarmed to the greatest degree for fear they must . . . be subject to the Legislative Authority of Providence, in which case they are unanimously determined to leave the islands."

The British government was unsympathetic. It frowned upon any trade slipping through the mercantilist net and in 1770 Lord Hillsborough told Shirley to legislate for the Turks and tax them, even though the islands were not represented in the assembly at Nassau. He declared that "as the whole body of People belonging to the British Empire are represented by the Commons of Great Britain, so are the inhabitants of the Bahamas in general represented in the Assembly of that Government."

This attitude the Bahamians resisted, not necessarily because it implied legislation and taxation without representation. Almost certainly some of them were engaged in the Turks Islands trade and clung to their fingerhold on prosperity. On January 25, 1770, Shirley asked the legislature to pass laws controlling trade, salt-raking, and the protection of property in the Turks Islands. The House declined, denying that the Turks were ever "before certainly known to belong to the Bahamas." Even when informed by Shirley of the orders of the privy council and the secretary of state, the assembly procrastinated. Explosion point was reached in October. In reply to an angry message from the Governor, the House refused to legislate, forwarding seven firm resolutions. These repudiated their right to legislate for the Turks, suggested that the islands apply for membership and expressed anger at Shirley's "threats and disrespect." Counter-attacking, Shirley dissolved the assembly the following day. "As I found by the Minutes of your House," he informed them, "that you are carrying on the Business of this Session in an unconstitutional manner, and in open defiance of the King's Instructions to me, it is my Duty to suffer such proceedings no longer."

Although a new session of the legislature passed the salt-raking laws and taxes were levied with partial success after 1771, the Turks Islands remained troublesome; a colorful rendezvous of lawless New Englanders, Bermudian salt-rakers, and French and Spanish *contrabandiers.* Shirley accused Symmer of complicity in the illegal trade, especially in liquor, and hinted that "while the Nights are dark and the Bar is smooth, you will not want your usual Night Cap." The outbreak of war stilled trouble for a time, but only because Nassau gave up all attempts at control. The Turks Islands always remained a safe place for smugglers.

Although no-one dared mention yet the quarter from which attack might come, the problem of defence was as severe as ever. Thomas Shirley found a garrison of a gunner and eight men guarding Fort Nassau and four men stationed at Fort Montagu. Only 13 guns were serviceable and those rusted, and the store of 300 barrels of gunpowder had been spoiled by the climate. The pitiful remnant of the 9th Regiment, consisting of two officers, two sergeants, two corporals, a drummer, and sixteen men, had been posted to St. Augustine, thus opening up a connexion which was to be remembered later.

Shirley made the usual plea for reinforcements, asking for 150 men and help for the fortifications. For once, something was done. In August 1769 the secretary of state wrote to mention that he had ordered General Gage, the commander in North America, to send an engineer with stores up to the value of £1,000. Captain Montresor arrived in 1770 and proceeded, with little of Bruce's energy, to repair the defences. It was a heartbreaking task. There were no suitable tools and labor was scarce and costly. The islands were so poor that even the £20 a month upkeep of the fortifications was beyond their means.

With poverty went apathy. In 1771 when Shirley tried to introduce bills for reforming the militia and instituting a night watch, the assembly refused to comply. Once more it was dissolved. "I am obliged to tell you," said Governor Shirley, "that your treatment of His Majesty's Council of the Bahamas is so indecent, illiberal and unjust, and shows such an intemperate spirit to prevail in your House that I despair of any business being carried on this session with any moderation or to any salutary purpose."

By 1773 distress was acute. Shirley wrote that the revenues were "almost annihilated, the Treasury exhausted, the Contengent charge of the Government will be unprovided for, the salaries to the officers unpaid, for want of which the Courts of Justice have long been shut up." Because the dead hand of the proprietors still discouraged settled farming, turtling, wrecking, and woodcutting were the only activities from which the islanders could scrape a living. Shirley pleaded that the British government help out, citing the example of Georgia, where prosperity followed the revocation of the royal charter. At least the Crown could assume the responsibility for paying some of the chief officers. The reply was as unsatisfactory as ever, and although some reinforcements in the shape of Captain Blackett's Company . . . arrived in July 1773, it must have been a relief for Thomas Shirley when he heard early in 1774 that he had been appointed to the Governorship of Dominica "as a reward for merit." It was only a small promotion, but one which took him away from troublesome Nassau and that much further from the events brewing in the north.

Montfort Browne, his successor, seems to have been a weak vessel more or less at the mercy of the tides of events. His Instructions of May 5, 1774, included an order to enforce the laws of trade, but this was difficult where the trade was practically nil. His first letter home described the dismal hopelessness of the islanders, to whom wrecks were a gift from providence and even illicit trade would have been a relief. But things were about to change. This letter was dated May 6, 1775; only two weeks before, the Massachu-

setts militia had fired at General Gage's troops on their way to and from
Concord and already the British in Boston were in a state of siege.

As early as August 1775, Gage wrote to Browne warning him that American ships were fitting out to attack New Providence and seize the military
stores there. He therefore proposed to send two merchant ships and a man-
of-war to carry off the guns and powder to a place of safety. Governor
Browne demurred, reminding Gage that the defence of the Bahamas was his
responsibility and he, and not Gage, was the commander-in-chief there. In
a footnote, Browne added that "the inhabitants of these Islands have upon
all Occasions given every possible proof of their inviolable attachment and
loyalty to H. M. Person & Govt."—an exaggeration that was to prove somewhat ironic later.

On February 25, 1776, Captain Andrew Shaw arrived in Nassau with news
that a fleet of eight small warships was gathering off Cape Delaware with the
intention of attacking New Providence. This was the first American fleet on
its initial operation, under the command of Commodore Ezekiel Hopkins.

Hopkins had received his orders from the Naval Committee of Congress
on January 5 to gather his fleet and sweep Chesapeake Bay. . . . Among his
varied band of officers with only privateering experience of naval warfare
was John Paul Jones. Later in his career, Jones, the American Drake, claimed
to have been the master-mind of this expedition—a wild exaggeration in keeping with the braggart side of his character. In fact, Jones was a mere lieutenant and, unlike Hopkins and Saltonstall, the second-in-command, was totally
ignorant of the Bahamas.

As soon as Philadelphia was free of ice, Hopkins slipped down the Delaware. The decision to attack the Bahamas was apparently his own, having
decided that Governor Dunmore's squadron in the Chesapeake was too formidable a foe. On March 1, 1776, the American fleet reached Hole-in-the-
Wall, Abaco, where two local sailors were impressed as pilots. Later the
same day a Captain Dorsett sailed into Nassau with the news. For some
reason Browne asked Dorsett to keep the information secret. Perhaps he
hoped that if he ignored trouble it would go away. At daybreak on March 3,
however, seven of the American ships appeared off the bar of Nassau.

The best contemporary account of the American "invasion" interpreted
the events in a manner unfavorable to Browne. In his own version Browne
accused many Nassauvians of entertaining the rebels. One thing is certain:
neither the Americans nor the Bahamians were very eager to come to actual
blows. At this distance of time the whole affair has an air of comedy.

Governor Browne was awakened and came to the door of Government
House in his nightshirt. The council was hastily summoned to Fort Nassau,
the militia drum sounded, and three cannon shot off as a general alarm. Apparently these were the only guns fired throughout, but they were enough to

deter the Americans, who began to sail for the eastern end of the island.

At 7 A.M. John Gambier, "who was so lame with the Gout he could not walk," rode into the fort to find the governor all of a dither. What should he do? Gambier asked what had been done. Nothing—should he send Captain Chambers away with the powder in his fast ship? Gambier suggested that the powder might be useful for defence. The governor agreed. Chambers was sent out to reconnoiter but he soon returned, saying that he could not beat up to windward. A detachment of militia was sent forward to Fort Montagu.

The situation did not look very hopeful for the defence. The roll of the militia was called and it was found that many were absent and most of the others unarmed. In the fort two of the cannon fired as an alarm had been blown off their mountings; the others were embedded to their axle-trees in drifted sand and required a dozen men to traverse them. One buttress of the fort was crumbling and there was a pitiful shortage of equipment such as rammers, sponge-staves, powder-horns, priming wires, and wadding.

At this critical juncture, Browne deserted the fort, "saying that he would just go home and make himself a little decent." While he was absent a report came in that an enemy ship had landed between three and four hundred men two miles east of Fort Montagu. This fort was in an even worse state than Fort Nassau, not having a single barrel of gunpowder usable and no guns properly mounted.

Once he returned, presumably now dressed out in his full uniform, Browne ordered Lieutenant Burke and then Captain Walker forward from Fort Montagu to engage the rebels. But Walker's men advancing tangled with Burke's men retreating, who, having found that the news of the landing was no rumor were now thinking of the defence of their own property in Nassau. Within minutes the militia had melted away without the exchange of a shot. Ordering two men to stay behind to spike the guns on the sight of the enemy, Browne also returned to Nassau.

During the afternoon about 150 men bustled around Fort Nassau trying to prepare it for a siege. They saw little of the governor, who spent most of the time getting his effects together at Government House. He did not call another roll, make a plan of defence, nor even order the gates shut, thus making it possible for "Spies and disaffected persons to come in and discover the Condition and State of the Fort and to Carry an account whereof to the Enemy." When he returned after an absence of three hours he complained "that he had had a violent fit of Cholick, which had detained him so long."

At 4 P.M. Lieutenant Burke went forward again to reconnoiter and apparently spoke with the rebels. He reported that they consisted of 250 to 300 marines "completely Armed" and ready to attack Nassau. At 8 P.M.

the council, militia officers, and chief inhabitants decided that the position was untenable and that the fort should be disarmed. At midnight the powder was loaded on board Chambers' sloop and at 2 A.M. he sailed for St. Augustine.

In the morning the Americans distributed leaflets promising security of life and property. The inhabitants needed no further assurance and gave up all pretence of defence. Montfort Browne was seized at Government House and the two forts formally occupied. The unfamiliar Grand Union flag, with its horizontal stripes and Union Jack in the corner, fluttered bravely over Nassau.

The rebels stayed in Nassau two weeks (not as is often stated for a single day). According to Browne, Hopkins and his officers were "contenanced by many of the principal inhabitants, and elegantly entertained at the Houses of some of the officers of the Government." The men caroused on captured, or surrendered, wine to such an extent that over 200 were seriously ill on the voyage home. But the chief business was the dismantling of the forts. When they sailed away on March 17, Hopkins carried with him no less than 88 cannon, ranging from 9- to 36-pounders, 15 mortars, about 5,500 shells, and over 11,000 cannon balls. With all this booty he was scarcely disappointed to find only 24 barrels of gunpowder. Montfort Browne and Thomas Arwin, inspector-general of customs for North America who happened to be in Nassau, were carried off as hostages, much to the delight of John Green, whom Hopkins released from one of his periodic spells in gaol.

The taste of their bloodless victory in Nassau went sour on the Americans, for off Block Island on their voyage home they were worsted in an encounter with a single British man-of-war, the *Glasgow*. Congress was torn between jubilation and shame and Hopkins was praised and censured in the same vote.

Montfort Browne was soon exchanged for the rebel Lord Stirling, but did not return to Nassau until 1778. He raised troops and fought in the siege of Rhode Island, bringing back four companies of "invalids" with him to the Bahamas. He found the situation in Nassau almost out of hand. Another party of American marines under Rathburn had invaded in January 1778, and had been admitted by Gambier, the acting governor, after threatening to burn Nassau. After two days they had spiked the remaining guns and left, but since that time many Nassauvians had deserted the island to join the rebel cause.

Browne found that the worst aspects of the revolution had infected the inhabitants. John Gould, the speaker of the assembly, had gone over to the enemy with eighty of the militia and the remainder he found "licentious, poor, haughty and insolent." In a telling echo of the American Declaration of Independence, Browne bewailed that "neither life, liberty or property was safe among them." John Gambier, like his brother in the Seven Years' War, had been guilty of issuing illegal letters of marque and now formed a

"Juncto" to oppose the governor. In January he asked Browne "to continue a Licence he had thought proper to grant to the merchants of this place to carry on an open and free intercourse with the Rebells, under the pretext of procuring Provisions." Browne refused but "five rich cargoes of rebel property" were landed nevertheless only one month later.

On March 30, 1779, Browne dissolved his council, an unprecedented step. A little later he dismissed Collector Hunt and Attorney-General Sterling. Although war with France and Spain had broken out and an attack was impending from Cape Francois, Browne complained that he was "totally deserted as well by the civil as the military power." The council members for their part complained to the board of trade that they were "now in a state of absolute Anarchy."

Despite the seizure of the *Young Cezar*, "a remarkable fast sailing Schooner" which, Browne claimed, was "Employed by the disaffected Inhabitants of the Government for the purpose of supplying the wants of the Rebels," the authorities in London listened to the complaints against the harassed governor. A governor without the support of his assembly was taken as a matter of course: a governor out of tune with his council must be in the wrong. In 1779 the board of trade recommended to the Privy Council that Browne be recalled "considering the animosities between parties" in the Bahamas. They stated that the "charges appear to be well founded" and that Browne's proclamations were "well-meant but ill-judged." Somewhat unfairly the governor was sacked in April 1780, though he was still in Nassau when his successor, John Maxwell, arrived later in the year.

Material for the last three years of the war is tantalizingly meager. One thing is certain: the Bahamas enjoyed their most prosperous period as a privateering base. On June 30, 1780, Governor Maxwell sent to London a list of 37 American vessels "Captured and Libelled in the Court of Vice-Admiralty in New Providence." In April 1782, an account brought up to date included the startling total of 127 rebel ships. So many American prisoners were brought into Nassau that Maxwell was unable to "keep or Victual them" and was forced to send them to the nearest American port and turn them loose.

Obviously Nassau was a base highly damaging to the trade between the rebel states and their allies in the Caribbean. Throughout the war the strong Spanish base of Havana fumed and threatened. Considering its defenceless state it is remarkable that Nassau survived so long. The pitiful ineffectiveness of the American fleet was one reason, but the seizure of naval supremacy by the French Admiral de Grasse in 1781, which was largely responsible for the surrender of Cornwallis at Yorktown and the practical end of the land fighting, meant that Nassau's days were numbered.

Warnings had been sounded ever since Governor Maxwell arrived in the

Bahamas. In his first meeting with the House of Assembly in April 1780, he had to warn the members of an impending invasion from Havana. He proposed calling out the local militia and sending to Sir Henry Clinton and Admiral Arbuthnot at New York for help. The aid was slow in coming, but luckily so were the Spaniards. There were further alarms in September 1781, which persuaded the assembly at last to pass the long-awaited Militia and Night Watch Acts. In April 1782, Maxwell was able to report to Clinton the arrival of two transports with stores, 170 men, 10 sergeants, and 2 drummers, bringing the garrison up to 346 men. Unfortunately, 25 of the new arrivals were wounded veterans and Maxwell reported that "to detain them here is Burying them."

None of the troops, however, were destined to stay long in Nassau. On May 6, 1782, the governor wrote urgently that he was "attacked by two American Frigates (large ones) some Galleys and 40 sail of Transports from Havana with Troops on board." This was a force of several thousand men under the command of the governor of Cuba himself, Don Juan de Cargigal. Optimistically Maxwell added that three British frigates might deter the invaders. He might as well have asked for an earthquake.

On May 7 Commodore Gillon, the commander of the American ships, sent Governor Maxwell a message of "gallant respect" urging the wisdom of surrender. Bowing to the inevitable, Maxwell hastened to agree and articles of capitulation were signed the same afternoon. In these savage days it is pleasant to read of the generosity of the terms granted by the Spaniards, which were remarkably similar to those dictated by George Washington to Lord Cornwallis five months later. The garrison was allowed to march out with all the honors of war, with arms shouldered, drums beating, and flags flying. Officers were to be permitted to keep their side arms. All troops were to be embarked for the nearest British port at Spanish expense. All officers and other inhabitants who wished to leave were allowed to take their families and Negro slaves with them and were given eighteen months in which to settle their affairs. Those who chose to stay were guaranteed protection of goods and property and freedom of worship. Finally, Governor Maxwell was to regard himself as a prisoner only as long as it took to land with the troops at the nearest British port.

The Spanish occupation lasted a little over a year, during which Don Antonio Claraco acted as governor. Unfortunately details are lacking, but from Governor Maxwell's references to "the insults and Calamities inseparable from Despotic power" on his return in 1784 it seems likely that the Spaniards did not stay closely to the spirit of the capitulation. In any case, subjection to a foreign power, however mild, is never congenial. It is likely that those Bahamians who could, deserted the islands and those who were forced by circumstances to remain envied their departure. After Rodney's brilliant victory at the Battle of the Saints in 1782 the British once more commanded the Caribbean and the Spaniards in Nassau became practically a beleaguered force. Supplies dwindled and only the recapture of Providence and the signing of peace in 1783 averted the threat of starvation.

One more interesting event occurred before the end of the war. Early in 1783 a French force seized the Turks Islands and defended itself successfully against an amphibious attack led by young Captain Horatio Nelson of H.M.S. *Albemarle,* then serving in Admiral Hood's West India Squadron. This petty setback was to be forgotten in the glory of Aboukir Bay, Copenhagen, and Trafalgar.

Article V of the preliminaries of peace signed at Versailles between England, France, and Spain on January 20, 1783, stated that "His Catholic Majesty shall restore to Great Britain the islands of Providence and the Bahamas without exception in the same condition in which they were conquered by the arms of the King of Spain." The return of the Bahamas and six small islands in the Caribbean was small compensation for the loss of the thirteen American colonies, and generally the peace terms were badly received in the British Parliament. In Nassau, however, there must have been rejoicing when rumors began to trickle in.

In Eastern Florida also there was interest. Loyalists who were no longer safe in the American states and heard that Florida was to be returned to Spain turned their eyes with desperate hope towards the almost unoccupied Bahamas. Among these was a certain Andrew Deveaux, lieutenant-colonel of the South Carolina militia, then in exile at St. Augustine. The islands were not to be restored until the definitive treaties were signed and there was no telling how long that would be. In fact, the formal peace was signed on September 3, 1783, but by that time Deveaux and several other adventurers had seized the initiative. In April, "a handful of ragged militia" set out for the Bahamas in two armed brigantines. Recruiting a few settlers and Negro slaves at Harbour Island they sneaked towards Nassau by night and landed just east of Fort Montagu.

Although the garrison of New Providence numbered over 700 men, the impending peace had rendered them supine. The single guard at Fort Montagu was easily disarmed and the sleeping garrison captured without a shot being fired. Before morning, Deveaux had seized the highest points of the ridge overlooking Nassau.

An almost contemporary account gives an amusing description of the events that followed. "Every artifice was used to deceive the Spaniards, both as to the number and description of the enemy they had to contend with. A show of boats was made continually rowing from the vessels, filled with men, who apparently landed, but in fact concealed themselves by lying down as they returned to the vessels, and afterwards made their appearance as a fresh supply of troops proceeding to disembark. Men of straw, it is said, were drest out to increase the apparent number on the heights; and some of the troops, to intimidate the Spaniards, were painted and disguised as their inveterate foes the Indians. One or two galleys in the harbour had been captured; and trusting to the circumstances in his favour, Colonel Deveaux summoned the Governor to surrender, with a pompous description of his formidable force. Some hesitation being at first discovered, the Colonel seconded his overtures with a well-directed shot at the Governor's House from a field-piece, during his deliberation, which produced an immediate capitulation. The Spanish troops, in laying down their arms, it is said, could not refrain from expressing their mortification and confusion as they surveyed their conquerors, not only so inferior in point of numbers, but ludicrous in their dress and military appearance."

The terms of capitulation offered to Claraco were similar to those dictated to Maxwell in 1782. Government House and all stores were to be given up but the garrison was allowed to retire with the customary honours, including "a piece of cannon and two shot per day, in order to hoist the flage of his Catholic Majesty." The enemy troops were to keep their baggage and effects and to be conveyed to Havana and the governor to Europe at British expense. All Spanish naval vessels in the harbor were to be surrendered but private property was to be returned, Spanish merchants having two months' grace to settle their affairs in Nassau.

Naturally enough, no-one gained more from this brilliant exploit than Andrew Deveaux himself. Carving out an estate of 250 acres in eastern New Providence and another 1,000 acres in Cat Island, he became a prominent member of the reconstituted House of Assembly. The first of the Loyalists to settle in the Bahamas, he gained immensely from his status as an already established landowner when the other Loyalists began to flock to the islands in 1784 and 1785.

NOTES

1. *Editor's note:* The Bostonian brother of Thomas Shirley who died at about the time of the Boston massacre.

HENRY C. WILKINSON

THEY BUILT SMALL SHIPS OF CEDAR: BERMUDA AND AMERICAN INDEPENDENCE

Although not a part of the West Indies, strictly speaking, Bermuda is the northern anchor in that great chain of islands curving across the Caribbean, and frequently referred to in the 18th century as "those jewels of a mercantile empire." However, Bermuda was a jewel with a questionable sparkle. As early as the Stamp Act crisis in 1765 Governor Bruere had announced Bermuda's policy, remarking that it had "no power to dispense with, mitigate, or alter any resolution of the British Parliament." Actually most of the inhabitants had no basic quarrel with this stand, but the strategic location of Bermuda was to make of Bruere a much harassed governor during most of the revolutionary period. The situation was made even more complicated by the petty bickerings which had always characterized the highly insularized politics of Bermuda.

By 1778 the American Revolution helped turn the waters of the western Atlantic into a great battleground for empire, and Bermuda faced the additional problem of near-starvation as it became increasingly difficult for England to supply its inhabitants. Lafayette, among others, had early suggested that the Continental Congress order the capture of Bermuda since it stood astride all the important sea lanes. But with no navy to speak of, and only privateers to depend upon, the Congress hoped that the Bermudians would bend their way.

Also, after 1778, the French navy had its work cut out in the West Indies. Bermuda was therefore forced to play the game both ways, capturing American shipping as well as supplying it. The depredations by American ships

From *Bermuda in the Old Empire.* Oxford University Press, 1950.

attempting to obtain British stores of powder and ball, and the friendly re-
sponse of the inhabitants, reminds the reader of some of the humorous an-
tics which took place in the Bahamas.

But there was nothing humorous in this response for Governor Bruere,
who hoped that this "undutiful" and "disloyal" behavior, as he expressed
it to the king, should "make no impression in your royal breast." And it
was with satisfaction that Bruere learned that one of the first tasks Jefferson
faced as the new governor of Virginia was to put an end to the depredations
of Bahamian privateers in the Chesapeake. Yet the good governor had to
face the threat of famine with the knowledge that the rebellious colonies a
short distance away largely remained the source for much needed staples.

Needless to say, Governor Bruere was finally a victim not of famine, but
mental and physical exhaustion. As the author comments, "George Bruere
tried to be an efficient officer in what he failed to recognize as an inefficient
system." Yet Bermuda survived both Governor Bruere and the "disastrous
commotion" of revolutionary disruption.

In influence, as Benjamin Franklin explained, "the West Indies vastly out-
weigh . . . the Northern Colonies." This strength sought to maintain itself
with the means at its command.

* * *

A Philadelphia merchant wrote: "The restrictions we are layed under by
the Parliament puts us at a stand how to employ our vessels to any advantage,
as we have no prospect of markets at our own islands and cannot send elsewhere." In other words, the trade with the Dutch, French, and Spaniards
would be much more difficult. "There is not a man on the Continent of
America," remarked another, "who does not consider the Sugar Act . . . as
a sacrifice made of the Northern Colonies to the superior interest in Parliament of the West Indies." The Bermudian version of these protests [was]
laid not against Whitehall, but against poor Governor George Bruere at the
outset of his administration; and not as a small colony objecting to the imperial policy but as individuals bitterly disagreeing with the governor.

The ministry, satisfied with Parliament's right to tax all Britons, decided
to proceed. The method chosen was to broaden the field of equitable and
light levies by imposing a series of fees under the terms of the Stamp Act.
It was presumed between £60,000 and £100,000 would thus be produced

in all America, and a half of it would be from the West Indies. Every colony regarded the measure with some hostility, though in Nova Scotia there was a "decent and dutiful acquiescence."

Even from the West Indies, those "jewels of a mercantile empire," came unwonted protests. In St. Kitts there was rioting and, while there was no violence elsewhere, nevertheless from Barbados, Dominica, Antigua, St. Vincent, and several of the smaller islands arose increasingly loud growls at their established export duty.[1] So thousands of written objections were directed to London, and English merchants hastened to intercede for the repeal of the law which had so distressed their "friends in America." The Commons called Dr. Franklin to their bar and questioned him but gathered from his witty answers that the colonists objected to internal taxes rather than to all taxes which Parliament might impose.

The Stamp papers were slow in reaching Bermuda, but when they did, in early November, the merchants paid for them in good spirit. The rumor spread, however, that the acceptance elsewhere had not been so complaisant The Bermudians accordingly, on second thought, felt that they should be careful and, with mock humility, expressed timidity at taking the papers. They asked Bruere if their ships could clear without these stamped papers, since the presence of such documents aboard might lead "refractory people in some of the other colonies" to burn or otherwise destroy their vessels. Bruere would not accept any excuse of this nature for an open breach of law, and said that he had no power "to dispense with, mitigate or alter any resolution of the British Parliament," adding that the merchants would find it their best policy to keep their ships fully employed till further word arrived from London.[2] Still, he informally advised the councilors, "with hearts full of duty and affection," to petition the Crown for redress since the stamps were "too great a burden" for little Bermuda.[3]

The repeal of the Stamp Act spread a wave of joy and thankfulness as instantaneous and widespread as the act had impelled dismay. For several weeks the hearts of all colonists were in transports of delight. Monuments were erected to George III and Pitt, now Earl of Chatham. Toasts were drunk to the king, Parliament, and the worthy Dr. Franklin. Bermuda shared in the good tidings, but in a milder way and with reservations. The people had hardly been excited enough about the stamps to forget their particular grievances over their trade, their ports, and their officials. George James Bruere was pleased to have something agreeable, albeit three months old, to tell the assembly. So he hastened to felicitate the House upon repeal, and did not fail gleefully "to commend the wisdom and moderation of the inhabitants during the late effecting crisis." The assembly, in reply, expressed its immediate pleasure "and the rather, as it is a full confirmation to us, that His Majesty's parental care extends to all his British subjects."

Thus, though the repeal of the Stamp Act had afforded a general respite and released so jubilant a mood throughout the colonies, the fundamental principle of the colonials providing for the expenses of government still remained to be solved. So, following a precedent coeval with the Navigation Act, and implementing Parliament's declaration which accompanied the repeal, an import duty was placed upon a series of articles, by the so-called "Townshend Act." America again became the scene of howling protests accompanied by violence, and in good time the ministry took cognizance. The Townshend duties had proved to be of minor consequence in Bermuda. After more than a year the governor wrote that the tax on glass, red and white lead, painter's colors, paper, tea, etc., had produced less than £23, but much trouble. Small and ineffective as the revenue was, these driblets proved nevertheless to be pinpricks. And a few weeks later Bruere was gratified to hear that the King proposed to drop them. Ebullient on such occasions, he wrote to Hillsborough that he hoped the royal clemency could "not fail to turn the hearts of the factious and seditious in America to good order and regulation."

Unfortunately incidents followed one another in quick succession and with increasing bitterness. Trouble arose over the troops who were in Boston in support of the customs and, though justice was impartial in this instance, the tempers were quickening on both sides, and there was a rapid resurgence of the radicals to the fore. The East India Company's tea became a special object of vengeance.

The news of this violence of the Bostonians reached Bermuda by way of the West Indies, but though thus belated it stirred Henry Tucker of Somerset, the rather vehement assemblyman, to write to his brother-in-law, St. George Tucker in Virginia: "I am as warmly attached to liberty as any man, but I cannot say that I like their proceedings." The same object, in his opinion, could have been achieved by declining to buy British luxuries, a procedure in which the Virginians had effectively cohered, but one in which the New Englanders, for all their cold restraint, had run to a gross excess. Incidentally, in this verdict the Bermudian Tucker had the endorsement of as great and moderate a Virginian as George Washington. Henry Tucker did not think the tax for Bermuda worthy of mention. And, as far as is known, it evoked no comment.

An effort at conciliation came from an unexpected quarter. The assembly of Jamaica memorialized the Crown, championing the rights of the colonists and beseeching the king to act as the mediator between his English and American subjects. This act, however, only riled Lord Dartmouth after the manner of Franklin's remark, though both by inclination and previous experience he was the most friendly and lenient spirit among the group who composed Lord North's ministry.[4] But the earl, caught off balance, as he not infrequently was in such a gathering, only fulminated against "so indecent, not to say criminal, conduct of an Assembly," and quashed the petition straight-away. Nevertheless the legislature of Connecticut and the young Congress extended their thanks to Jamaica for its kind intention.

If the news of the war brought a general depression in England, it wrought some elements of consternation in Bermuda. Among the islanders the opinion had been that the squabble was not much more serious than their own, and though few liked the governor, all were applauders of the king and constitution. They had accordingly thought a solution possible. Individually some held to one side and probably almost an equal number to the other, while the majority, in their perplexity, tried to steer between the two. Now, however, they all suddenly found their food supply cut off and their slim trade ruined. They had perforce to turn even wider afield and seek what they could in distant seas. For some years they had been sailing into the South Atlantic to Ascension, St. Helena, and the Cape of Good Hope, carrying turtles to barter with returning East Indiamen. Hence it came about that Captain James Cook, on his third voyage in 1776, found them established at Ascension. Others turned elsewhere, and soon a few went to the banks of Newfoundland to fish.

The cry of Bermudians was for food, and that of the Americans for munitions of war. The defiant colonists, as a reprisal for the British blockade of their ports, laid an embargo on all provisions consigned to other parts of the empire and threatened to capture or destroy any vessels arriving thence within their waters. The report of these measures spread like wild-fire and with the greatest dismay to Bermudians, who, not knowing what to do, held 120 of their ships in harbor, thus paralyzing their commerce and endangering their own lives with starvation. Under these trying circumstances, representatives from the parishes met early in April (1775) and, at Colonel Henry Tucker's suggestion, decided rather precipitately, but not without one or two faintly dissenting voices, to send delegates immediately to the Continental Congress at Philadelphia to beg for food.

Colonel Tucker was unanimously chosen as head of the delegation, but was hardly of one mind as to the procedure, and rather less certain of the prospects, knowing as he did, something of the political feeling on both sides of the Atlantic, and having his family so conspicuously divided. For his eldest son, Henry, who had remained in business in St. George's, was both a loyal councilor and son-in-law of the governor; and his third son, once clerk of the council, was now completing a course in physic at Edinburgh; while his second son was a physician in South Carolina; and his fourth, St. George, a fledgling lawyer in Virginia. But both of the Americans, as was so generally the custom on the continent, were politically-minded. Still, however hesitant the colonel may have been on the impending question of statecraft and his duty to his impoverished people, he was quite sure, as a father, that some

155

economy was necessary for his far-flung and imaginative sons, so he instructed St. George to return home. So dutiful a son could hardly demur; nevertheless, he did not sail before he had exchanged some words with Peyton Randolph and probably with Thomas Jefferson, Virginia's representatives in the Congress, on the possible bearing of Bermuda in the great crisis which they were so inexorably approaching.

The colonel's doubts on the empire's policy were not assuaged by the assurances of continental hardihood as voiced by Silas Deane, a young, fashionable, and enthusiastic agent of Congress who arrived on the island in the second half of April 1775. Deane was on his way to France, and saw fit to transship at Bermuda in order to get a faster vessel and one likely to stand in better light on the British register than that which had brought him from Philadelphia. He thought the latter could be utilized for a shorter but equally necessary trip to the West Indies.

Now it happened that Deane had held a Berkeley scholarship at Yale, and perhaps in part because of it, brought a sympathetic ear to Bermuda. At any rate he immediately caught the mood of the people and the friendship of the Tuckers, and made certain of his own general popularity by disposing of his available provisions. The island's corn supply was already exhausted and, with flour running low, he could see inevitable famine for the inhabitants if the continent did not befriend them; and he suggested to Congress that such friendship might bring its own reward. For the islands, standing as they did within 100 leagues of the course of every ship sailing between the British Isles and the West Indies, furnished an excellent advance base from which light frigates and sloops could issue to harry or destroy Britain's richest commerce. Furthermore, if the islands were seized at once, many vessels suitable for such forays could be found, and armed on the spot, and the whole project be launched before the British, bent on blockading continental ports, could change their plan to meet the altered circumstances. The success of the whole enterprise could be the better assured and facilitated by the cooperation of the Bermudians, who could receive the Americans as "their best friends."[5]

Such was Deane's hopeful suggestion to Congress before he left Bermuda at the beginning of May in the new, smart little ship which John Jennings sold him, and Captain Morgan commanded. Congress, however, was not in a position to act on this advice, though it was valid and was repeated by others on several occasions.[6] In the meantime the American hunt for powder was being vigorously pushed. Two Boston men had already spent a winter in Amsterdam buying quantities of it and shipping it in rice-barrels or tea-chests or any deceptive receptacle, by way of St. Eustatius, which became a veritable and most profitable entrepôt for contraband goods. The bulk of the supplies, however, came directly or indirectly from France, the indirect route being by way of the West Indies, especially St. Eustatius. Probably about 90 percent of the powder used by the continental troops during their first two years in the field was brought from overseas.[7]

In the spring of 1775 Washington left the Continental Congress to become commander-in-chief and took over the army before Boston two days before the engagement at Bunker Hill. Arnold, at the same time, was pushing into Canada. In both places the dearth of powder was "incredible." On August 3 the commander-in-chief noted that there was not enough "in the whole army to furnish half a pound to each man exclusive of what was held in the horns and cartridge boxes." Next day he wrote to the governor of Rhode Island: "No quantity of powder, however small, is beneath notice," and reported having heard indirectly that there was a considerable magazine at Bermuda and the people there well disposed. "The voyage is short; our necessity is great," he added, and the powder is not privately owned and so to be purchased in the customary way, but "is publick property," so that payment "may be settled with our other account."[8] He suggested that one of Rhode Island's two armed vessels be sent thither at once, and added that the "risk must be run," for the best chances lay in "a sudden strike." From Providence came the reply that some French powder was expected from Cap Français, but Captain Abraham Whipple nevertheless would be dispatched to Bermuda in the larger vessel. The Captain thoughtfully requested a note from the General to assure the Bermudians that their cause would not be forgotten by the Continental Congress, but promised to use the document only if necessary, and as events turned, it was never presented.[9]

In the meantime Colonel Henry Tucker led the parochial delegates to Philadelphia in furtherance of the principle of self-preservation. He carried with him a petition drafted in such moderate terms that its sentences seemed to alternate between the contending parties and invoke the best attainments of both. The petition was presented on July 11, 1775, in a relatively unexciting period for the Second Congress. It set forth the belief of Bermudians in national liberty and the abiding loyalty to the royal family, but also their acknowledgment of sufferings from ministerial vengeance and the futility of expecting any redress from the administration. As affectionate fellow subjects, therefore, they turned to the wisdom and humanity of Congress to recognize their desolation and hear their prayer for food. They cherished the American cause, and regretted that they must be prevented, by numerical insignificance, from giving any substantial reciprocal help to their continental brethren. Nevertheless, there was some verbal mention, or at any rate acknowledgment, of a little royal powder stored on the island, and Congress responded four days later with a resolution that any vessel which the Bermudians should send northward with munitions of war would not return to their island empty.

The details of the matter were turned over to the *Committee of Safety* of Pennsylvania of which Benjamin Franklin and Robert Morris were leading members. As negotiations proceeded, Colonel Tucker found himself in difficulties, for he had gone to Philadelphia as a loyal subject of the king, hoping and expecting that some conciliation would soon be found by both the Crown and the colonists, as the First Congress had asked and the Second was repeating in the humblest terms, assuring George III that it sought not independence but reconciliation. But with Washington already in the field the purposes of gunpowder were only too obvious and, besides, Franklin had no faith in the Crown granting any accommodation. Some of the colonel's fellow delegates were less given to theorizing, but were wholly aware of their own islanders' approaching starvation, and the sympathy of the Americans for them, so that it seemed an abnegation of the truth not to leave a list of the island's requirements. This, accordingly, they did, before starting on a speedy return voyage.

Meanwhile, the news of the gunpowder in the magazine at St. George's was dispatched to Washington, but Congress knowing full well the difference there might be between words and performance, made no definite commitment. None the less Franklin wrote a note to the Bermudians for Captain Trimingham to deliver, stating that Congress was inclined to help the Bermudians as soon as assurances could be given that the provisions would not be reexported to the West Indies.

A few weeks before these events, St. George Tucker in Williamsburg, having reached the end of his financial tether, responded to his father's behest and started homeward, after giving his advice about the Bermuda powder to Peyton Randolph, who had since been elected president of the Congress. During these same weeks St. George's brother, Thomas Tudor Tucker, had been no less thoughtful in mentioning this same supply to his officials in the Carolinas.

When, however, the family had talked over this risk, it did not seem as great as presumed. Accordingly there was no reason to keep St. George's visit secret or to restrict his movements. And Colonel Henry, back from Philadelphia by July 25, and moderately optimistic, told him to see the Brueres and express his thanks for the letters and presents they had sent him in the better days, but warned him to expect no tolerance from the old man. St. George started upon his errand at Government House in a somber mood, but found the atmosphere less heavy than he expected, and soon had the official permission to practice his profession on the islands. For the governor was in a good frame of mind, having seen nothing of the assembly for a month, or of the council for two, and was feeling a pleasant relief from both. Furthermore, the return of the delegates had eased the political tension somewhat, and cheered him enough to recall the assembly to consider some lightening of the food restrictions.

That night, however, when stillness had fallen upon the town and Government House settled into a more comfortable mood than usual, several dozen men scurried noiselessly over the northern hill to the powder magazine only a few hundred yards north-east of the house, and actually on land owned by the Bruere family, on which the governor, in his generosity, had allowed the magazine to be built. There they stood anxiously catching their breath while the roof of the vaulted chamber was boldly and quickly pierced with muffled blows until a sufficient breach was made for a man to be lowered within. As soon as the door was unbolted 100 barrels of powder were grasped by ready hands and trundled down the hill to a fleet of small boats in readiness to receive them. So adroitly was this audacious theft executed that the boats had time to get miles off shore in darkness—so silently, in fact, that the slumber of no single noisy dog was disturbed.

An alarm, nevertheless, was raised at daybreak. The town, hitherto so quiet, was immediately in turmoil. The customs boat put out as soon as a crew could be mustered. The sloop *Lady Catherine* of Virginia, under the command of Captain George Orde, a gentleman who had been in Bermuda four months before and was well known to Silas Deane and the Tuckers, was understood to be at the West End with clearance papers for Philadelphia. The customs officials, however, found that the sloop had sailed betimes and could not be overtaken. But to their surprise the schooner *Charlestown and Savannah Pacquet* of South Carolina, John Turner master, was spied in much the same quarter, though she had left St. George's four days earlier with a load of stone for Barbados. She too was under full canvas and sailing admirably, and what was more the local whaleboats were returning from her.

The situation was of the utmost gravity, for many people must have been implicated, and many more must have known. The latter, however, seemed to be sharply divided between those who knew too little and those who knew too much, since extraordinarily little was said at the time and almost nothing thereafter. General [Gage] ordered Captain Tollemache of the *Scorpion*, who was about to convoy a transport to the Carolinas, to put in at the island to assist the governor as best he could. So it happened that the ships reached St. George's early in October (1775) and gave the governor a short respite from his nervous tension, with the preponderance of strength for the moment on his side. . . .

In due course Lieutenant George Bruere, wounded and invalided from America, took up the function of agent in London, with the filial duty of palliation for the acts and omissions of his unfortunate and bewildered father, the governor. He reported that many assemblymen and even some councilors were implicated in the powder exploit. So it had been in Barbados too, where the president of the council was impugned for selling powder to the rebels. There was no doubt in his mind that widespread dribbling occurred from many British outposts. He went on to say that most of the American privateers were Bermuda-built, and that there were some twenty Bermudian craft at the Bahamas helping the enemy in various ways, fetching them salt when not more flagrantly transgressing. It was a wonder, he added, that the rebels had not yet seized Bermuda, defenseless as it was and without a garrison for eight years past. George Bruere was right. Bermuda was becoming increasingly important to the American cause both strategically and commercially, and so Silas Deane was representing it to the versatile Beaumarchais.

The paramount need of salt rendered Bermuda almost as important commercially as it was in naval strategy, especially now that armies were active and food had to be pickled for them. So Congress in its "maturer judgment," having learned that George III had refused even to read their second humble petition, turned more industriously to a protracted war, and hearkened to the expediency of encouraging Bermudian shipping and that of the Bahamas with it. Furthermore, since the powder from St. George's had reached the continental armies, Congress felt better disposed and spent all of November 22 (1775) unbegrudgingly, in committee of the whole, considering the needs of the island. As a result, it authorized the shipment of a year's provision by the colonies from and inclusive of New York to South Carolina. . . .

The Congress, at the insistence of Washington, gave maritime affairs the utmost attention. It set up a standing committee for the purpose, and commissioned four cruisers, with others to follow as soon as possible. One ship was commanded by John Paul Jones, and on August 6 he was instructed to cruise about Bermuda, which the commander-in-chief intended to make "a nest of hornets to annoy British commerce," and to that end had already sent the gallant Nicholas Biddle in the *Andrew Doria* into those waters.

The Marine Committee gave word for two sloops of war to be bought, fitted, and manned at Bermuda. It wrote to Henry Tucker of Somerset and Thomas Godet asking that five or six large vessels be chartered to fetch salt to American ports, and then be reloaded with provisions. Poor George James Bruere was kept humiliated, aghast, and chagrined. Misunderstood as he had always been at Whitehall, his failure to secure his most sacred trust could hardly be condoned, and he was now even further lacking in means to maintain the royal prerogative and only too often was being outwitted by rebel sympathizers. In fact he could do little but grit his teeth and hold on.

Meanwhile the legislators, not knowing how events would turn, decided it was their part to propitiate both sides, and in the week of the Declaration of Independence, though slightly in anticipation of that document, assured their gracious sovereign of their loyalty and zeal for him and his family, their admiration for the Constitution, and their "unfeigned solicitude for the happiness and prosperity of the Parent State." They explained that self-preservation had driven them to seek their food at its habitual source and address the Continental Congress at a time when they still hoped an honorable reconciliation possible. No sooner was this hope blasted than the prohibition of all intercourse with the American colonies again threatened them with famine. And, they added: "From various concurring circumstances . . . we apprehend that some unfavorable representations of [our] people have been made, and their conduct stigmatized as undutiful and disloyal. . . . We humbly trust that such statements will make no impression in your royal breast. . . ."

During the interval, St. George Tucker perceived that the war had to be fought to a conclusion, and decided to return to Virginia. But to do so he had to wait until Lord Dunmore had been subdued, and the Chesapeake opened. By November (1776) these obstacles had been cleared and, with his father's help, he bought a vessel and "without taking leave of the governor or the chief justice," sailed for Turks Island. From there, with a cargo of salt, he made for Yorktown, which he reached about the hour when the Battle of Princeton was being fought. He went on to Williamsburg to join in a ball given to celebrate the capture of the Hessians in that engagement.

The Bermudians had many shipping grievances of which to complain, for their tempers and allegiances had been unduly strained from the outbreak of the rebellion. The sloop *Thomas and Stafford,* loaded with South Carolinian provisions for Surinam, had been held by the embargo throughout the summer of 1775, and when at length allowed to proceed, found too good a market at Martinique to venture past it. But on the way back she touched at St. Christopher (St. Kitts) where, by mischance she encountered Captain Tollemache in the *Scorpion* [who] promptly seized her. In the same way a naval cutter chased Captain John Seymour's sloop *Dick Cole* to Turks Island and then sent her to Jamaica as a prize. Though there had been losses to the Americans there was also, at times, some justification for that course, for not every Bermudian sailor was circumspect. But the Americans never failed to give due consideration to every ship which they saw fit to question.

As though troubles were not accumulating fast enough, the summer of 1777 was unusually hot and dry, and famine was imminent. The assemblymen were truly apprehensive and begged Bruere in respectful terms to give up his futile notion of drawing provisions from Britain or Ireland and, working in agreement with them, relax the embargo against the continental colonies to enable them all to live. But, though Bruere's heart was ready to yield to such pleas, a request came from Lord Howe that no West Indian produce be released. And as Bruere cogitated on these intricacies, and the weakness of his own position, he could not help thinking that the cry of

Bermudians for trading privileges was primarily to "run" provisions to the rebels, and the assemblymen's real motive was to usurp authority. So it seemed only too evident that none had pity on the wretched, though in reality the War Office was not without sympathy and instructed the governor of Barbados to release some of the government stores there to relieve the Bermudians. Nothing, however, came of this, and famine hovered closer to the island than ever. So Colonel Tucker begged his son in Virginia to get some food off by any method he could.

In October, only in the nick of time, 1,000 bushels of corn arrived, as the first importation in six months. It could afford only temporary relief and the islanders had still to rivet their minds on the best means of averting the grisly prospect ahead of them. They could see no way to help themselves but to carry salt to the struggling colonies, especially the southern, where that commodity was becoming more important than ever. They accordingly plied themselves to the trade and with enough success to be reported to the Admiralty.

To understand the next legislative move we must take a little time to separate the ever-tangling threads of the island's affairs. This may be dated from the autumn of 1777 when the Goodrich brothers returned to the island one by one, to be followed by their father and a couple of dozen Scottish and Irish adventurers, but Loyalists all of them, mostly from New York. Bridger Goodrich made it clear that, except for authorized provision ships, he had no intention of letting Bermudian vessels go unmolested to the Continent. Indignation kindled to an intense pitch. The advent of the troops had synchronized with this subjugation of the island's shipping, and turned the tables upon a politically-minded group which had long had its own way. This commissioning of privateers and fetching of prizes, wrote Henry Tucker of Somerset, has become obnoxious to the more thoughtful inhabitants, without a way being found to stop it.

The Bermuda privateers continued to sail, and with enough effect for the governor of Maryland and Governor Patrick Henry of Virginia to implore, and for Congress to assure them that the trade of the Chesapeake would be safeguarded and a speedy end put to the Goodriches with their roving fleet. So one of Jefferson's first duties upon assuming the governorship of Virginia was to work diligently for the destruction of these marauders. He wrote to John Jay for several of the letters of marque recently granted by Congress, adding "our trade has never been so distressed since the time of Lord Dunmore as it is at present, by a parcel of trifling privateers under the countenance of two or three larger vessels who keep our little naval force from doing anything."[10]

This privateering had produced other than the direct effects, for in the late autumn, when Congress further regulated the exportation of provisions, it omitted as heretofore to exempt the British colonies, in which list Bermuda had held first place. Captain John Lightbourn was in Philadelphia at the time and, in spite of his exertions to get the new regulation reconsidered and his pleas for "the starving and distressed" island, he failed even to get a hearing.[11] Thus the rebellious American colonies remained the sole source for replenishment of the exhausted food supply of Bermuda, and the obtuse old governor clung literally to his instructions to have no traffic with any belligerent subjects of Great Britain and abetted privateering to molest them. Naturally there was a considerable revulsion of feeling on the Continent against Bermuda and its plight now became extreme.

In January (1779) the assembly met in a milder mood and implored Bruere to relax the embargo against the Continent so that their fellow islanders could fetch themselves some food. As the assemblymen expressed it: "To Your Excellency alone we must look for relief, if you refuse to attend, we are undone." This time he heard them and promised to allow a vessel to sail for the relief of each parish. But the food situation became graver. The first ray of relief appeared in February when Thomas Forbes's brigantine *Superb* arrived from St. Eustatius with a cargo of rice. The governor was prevailed on to receive her, the public faith was pledged for her safety, and she was quickly unloaded, when Captain Collins pounced upon the empty ship and, in spite of all the governor could do, took her to New York. In April another cargo of rice arrived and was duly entered and landed at the West End after the people had solemnly promised to respect the vessel and divide her cargo among the nine parishes. The governor was well satisfied, but the collector unexpectedly tried to seize the sloop with the aid of soldiers and sailors. He proved to be too slow in this instance; nevertheless troops marched to the West End in time to drive off several other ships. Colonel Henry Tucker felt sorely tried, and wrote: "This is most shocking to us to have bread brought to our doors and not [be] permitted to get it."

Necessity impelled some action, and this year, as in 1776, the political leaders decided that they must put forth their best efforts both in England and on the Continent. They agreed that their start should be at Philadelphia, and would require their undivided attention. So they put off any meeting of their assembly, ostensibly because of the lack of food at St. George's.

Accordingly the Tuckers and others to the number of twenty sent a petition to Congress, recalling the favors previously afforded them, and begging for reconsideration of the embargo now placed upon the island. But Congress was of two minds, and thought it inexpedient to relax its embargo on Bermuda. By the further efforts of the [Bermudians], however, and after presenting more ample proof of the effective services of Bermudians in fetching salt, the question was reopened on May 18 with the result that this time the members became convinced of the island's great need. So Congress, with the concurrence of the minister of France, authorized the Executive Committee of Delaware, Maryland, and Virginia to ship 1,000 bushels of corn to the famished islanders, as North Carolina had already done, and as St. George Tucker had asked of the Virginia Assembly. Thereafter many shipments were made, and Bermudians were again exempted from capture in all commissions issued by the Marine Committee.

But the food situation hardly improved. Though seventy-nine, Eliza Tucker reported: "Our unhappy country feels the severest of ills, thousands have suffered and many more have perished for want of bread. We have had several providential but temporary reliefs and our prospect is now as bad as ever . . . scarce one letter in twenty . . . gets to hand in running the gauntlet not only of belligerent action and the turbulent waves, but to no less a degree of the prying eyes of impertinent curiousity and of inattention." The council and assembly joined in this verdict.

The weather during this winter of 1779 to 1780 was foul beyond the memory of living Bermudians. At the same time the redirection of the British thrust in America from north to south, improving as it seemed the chances of success, greatly increased the volume of shipping in the latitude of the island. Many vessels failed to keep their place in convoy and collided, so that they had to put in for hurried repairs. Not a few were captured by continental cruisers only to be recaptured by Bermudian privateers.

After all that had passed and been stoically endured, there was no occasion for George James Bruere to feel crestfallen. . . . His repeated pleas had at length been heard by the Lords of Trade, and as a result he was to be reinforced with a lieutenant-governor, and none other than his eldest and meritorious son, to sit in the council and help in coping with the local difficulties. Likewise, as an old soldier, he was invigorated by the fall of Charleston to Lord Cornwallis, and at the same time relieved of the tribulations of his own small command by Colonel Donkin, who quickly brought order out of chaos. It made for an equally mellow twilight for this old warrior grandsire. For after mid-July the governor's health steadily declined, and he died peacefully on September 10 (1780), a victim, in the eyes of his family, of five years of incessant strain and foul play.

. . . Now it happened that new situations had brought fresh devices. For the time had come when chaos in American finance was bringing engrossers, forestallers, and regraters into unimagined prominence and the price of meat in Boston was climbing to $10 a pound and butter to $12. Small wonder is there that such inflation stimulated the cupidity of a good number to run the chief preservative to such a market, and that salt reached New England at the price of dishonor. There was, in truth, regrettable evidence that a dozen Bermudian ships had actually supplied the French fleet, under D'Estaing, with salt during his ten burdensome weeks at Boston, for two craft bringing thousands of dollars in payment, fell into the hands of the loyal privateers.[12]

[In the meantime] St. George Tucker wrote to Washington of the feasibility of capturing Bermuda, so beloved by him and so important to the American cause, and now, as a result of British "tyranny" with its people, almost united in ardor for the success of the United States. "The reduction of Bermuda," wrote Tucker, "would open again those resources for the supply of salt to the Continent, the obstruction of which has been severely felt by the inhabitants of [Virginia] in particular, who not being furnished with vessels of their own, have been obliged to depend on the fortuitous arrival of Bermudians driven hither by necessity, or allured by the advantages of our commerce, to brave even the horrors of a prison-ship, which many of them have fatally experienced."

Washington was definitely interested, so Tucker elaborated the plan over many pages, suggesting that the whole scheme be considered by "some respectable gentlemen" resident at West End. He knew of competent pilots who were available and thought the time suitable for action, and, he continued, in the event of success Bermuda could remain a neutral island until the end of the war, when a disposition of it could be made in accordance with the wish of its own people and the best interests of the United States and her allies. From the island's point of view there was as great a chance of invasion from the French and Spaniards who were demonstrating in such force in the West Indies.

* * *

George Bruere, with soldierly courage and faith in his cause, dispelled those forces of opposition which his father's death had released to their own devices. And soon he was gratified to see a marked diminution in the rebel salt trade, more Loyalist privateers putting to sea, and their list of prizes mounting rapidly above 300. His intelligence system kept him informed of the sallies of his sly opponents, who, cut off from their illicit entrepôt at St. Eustatius, turned quite nimbly into the Danish islands of St. Thomas and St. Croix, whence they returned with sufficient quantities of American contraband produce to keep their small boats busy on the horizon every week. This "rescuing" of forbidden goods, under the pretence of saving the people from starvation, had become habitual and had been expanded to luxury wares.

Bruere wrote Lord George Germain of his difficulties, as he had previously written Rodney, explaining the artifices at which the assemblymen were such masters, and their too frequent practice of side-stepping oaths while "making the most loyal professions at home" and then doing the exact opposite. George Bruere, throughout, had tried to be an efficient officer in what he failed to recognize as an inefficient system. For the empire, which had been his glory and the pride of every Britisher, had been brought, by an unnecessary war, to its lowest level and to the point of disruption.

But a policy of retraction had already set in, not from any conviction that the former procedure was wrong, but to gain time and divert the smaller colonies, if possible, from any petulant action in joining the American rebels. So while Lord George Germain continued to uphold Bruere and to commend his energetic action, in reality before the end of 1780 a governor had been appointed to supersede him.

The next governor was William Browne, a Loyalist of distinguished family from Massachusetts. He had been valedictorian of his class at Harvard in 1775 and stood third in order of social position. Seven years later he had been elected to the assembly and in 1764 appointed collector of customs at Salem. But he lost this office two years later for leniency in enforcing the sugar duty. Nevertheless he was made a judge of common pleas, and in 1774 was raised to the Superior Court of Massachusetts. Years later his friend and classmate John Adams said that he was "a solid, judicious character," and he added, "they made him a judge of the Superior Court and that society made him a refugee. A tory, I verily believe, he was never." But the times would not permit of a doubt, and the explosion of the Revolution forced him to flee from Boston in the company of all the officials and more than half the university groups.

Lord North approved of this appointment and the royal confirmation came in February 1781. The governor-designate was then personally instructed by Lord George Germain to adopt a conciliatory attitude towards Bermuda so that the island would not become wholly alienated in sympathy from the Crown. In the official view Bermuda had stood as a moderate among the colonies throughout the disastrous "commotion" and taken sides as little as possible. Indeed, the islanders appeared to their sympathetic governor to be a "simple people" wholly "bewildered" by the contortion of events about them. They had questioned the authority neither of king nor Parliament. It was true that individuals had shown preferences, and no doubt most of the delegates to the Continental Congress had returned as confirmed separationists to spread their beliefs as widely as they dared, short of tangible treason. Still they had become, in fact, only the opposition to the governor's party, stepping-up their resistance, as in generations past, when his stupidity or willfulness seemed to demand it.

When in turn these same men reflected on the preceding decades they could see some justification for their obstruction in that it had brought them, at this late stage, a model governor who understood them and identified himself both with their difficulties and their aspirations. Moreover, they could not help being impressed by one who had suffered as much as he for his loyalty to the Crown, and they were quick to respond to his leadership, especially as the conflict was not at an end and the navy again stood unchallenged on the seven seas.

NOTES

1. Lowell J. Ragatz, comp., *A Guide to Official Correspondence of the Governors of the British West India Colonies, 1763-1783* (London: The Bryan Edwards Press, 1923).
2. In North Carolina the people forced the commander of H.M.S. *Viper* to release two vessels which he had seized for sailing without stamped clearances.
3. Wilfred B. Kerr, *Bermuda and the American Revolution: 1760-1783* (Princeton, 1936). Reprinted by Archon Books in 1969.
4. *Editor's note:* Franklin's remark: "Every man in England seems to consider himself as a piece of a sovereign over America; seems to jostle himself into the throne with the King, and talks of our subjects in the colonies."
5. Silas Deane to Robert Morris (April 26, 1775) in Library of U.S. Naval Academy. Deane took a keen interest in Bermuda. "In some companies," the British Ambassador at Paris later reported, "Mr. Deane calls himself a native of Bermuda."
6. *Editor's note:* Notably Lafayette who persistently pressed Vergennes to take Bermuda for the Americans and to start "a party of liberty there."
7. Orlando W. Stephenson, "The Supply of Gunpowder in 1776," *American Historical Review,* XXX (1925), pp. 271-81.
8. *Editor's note:* Rhode Island had early taken the lead in privateering, and with its list of experienced sea captains, provided a revolutionary "navy" in embryo.
9. *Editor's note:* When Whipple finally arrived at Bermuda, he found H.M.S. *Scorpion* in St. George's Harbor and wisely sailed away.
10. Robert A. Stewart, *History of Virginia's Navy of the Revolution* (Richmond, 1934), pp. 53-54.
11. Wilfred B. Kerr, *Bermuda and the American Revolution: 1760-1783* (Princeton, 1936).
12. In 1781 to 1782 merchants of Kingston, Jamaica, supplied the enemy with stores, using false clearance papers for New York. From 1784 to 1786 they carried on an extensive illicit trade with the thirteen states, which Captain Horatio Nelson endeavored to curb.

E. ARNOT ROBERTSON

THE SPANISH TOWN PAPERS: SOME SIDELIGHTS ON WEST INDIAN PRIVATEERING

The story of revolutionary privateering more properly belongs to the formative history of the fledgling American navy during the war for independence. The selection which follows was written by someone who kept one eye on the goddess Clio, but whose second eye is truly the eye of a poet. E. Arnot Robertson will be remembered by some readers for her delightful mixture of past and present in the beautifully illustrated Thames Portrait. *Historians are in debt to her sensitive handling of the Spanish Town papers, those crumbling bundles of the history of courage, bravery, and dedication. Selfishness, greed, and ruthless ambition were not absent. The division of spoils attracted many adventurers who were not seamen and who were ridiculed as "gentlemen sailors." As that great historian of America's navy, Edgar Maclay, remarked: "all seaports sending out privateers were thronged with these tars of exalted degree, and, in many cases, of long pedigree." But this aspect is kept in its true proportion as Eileen Robertson keeps a steady eye on the true elements in a dramatic story of patriotism and sacrifice.*

In the first three years of the war perhaps less than ten percent of the powder needed for the guns of the Revolution was produced in America. The balance was imported chiefly from the French and Dutch—and mostly through their islands in the West Indies. Including both state and continental privateers, probably more than 2,000 ships were put into service between 1775 and 1781. And they brought not only powder, but such items as salt without which Washington's armies could not have survived to use

From *The Spanish Town Papers.* Cresset Press, 1959.

the powder—together with many "essentials" required by the people of America (including the favorite wines of the founding fathers).

Some sixty of the privateersmen became captains in the new American navy, and one of them fathered a hero for a future war, Stephen Decatur, Jr. All in all, the Spanish Town papers are the story of human courage, "courage," in the words of the author, "magnificent and wholly unaware of its own splendor."

By day, bats keep up a soft, insistent twittering in the eaves of the Old Armory in Spanish Town, Jamaica's former capital. It sounds as if they are impatient for the return of night, when they can have the huge building to themselves again, and flit and swirl among the records of dead men's courage and efforts and disasters. Here are stored the island's Vice-Admiralty Court records, an extraordinary cache of eighteenth- and early nineteenth-century naval documents, many of them, unfortunately, in an advanced state of decay.

Among them are nearly a thousand bundles of ships' papers, each bundle representing a vessel captured during the American War of Independence, 1776–1783.

They were seized either by the British Navy, patrolling in force in the West Indies, or by the many privateers who rushed joyously into what was really legalized piracy: Letters of Marque were freely granted as the war went on, by the angry George III, to practically any merchant in his possessions who owned a fast ship carrying guns, and was willing to harry the disaffected colonists and his other enemies. (In Caribbean waters such craft were likely to be ex-slavers: they were always well-armed with swivel-guns which could be turned either on to the holds or against other vessels.)

Captured merchant ships taken in the South Atlantic or Caribbean seas were brought into Kingston Harbor, to Port Royal, the naval base, to be tried by the Vice-Admiralty Court on a charge of "Trading with the American Colonies in Rebellion," or of being American owned, in hull or cargo. In the later years of the war, when France, Holland, and Spain had joined in—less, on the whole, as allies of the Americans than in order to annoy the British—the charge was widened to include ownership by any of their nationals. More and more American merchant-captains took to adding to their Ship's Passport, or Clearance, the declaration which had been no more than a proud flourish of defiance at the beginning—*"that no Subject of the King of Great Britain directly or indirectly hath any Share, Part or Interest there-*

in": it became a practical but somewhat pathetic effort to avoid capture by their own privateers—pathetic because usually unavailing.

Predatory ruthlessness appears to have been level between the Letters of Marque ships on either side, and from these Spanish Town documents rises constantly the outraged cry, *"We never deviated from our Course, not apprehending the least danger of being made Prize of by People we esteemed our friends,"* recorded by the Master of the brig *Penelope.* She had been captured and recaptured so many times that it was hard to disentangle her ownership. Though she still carried many of the English seamen who had signed on as crew when she was a West-of-England craft, she was taken into Port Royal and condemned as French property. This meant that the ship and cargo could be sold "by public outcry" (auction) for the benefit of the captors; and the unlucky seamen lost their wages, unless they had prudently persuaded their owners to pay part in advance.

* * *

Ships changed hands with remarkable rapidity during the war of independence: it is not unusual to learn that a particular vessel had twice sailed as an American ship, and twice as a British ship, in the course of one year. Neutrals were rarely luckier; if one were stopped by an American privateer, and found to have an Englishman among the crew, this was sufficient excuse for taking her into Salem and selling her up there; the blockaded colonists were desperately in need of ships almost from the start, and of cargoes of all sorts. Flying American colors, the ex-neutral would then creep out of port, one dark night, to run the blockade under a new name, fall in with an armed British merchantman and be made prize: both might well be taken, on the way to Jamaica and the Vice-Admiralty Court, by a French privateer. At this point the rechristened and lately American ship could be considered British, as prize to a British ship, and plundered by the Frenchmen, along with her captor, with no more than the customary ill-feeling between allies. Nelson was on the prowl along these sea roads, first as a captain aged twenty in H.M.S. *Badger,* and later in the *Hinchinbrook*; and there were many other Ships of the Line about: the odds were that the French privateer and both her prizes would fall to one of them, within the next few weeks, and be taken into Kingston Harbor. Once there, the ex-neutral had no more chance than at Salem of escaping confiscation and forced-sale, but in Jamaica the charge against her would probably rest not on her crewlist, but on her cargo-manifest: it mattered very little what nationalities were among her sailors if she had salt in the hold. Salt was known to be in great demand—increasingly great demand—by the inhabitants of the thirteen colonies in revolt: food grew scarcer there as the war dragged on, and what means of preserving it was there excepting salting, for winter use? Turks Island in the West Indies was a well-known source of salt: several ships were condemned in the Vice-Admiralty Court as intending to trade with the colonists, even though they had not already done so, on no stronger evidence than that they had touched at Turks Island, and had salt on board.

When a cargo of salt did get through to the fighting Americans there was jubilation: by what chance the advertisement of a sale of salt in Baltimore got among the papers taken off a prize at Port Royal it is impossible to say, but it is significant that already, by the date of the advertisement, 1778, money was giving way to barter as an inducement to buy large quantities: money was plentiful, but growing discredited in the eyes of ordinary citizens: other goods made a better exchange for this invaluable commodity.

The shocking fact which emerges from a study of these Spanish Town papers—shocking even by the standards of the century in which they found their way to Jamaica—is that the presiding judge of the Vice-Admiralty Court was allowed a very small sum for his trouble in holding the trial, if the ship were declared innocent of the charge against her and freed, but a substantial cut in the proceeds of the local sale if she were condemned. In consequence, the records of ships being acquitted are very few indeed.

And yet, despite the smell of wickedness, greed, and brutality which comes up from these brown, damp-stained, insect-eaten papers, there comes, too, movingly, across the years, a sense of the good, enduring human things: men in danger writing tenderly to their wives, in the hope of falling in with a ship of their own side on the homeward run which might successfully take the letter back through the blockade. *"My dear and affectionate Wife . . . My dear Betsey, kiss the children for me and Keep up your Spirits. . . ."* This was from Captain William Luce, writing in April 1776 by the schooner *Dolphin* bound from Hispaniola (now Haiti and Santo Domingo) to Charleston, North Carolina; but the *Dolphin* was intercepted by H.M.S. *Southhampton* and the letter was never delivered; nor was another from him to his brother-in-law, Andrew Gautier in New York, written at the same time:

Since I left New York I have Not Had a Single Line from any of my friends which makes me Very Uneasy, and I fear the time is not far Distant when you will have a large Fleet and Army on the Continent from England— should New York meet with any disaster which god forbid, you must with yours go to my house in the Country, and should that once happy Retreat be made the scene of Warr I shall leave it to you to take Refuge where peace is most likely to Reign until some Change in Affairs happen, taking my dear Wife and two poor Children with you, I think some place on the Sea Shore about the South side of Staten Island or the South side of long island would not be amiss as there you might always at the worst of times procure a little fish which would be agreeable.

The anxiety of mind I have undergone since I left you is beyond your Conception. When I think of home and what may happen there it almost overcomes me, those thoughts with other Matters relative to my ship which I fear I shall be put to my Trumps about loading almost at times Gett the better of me.

A touching fragment only survives among the papers of another vessel: *"my dear Husban i woud like to wash your dirty dirty shirts agen."* The termites have taken the rest, and the long years of neglect during which these bundles were, literally, kicked about on the floor of a damp storehouse before their move to Spanish Town.

Courage—magnificent and wholly unaware of its own splendor—this is the savor which rises more strongly than any other from these bundles: the men of the time had an enormous capacity to face with equanimity what must be endured because it could not be helped. They were tough almost beyond belief, the crews who sailed the small, ill-found, and frequently (as the records show) rotten boats which made the relatively enormous voyages mentioned in these court records. Interrogated, one of the seamen of the *Désirée*, captured by the privateer *Lord Sandwich*, stated that he thought he had heard from his messmates that the next destination of his ship *"was England, but whether England in Europe or England in America could not say."* And probably he did not care; not, at least, enough to inquire further. He was a man of the sea, not at home on the solid earth: landfall meant little to him, unless he happened to be a family man, putting into his home port: it was the immediate voyage which mattered, its vicissitudes and the men who shared them with him. This attitude of indifference towards the land appears again and again in the depositions of the seamen, who frequently contradicted their captain after he had given evidence on oath, as part of his defence of his ship before the Court, that everyone on board knew she was bound for some lawful neutral port. They had no idea, they said, where they were going. They had signed on for one trip, and then for another, not asking what risks they were likely to run.

The Vice-Admiralty Court was originally set up in the West Indies in the seventeenth century to deal, in peacetime, with affairs of piracy or murder on the high seas, the Oyer and Terminer cases (from the French "Ouir et determinar," to hear and decide). The court did, indeed, hear, but had generally decided beforehand, on the side of authority. This was the court which in 1776 took over the task of deciding, when a prize was brought into Port Royal, what should be considered the nationality of the owner or owners, the past activity of the ship, and the intentions of the captain. A number of ships were condemned, despite their masters' declaration on oath (often supported by documents) that they were bound for a neutral port where they had every right to go, because the state of their hulls was adjudged too leaky to allow them to make such a destination: they could therefore be assumed to have been sailing for one of the nearer ports of the thirteen colonies in rebellion. An example of this is the case of the brig *L'Elizabeth*. Plainly she was owned by merchants in Hispaniola. This is an extract from evidence by the court from the captors:

The said brigantine sailed from Cape Francois bound as the Master of her stated for San Pierre de Miquelon but . . . from the condition she was in, she never wuld have been able to have got there (not being) by any means fitted or calculated for such a voyage and particularly at this tempestuous Season of the year. . . . She must from necessity have desisted . . . and stood away for some port in North America.

Despite the clarity of her papers from Hispaniola, she was condemned as American property, in January 1776.

A peculiarity of a Vice-Admiralty Court was that it proceeded against a ship, not a person. What happened to the captain and crew, when their vessel and cargo were condemned, was always doubtful. There are references in letters found among these papers to *"American prisons now full of English mariners,"* but the prisons of Jamaica could not possibly have housed, in any year of the war, the thousands of men brought into Port Royal in the prizes.

The outbreak of the American War of Independence coincided with the first recognition, by service authorities, of the fact that any scrap of paper written by an enemy might prove a weapon to be used against him. The order went out from the Admiralty in London that nothing written, however personal or trivial, should be left aboard a prize: every paper was to be handed over to the Register of the court. The American colonists were plainly unaware of this new tactic: their letters to friends abroad, entrusted to captains of their acquaintance—there was no other way of sending them—were extremely indiscreet in detail about the disposition of troops, military plans and any information which had come their way: 4th January, 1778, *"Count d'Estaing lays in Boston refitting, he met much damage in a hard gale. . . ."* This was taken off the schooner *Agnus* captured by the privateer *Surprise*.

The lulling of an intended victim's suspicion by approaching her under her own colors, until the last moment, may seem a somewhat liberal interpretation of the instructions given to American privateers in the Letters of Marque signed in his own handwriting by John Huntington, as president of Congress, a copy of which was found aboard the privateer brig *Ranger* of Newburyport, Massachusetts, when she was captured by H.M.S. *Pelican* off

Hispaniola in 1781: *"You may also annoy the enemy ... by all means in your power, taking care not to infringe the laws of humanity and the usages of the sea."* But in action the privateers of both sides knew few qualms of conscience, the Jamaican privateers least of all: they fought without mercy on the British side despite the West Indian sympathy with the other colonists.

As the war progressed, the practice of sailing under false colors became more and more general. In the first year of the war the behavior of the Charleston brig *Rebecca* was noted as exceptional. She was out from Sunbury with a cargo of rice, bound for Cap Français and then back to South Carolina, when she was captured while flying British colors, according to the libel against her. A few years later not only the ships of the colonists in revolt, but French, Dutch, Spanish, Portuguese, and some British vessels, illegally trading with the colonists, were all condemned for having on board and having used—according to the admission of the crews or the testimony of the captors—an assortment of national flags to which they were not entitled.

The bitter feelings of the American War of Independence were shared, as has been indicated, by many planters in the West Indies: here, too, were colonists taxed without adequate representation in London. When the island of St. Kitts was taken by the French during the war, it was recorded at the time by a local historian that "the planters feared lest their good relationship with their captors should be endangered by the patriotic indiscretions of the negroes and poor-whites." Sympathy with America might even have found an active outlet had not the British navy been in such strength in Caribbean waters. George III and Lord North between them could alienate men of high temper anywhere. There were plenty of signs of dissatisfaction. One small but pleasing act of defiance lurked among the papers of the schooner *Dolphin* from Boston: she took on part of her cargo at Montego Bay, on the north side of Jamaica, as far as could be from Port Royal, and with it a printed clearance paper with one most unusual feature. At this period the king was still officially styled, within his own possessions, "King of Great Britain, Ireland and France"—the last, a claim which had never been relinquished from the days of Henry V and the quarrel over the Salic Law of succession. His subjects at Montego Bay, in 1777, referred to George III as "King of Great Britain, Ireland and so forth." The long initial "S" of those days adds considerably to the contemptuous appearance of the words on the *Dolphin's* clearance: "... and so forth."

One of the unforeseen effects of the outbreak of war between Britain and America was the dearth of reliable sailing directions in the colonists' ships—these directions had almost all been printed in England and suddenly the supply was stopped. The cumbersome little merchant ships, mainly square-rigged, could sail hardly closer to the wind than 60 degrees; only the fast sloops and ballahous, with fore-and-aft rig, were handy vessels in narrow passages between reefs, and the Caribbean is strewn with difficult fairways between underwater shoals. Yet the captains found their way by faith, hope, and remarkably vague handwritten sailing directions, copied out from memory for themselves or one another, to replace the printed documents from England. These well-thumbed pages of awkward handwriting, which must have been consulted so often by anxious eyes, by poor light in the night watches, are none of them fully legible now, they have been soaked and dried too often. Some of them may have been almost in their present poor condition before they were taken from the prizes; they have kept a personal feeling about them which defies time.

The owners of the merchantmen were often old captains themselves, and as such, naturally and obviously distrustful of the sea-sense of the younger men who took over their ships. In their letters to their captains they interspersed technical sailing instructions, which the young captains could not afford to throw overside, with counsel which must occasionally have been extremely irritating in its assumption of greenness in the new command. One such letter, giving the course from Turk's Island to Cap Français, ends on a note of unexpected poetry. It is to Captain Sandford Munro, of the sloop *Elizabeth,* bound from Woodstock, Connecticut, to "Hispainlore" in 1777, with tobacco, hog's lard, barrels of salt pork, cask-staves, a thousand feet of board and seven thousand bunches of onions.

Some advice I have to Give to you. . . . Keep a Good Look out from your Masthead Every half-hour for Your own Safty . . . if any Vessel should give you chase make from her with all hart. Don't speak with any Vessel on your Safty if you can Healp it. Don't trust to no one at the Danger Times. . . . Don't run after Night for Night has No Eye. . . .

No one, on either side, expected to win the war—this is the impression given by all the letters which touch on the subject. Among the Spanish Town papers, not one expresses hope of the outcome, until just before the end. The *Dolphin,* a Charleston schooner . . . carried a letter from *"Thomas"* to his *"dear Brother"* in Jamaica:

The wish of us all is to see you. But if you are in good Business I think you had Better Stay one year More Until you hear how this War will likely go with us poor Americans for I Beleave that the next summer their will (be) More Blood Shed here on this Side the Water Than Ever Was Shed on this Contanent in One Year Before . . . How it will go with us in an Other Summer god only knows.[1]

Fragments from other letters run: "The king's men cut us to peeses like we are a parcel of snakes." "We poor Americans, what will become of us?" "I dare not think to the future." "We air Bled by the British, we air Drove by the French, and by the Dutch we air dragged over the Devil's Own Bench." "Can see no Escape from Disaster except other George Washingtons arise to lead us, and where are they to find?" "Our flag is about as much Respected among the Different Nations as an old Rag thats hung up in a Corn field to Scare Crows." "The British Army gains ground, but with little Credit, they have possession of New York and long Island." The writer of the last is exasperated: "I seldom go now to Town.... I'm quite tired of America and shall quit with more pleasure than when I came in."

* * *

Probably a truer picture to emerge from these letters is that of the discomforts and shortages borne by the colonists at home: women beg constantly, like little Sharlot Ostermans, for "Linning and cloathing" to be sent to them by friends and relatives abroad. Sarah Rolland of Newport writes in June 1780 to her husband at sea, addressing the letter to Cap Français, where his ship is expected to call: "I go out for my Daily Bread times was never so hard and Difficult as at this present." Her letter is, incidentally, a touching example of how long it often took to get family news to the merchantmen. It begins: "Dear Husband I have the hapness ons more to haar that you are in the land of the living by Mr. Shiffal who tells me you are in Good health and be praised for it our Daughter is happely married to Mr. William Thurston, and his mother and they live together, they have got a nice child and call it by the name of Margaret.... Witching you health and hapness I remain your Loving Wife till Death."

Money, judging by these papers, was the only commodity not scarce in the fighting colonies throughout the struggle; because there was so little to be bought, merchants could raise their prices to astonishing levels, and by 1779 it was reckoned—as mentioned in several letters—that if only one cargo in three got through the British blockade, the owner made an excellent profit, despite the loss not only of his other two cargoes but of the ships as well.

* * *

At this stage of the struggle in their efforts to get crews for their merchant ships, American owners were offering the captains as much as half the profits on the cargo, per voyage, in some cases. The captains, engaging the crews, made their own bargains with the men. From 1780 till the end of the war wages became fantastic, in relation to those paid at the time in other than American ships. Among the papers of the *Fanny* are receipts signed by the seamen, paid in advance before they would sail from Newport. Comparison with pay on British merchantmen at the same period is afforded by the court records of claims for unpaid wages. These are some of the saddest documents in the archives: the men earned so little compared with the fat profits of the owners; their wages did not increase at all during the war, and to be deprived of even the small sums due to them was hard indeed.

Vast sums, for those days, were paid by the Americans for unseaworthy craft, as their need for merchantmen became more pressing while the war casualties mounted. The *Friendship,* a 65-ton schooner, registered in New London, captured by the privateer *Who's Afraid* in 1780, had been purchased in North America for £2,200 (Continental paper-money) only a few months before she was seized, though she was described in the evidence before the court as "somewhat leaky in her hull and much leaky in her upper-works"—worth nothing like that sum. . . . A 35-tonner, the *Two Brothers,* went for only £75 "being without most any materials . . . leaky and worm-eaten." But her cargo was valued at £1,007 (351 bags of coffee). The brigantine *General Heath* of Boston, captured off the West Caicos Bank in 1779, when she was bringing back from Hispaniola 25 hogsheads of sugar, was in miserably poor condition: the prize-master . . . remarked in court that "from the Poverty of the Brig he did not conceive he would be much Benefited by the Capture."

Not surprisingly, by the second year of the war it seems to have occurred to the fighting colonists that it would serve them handsomely to have agents of their own in Kingston, buying back, for the small sums which forced-sales fetched, the prizes which had recently been captured from them. Transferred to the ownership of a Jamaican mercantile firm, such ships could then be fitted out for a voyage to a neutral port, and either be captured on the way by an American privateer, as often happened, or else discharge one cargo at the neutral destination, pick up another with the help of a second agent there, and bring it back to America.

Again and again in the transactions recorded in these papers, the same names crop up as agents, sometimes acting for the colonists against the captors, sometimes for the captors against the American owners, when a Ship-of-the-Line, off on a cruise, was forced to leave a prize behind in Port Royal with her fate still undecided, and needed someone to press her claim. Occasionally they combined with one another and acted on both sides, one as assessor, marking down the value of a cargo, another as bidder, taking commissions all round. Commercial morality, afloat and ashore, was at its lowest ebb towards the end of the eighteenth century, if it can be said ever to have had a flood from which to ebb. The American agents, introduced with some difficulty into an enemy-owned island, cheated the American colonists;

the English merchants in Liverpool traded briskly with the colonists in revolt throughout the war—money knows no patriotism.

Like the wages of the seamen, the rates for insurance went up, on American vessels and cargoes, not steadily, but in sudden leaps, as the Royal Navy
and the privateers met with a season of particularly good hunting. With
ships captured during the first year and a half of the war, correspondence
was also taken between captains and owners arranging for insurance at 3
percent for sailing in convoy. Convoys became more difficult, then almost
impossible to organize, on the Americans' main trade routes. By April 1778,
when the ship *L'Aimable Marie Anne* was captured, carrying provisions, dry
goods, and salt from France to Port au Prince (Haiti) and then Salem, her
insurance, effected partly in France and partly in Spain, had risen to 30 percent of the value of cargo and vessel combined. Yet still it was profitable to
the merchant-owners to run the cargoes.

The slave-trade was known in the West Indies, in those days, as "the nurs-
ery of seamen," because of the size of the crews required. Slaves were one
of the commodities in short supply, and greatly increased demand, because
of the war, not only in the southern states of America but throughout the
Caribbean. In Barbados, where the price of flour doubled in the first year
of the struggle, through losses among the merchantmen, the slave population fell from approximately 68,000 in 1773 to less than 57,000 in 1778,
through malnutrition, and corresponding losses occurred in other islands.[2]
Fifteen thousand died in Jamaica, from hunger and the diseases following
on hunger, mainly in the first two years of the war, before the cheap sale of
prize cargoes of all sorts, when these were condemned by the court, compensated somewhat for the cutting down of the usual imports of food. The
dying off of slaves was crippling to the plantations. Many ships like the Massachusetts schooner *Sally*, captured by H.M.S. *Bristol* in 1778, carried in
their cargoes a horrible substance with the trade name of "Jamaica Fish."
This was a low-grade salt fish considered unfit for any white person to eat—
even mariners. For many years the planters had relied on it as a staple of
the slaves' diet: despite its name, it came mainly from America, and as food
in the plantations had always been poor, the lack of this wretched source of
protein reduced it to starvation level. American shipowners and captains
knew that if they could get through with a cargo of Jamaica Fish to any of
the West Indian Islands, they were assured of a quick sale and good profit,
with which to buy what the colonists at home were clamoring for—arms,
ammunition, clothing, and better food.

Vessel after vessel was caught on the outward journey carrying "alewives,"
a cheap pickled herring, which if not quite as nauseous as Jamaica Fish, was
not likely to be far off it, after a tropical voyage. Another Massachusetts
schooner, the *Ipswich*, carrying a mixed cargo to Haiti, had a crew of five,

all of whom were allowed to take "private adventures" from their home port. They all chose fish, as the most certain source of a good return.

It is curious that the American War of Independence, in which the West Indian slaves suffered incidentally as much as anyone, should have happened, also by accident, to improve their diet considerably in the end. In 1782 the British Admiral Rodney captured the *St. Anne,* a French vessel carrying from Mauritius to the French West Indian colonies a cargo of useful food-plants, among them the achee and the mango, one African and the other Asiatic in origin. Realizing their worth to Jamaica, he sent with the ship instructions to Port Royal that the cargo should not be subjected to the usual delays of the court, but delivered at once "to Mr. East's garden at Gordon Town," where the plants were tended and flourished. Achee and mango soon spread through the West Indies, and with the breadfruit, imported earlier by Bligh of the *Bounty,* did wonders for the miserable feeding of the slaves.[3]

NOTES

1. The recurrence of certain popular names among the prizes is confusing; there were ten *Dolphins.* Nineteen *Pollys* were brought into Port Royal; seventeen *Sallys,* sixteen *Hopes, Nancys,* and *Betseys,* eleven *Adventures* and—this has a sad ring—five *Happy Returns.*
2. *Editor's note:* None of the islands with a heavy slave population was self-supporting.
3. *Editor's note:* The fact was, however, that it not only took decades for these plants to spread and prosper among the islands, but that it took at least a couple of generations for the slaves to adjust to the breadfruit as a staple of diet.

AFTERMATH

The full story of the aftermath of the American Revolution with respect to the West Indies has not yet been fully written. Yet there are several areas which have received deserving attention. If the revolt of the thirteen colonies did not immediately bring an end to the mercantilist system, still so tenaciously clung to, historians are in agreement that it did bring an end to the *first* British Empire if only because English leadership tried to hold it all together "with ropes of pounds, shillings, and pence." William Pitt and Adam Smith were not alone in suggesting that this mercantile empire was doomed in that its welfare was always measured in terms of profit and loss.

Lowell Ragatz has traced the immediate problems which were faced by the English possessions in the West Indies. That the islands were bound to suffer from peace as much as war was clearly acknowledged not only by Englishmen at home, but by such enlightened leaders in the West Indies as Bryan Edwards. West Indian trade with the mainland was part of the natural order of things in the eighteenth century. In the words of Adam Smith: "Any interruption or restraint of commerce would hurt our loyal much more than our revolted subjects."

The West Indian reception of Pitt's bill in 1783, to enable the American people to enjoy the commercial privileges held before the Revolution, was generally so favorable that some of the island governors freely admitted American vessels into their ports. As the editor of this volume relates the post-revolutionary story, between the followers of the high-priest of mercantilism, Lord Sheffield, and those who were opposed to extending privileges to "ungrateful recusants," an *Order in Council* effectively closed the West Indian ports to American ships for a whole decade—and postponed the controversy regarding the policy of mercantilism until after the Napoleonic wars.

In the meantime this obstinacy on the part of British leadership provoked years of diplomacy after the Revolution as Americans tried to obtain the "natural right" of entry into the ports of the West Indies. This diplomacy was sustained with a single-mindedness which led Phineas Bond to remark after Washington's inauguration that "the present views and objects to a commercial treaty with England extend no further than to the opening of trade to the West Indies."

In the meantime the war's end sent thousands of refugees into exile to all islands of the West Indies, but especially to Jamaica and the Bahamas. This "loyalist exodus" is described in all its rich detail by a foremost authority, Wilbur Siebert. And he effectively traces the impact of the southern exodus, since so many who went to the islands were forced to go there because they were planters with slaves. Besides there was the matter of geographical proximity. Thus the loyalist "invasion" either introduced slavery as a system, as in the Bahamas; or reinforced it, as in Jamaica. Within a decade the estimated number of slaves in Jamaica had jumped from 191,000 to 250,000.

All in all, the story of this exodus from America was, at the least, one that was bittersweet. And it is a story still to be told in full both with respect to America and the West Indies.

LOWELL J. RAGATZ

"UPON EVERY PRINCIPLE OF TRUE POLICY": THE WEST INDIES IN THE SECOND EMPIRE

The distinguished author of the following selection remarked at the fiftieth anniversary celebration of the American Historical Association that among historians "the mischievous concept of 'thirteen colonies' has become firmly rooted and has been permitted to distort the picture for generations." What Ragatz was attempting, of course, was to prevail upon those concerned with the Revolutionary period to recognize that the British Empire, or the disruption of that empire, involved more than just a baker's dozen of territorial possessions.

The loss of the "baker's dozen" from the mainland did, indeed, bring an end to the so-called First British Empire. But it did introduce what historians call the Second Empire. The first was already immense: the second was to sprawl across the world like no other empire in history. And this time around the British did not try to hold this imperial conglomerate together, as Reginald Coupland so charmingly expressed it, "with ropes of pounds, shillings, and pence." In other words the constricted vision of empire, dictated by the old navigation laws, was jolted into a new reality which eventually introduced the era of free trade.

But this was not to be overnight. The popularity of Lord Sheffield's Observations on Commerce *showed that Great Britain was not about to abandon its ancient traditions. The mercantilist practice was still considered an essential ingredient of commerce and empire, and a practice still common among England's European rivals.*

From *The Fall of the Planter Class in the British Caribbean, 1763–1833.* The Century Co., 1928.

After the Treaty of Paris of 1783 there was a reluctance to follow Pitt's suggestion that any interruption or restraint of commerce would hurt England's loyal subjects much more than those who had revolted. He was, of course, reciting from Adam Smith who had consistently urged that something be learned from the experience of the American Revolution. But to no avail. The fear of American rivalry, together with the reluctance to restore privileges to "ungrateful recusants," produced an Order-in-Council which closed the ports of the West Indies to American vessels for a decade.

But the ports were not closed to American products—only to the carrying trade. Although there were restrictions on certain goods, it became increasingly obvious that John Adams spoke for all in remarking that "the commerce of the West India islands is a part of the American system. They can neither do without us, nor we without them." Between West Indian petitions and sustained American diplomacy, trade and commerce again began to flourish.

And thus the Second Empire was launched. To quote Coupland again, "the American Revolution enabled British statesmanship to examine what was left before it was too late, to discover the new nourishment which the imperial system needed, and thereby to achieve a revolution without schism."

Recognition of the United States as a sovereign nation raised a question of momentous import for the planters in the British Caribbean. With the old political relationship between the late mainland colonies and the one-time common mother country dissolved, would they be suffered to enjoy free access to their natural source of supply for essential stores as in antebellum days or would imperial commercial policy demand the erection of barriers to check the normal flow of trade between them and the Americans?[1]

There was no question regarding the attitude of the West India interest in England, the residents of the sugar islands and statesmen of the new republic. At a meeting of a committee of the Society of Planters and Merchants, held in April 1783, a straightforward representation was made to the ministry.

Under a just and reasonable attention to mutual Interests, the Committee entertain no doubt but such a share of the American Trade may be preserved to the Sugar Colonies as will greatly tend to their support, and, upon every principle of true Policy and proper regard to the views and purposes of rival Nations, be highly deserving of the utmost countenance and assistance from the Mother Country. . . .

The council of Jamaica in the same month unanimously urged that commercial relations with the United States be placed upon a liberal footing, and, on its recommendation to the governor, American vessels were provisionally allowed to enter local ports with supplies and to clear out with cargoes of tropical produce exempt from the payment of any duty.

"Without a free admission of all kinds of provisions into the Islands," wrote Robert R. Livingston, first American secretary of state for Foreign Affairs to Benjamin Franklin in 1782, "our agriculture will suffer extremely."[2] John Adams, in correspondence with Livingston from Paris under date of June 23, 1783, held similar views:

The commerce of the West India Islands is a part of the American system of commerce. They can neither do without us, nor we without them. The Creator has placed us upon the globe in such a situation that we have occasion for each other. We have the means of assisting each other, and politicians and artful Contrivances cannot separate us. Wise statesmen, like able artists of every kind, study nature, and their works are perfect in proportion as they conform to her laws.[3] . . .

But ship owners in Great Britain, the large body of Loyalists who had taken refuge in the remaining North American colonies, a notable part of the British public which sympathized with them, and exponents of mercantilism united in opposition to the slightest relaxation of commercial laws in favor of citizens of the United States. John Baker Holroyd, Lord Sheffield, a recognized authority on trade and agriculture and a rigid doctrinaire, became spokesman for these groups and in a forceful work, *Observations on the Commerce of the American States,* piled argument upon argument for maintaining the navigation system inviolate.[4]

The American nation, declared he, was foreign and must be treated as such. The admission of its nationals to West Indian ports under any conditions whatsoever would lead to their gaining complete control of the island carrying trade, would place the planters in dangerous dependence upon a rival power, and would encourage the late enemy's shipping while at the same time ruining the British merchant marine and menacing Great Britain's command of the seas. The mother country bore the heavy expense of protecting her Caribbean colonies in order that she alone might engross the gains from transporting their freight and could enjoy the exclusive right of purchasing their produce. If the Americans were allowed to participate in the trade with them in any way, it would be unprofitable for Great Britain to longer retain them.

Congress, he continued, might well close the ports of the United States to British ships if its citizens were not granted the right of direct intercourse with the West India possessions, but such a measure could only deprive that country of the best market for a large portion of its produce and would not prevent British ship-masters from securing cargoes of American products. The mainland traders' self-interest would lead them to engage in extensive smuggling operations in defiance of any prohibitory law. Furthermore, it would be difficult for the thirteen states to present a united front on such a question.

The monopoly of supplying the home market, enjoyed by the Caribbean proprietors, increased the prices of tropical produce sold in Great Britain from 15 to 30 percent above those which would prevail if free importations from the foreign West Indies were permitted. The estate owners of the sugar islands owed their prosperity to the British connection and could not justly feel aggrieved at increased costs arising from the adoption of a new policy dictated by imperial interests. If they should proclaim their independence they could not defend themselves, nor could they find protection in the small American army. If the British possessions fell under French control, the planters would be ruined by the lower selling prices prevailing in the markets of France. The excessively high prices received for their produce by the British planters was a matter which should be taken under serious consideration.

The Navigation Act, the basis of our great power at sea, gave us the trade of the world. If we alter that Act, by permitting any state to trade with our islands . . . we desert the Navigation Act, and sacrifice the marine of England. But if the principle of the Navigation Act be properly understood and well followed, this country may still be safe and great.[5]

Publication of this exceedingly able work gave the sign for the spilling of huge quantities of printer's ink. The foremost attacks on Sheffield's representations were made by members of the London West India group. Bryan Edwards, recently returned from his properties in Jamaica, made his début as author through penning a pamphlet designed to demonstrate that Caribbean estate owners could not prosper without supplies at the cheapest rate from the United States.[6] His friend Edward Long, historian of the colony, adopted the same argument in a well-reasoned statement of the island point of view.[7] More important, however, was a work of several hands issued under the signature of James Allen, secretary of the Society of Planters and Merchants, *Considerations on the Present State of the Intercourse Between His Majesty's Sugar Colonies and the Dominions of the United States of*

America, given over largely to a refutation of the claim that British North America could supply the planters' needs.

Lord Sheffield, however, had many and capable defenders. Replying to the declaration of Bryan Edwards, that restrictions would result in an inequitable increase in the cost of supplies, John Stevenson argued that planter products should then be sold for more so that the consumer, not the producer, would bear the additional cost. If it was true, as stated, that American ships could operate more economically than British ones in supplying the West Indies, then those of the remaining mainland colonies could most certainly do likewise. If citizens of the new republic were allowed to enter the Caribbean trade, they would soon be competing with Great Britain in supplying European markets. The planters and Americans would doubtless be mutually benefited by free intercourse, but this would work such injuries to British trade as to make it altogether impermissible.

* * *

Americans with one accord naturally opposed any modification of the old relation. Indeed, it was one of them, William Bingham, commercial agent for the Continental Congress, writing anonymously, who first answered Sheffield. Residing in England, he shrewdly enough stressed the advantages which that country would derive from uninterrupted intercourse between the late colonies and the British Caribbean. If the planters were obliged to pay more for their supplies, the prices of tropical produce must be increased and the public would suffer. With cheap stores from the United States at their command, a greater portion of the proprietors' incomes would be available for spending at home and manufacturing there would be stimulated. If direct trade were not permitted, Great Britain would be put to heavy expense to curb smuggling. Common opposition to British policy would draw all the American states together. Retaliative measures on the part of Congress would inevitably follow any attempt to close the West India trade. British industry and commerce would suffer heavy losses; a powerful merchant marine would be established beyond the Atlantic and this would take over the carrying trade between Europe and the New World until then so largely in British hands.[8]

While the controversy regarding the policy to be adopted towards the late trans-Atlantic possessions was at its height, action of some sort was necessary. The ports of the United States were opened to British shipping without discrimination and William Pitt, then chancellor of the exchequer, proposed the temporary institution of a liberal system of commercial relations giving vessels under American registry the right to import stores freely from the new country into the West Indies and to depart from there laden with tropical produce.

There was, however, a practical problem—the powers claimed by the legislatures of the thirteen states were so extensive that the competency of Congress to conclude a general commercial treaty was seriously doubted.[9] Furthermore, with a change in ministry, Pitt went out of office in April 1783, and was no longer in a position to carry through his project. Arrangements of a different nature were therefore made. An act of Parliament passed the following month "vested the king in council with power to regulate the American-West Indian trade for the time being."

Three orders of July 2, September 5, and December 26, 1783, issued in accordance with this measure, set forth the conditions under which American supplies might enter British Caribbean ports. His Majesty's subjects were permitted to import all kinds of lumber, livestock, grain, flour, and bread from the United States into the islands in British bottoms. They were likewise allowed to export rum, sugar, molasses, coffee, cacao, ginger, and pimento from them to the United States upon payment of the same duties and conforming to the same regulations as if those products were cleared out for a British colony. American vessels, on the contrary, were wholly excluded from any share in the trade, and American meat and fish were forbidden entry in the interests of pork and beef producers in Ireland and the Newfoundland fisheries.[10] Meeting the challenge of the July 2 order in council, Congress, in April 1784, asked the states for the right to prohibit all importations or exportations in vessels owned or navigated by subjects of foreign powers not having commercial treaties with the United States, for a period of fifteen years. The proposal fell through for lack of unanimity.

These orders, intended merely to meet the needs of the moment, were subsequently continued in force under the authority of various enabling acts until 1788 despite attempts at retaliative commercial legislation on the part of Congress and the several state legislatures and loud West Indian remonstrance. The regulations were then made permanent by statute.[11]

The government's policy, evinced by these orders in council, was subjected to attack by both the London West India group and the islanders. In the spring of 1784, the Society of Planters and Merchants secured a privy council hearing and there brought forth evidence designed to demonstrate the dependence of the islands on the United States, and the inability of British North America to supply their needs. But the committee named to consider their representations was in no way convinced and supported the new arrangement. The Jamaican legislature about the same time expressed astonishment that the Americans should be denied entry into British Caribbean ports, while they were being freely admitted to those of Great Britain, Ireland, and the North American colonies, and denounced such distinctions between Englishmen as being invidious. Prediction was made that if the direct trade remained closed, large numbers of planters not too heavily involved would depart for neighboring foreign possessions, while those finding emigration impossible because of debts must suffer total ruin of their property and sink into indigence.

In a memorial to the ministry, Stephen Fuller, agent for Jamaica, urged that American citizens be allowed to enter at least lumber, cattle, and such provisions as could not be supplied by Great Britain, Ireland, or British North America in small vessels which should be permitted to load up only with clayed or refined sugar. The government was, however, entirely unmoved by such pleas. Failure to secure a reopening of free commercial relations between the United States and the British West Indies at the close of the Revolution was the first great defeat suffered by members of the planter interest.

Large-scale smuggling was an inevitable result of placing restraints on trade with the mainland. Such activities were especially common in the Leeward Islands and Jamaica due to their proximity to the continent. "A great deal of American produce is introduced into these Islands, by methods which are contrived to evade the restrictions of the late order in Council," wrote Governor Shirley of the Leeward group to Lord Sydney in the summer of 1784. A report from Jamaica, made a year and a half after the new regulations had gone into effect, stated "There is every reason to believe that the fraudulent importation from the United States of America is very considerable . . . ; the Amount . . . is probably equal to that which is imported legally."

The experiences of Captain Horatio Nelson, assigned in November 1784 to service on the ship *Boreas*, off St. Kitts-Nevis, are illuminating. . . .

The future victor of Trafalgar found the harbors filled with their vessels and promptly forced them to depart. In consequence, he was not shown the respect due his rank and was denounced as one injuring the colonists. Despite his ordering away such American ships as approached the islands, they frequently got into port a short time after while he was procuring wood, water, or provisions elsewhere. Ten were unloaded in Basseterre Road during one such absence alone.

* * *

When Nelson seized four American vessels flying the Union Jack in the road of Nevis in the spring of 1785 and secured their condemnation, the local merchants prompted the several ship masters, one of whom the captain had never even seen, to procure writs for his arrest. . . . Feeling in the island was so against Nelson that the attorney-general advised him not to appear for trial and he was obliged to remain on board ship for two months to keep beyond the reach of colonial law officers. . . . Some time later he coolly accepted for himself the thanks of Treasury officials for his zeal in protecting British commerce![12]

Returns covering all ships entering British Caribbean ports, required by the home government after July 1783, prove conclusively that the lumbering and fishing industries in British North America were greatly stimulated by the new commercial policy towards the United States. No small part of the wood and sea-food products thenceforth marketed in the islands were of British origin. The increase in imports from Canada, Nova Scotia, and Newfoundland over those preceding the Revolution was marked from the first, and, from the imperial point of view, afforded ample justification for the prohibition placed on American participation in the West India trade. But it is also evident that the Loyalists' ability to provide plantation needs had been overestimated, especially as regarded grain. The thirteen states still remained the principal, though no longer the almost exclusive, source of supply they had been in the colonial period.

* * *

But, however warrantable in imperial interests American exclusion from the West India trade may have been, it bore heavily upon the planters. Their fellow-colonials on the mainland were unable to provide supplies as cheaply, and British carriers could not deliver them from either the Continental possessions or the United States at as low rates as the Americans. These differences in costs are to be explained in several ways. The distance from British North America was greater than that from the United States, resulting in fewer trips and greater charges. Whereas the Americans employed small coasting vessels in their commercial operations in the Caribbean, the British used trans-Atlantic sailers, operated at more expense, almost exclusively. Ships built in Great Britain cost more than those constructed in the United States and higher freights were necessary to afford adequate returns on investments.

Furthermore, the price of labor in sparsely-settled Canada, Nova Scotia, and Newfoundland was higher than in the more fully developed states to the south. Largely due to this factor, stores could be procured in the United States for a third less than in British North America. The increased cost of supplies to the planters after the Revolution, [arising] in part from the institution of new trading regulations and in part from a natural rise in values following the conflict . . . Peace brought an end to scarcity and wartime quotations, but the prices of essential commodities failed to return to antebellum figures and the proprietors were not afforded the much-needed relief they had anticipated.

Considerable quantities of goods originating in the United States reached the British West Indies indirectly by way of the foreign islands after 1783. "The old intercourse with the Dutch Island St. Eustatius is again opened, and through that medium we get many American Commodities, but [at] an advanced price," reported Governor Shirley of the Leeward Islands government early in 1785. Such large amounts of produce were received in this manner in Dominica that somewhat over a year later vessels arriving from Nova Scotia were unable to dispose of their cargoes. Governor Lincoln wrote to Lord Sydney from St. Vincent: "The Commerce among the Islands is carried on by Sloops and Schooners navigated according to Law. These vessels trade to Martinico, Guadeloupe, but in particular to St. Eustatia where they are laden with Lumber, Provisions &c., from the Americans purchased at nearly the same price as before the War & retailed to the Planters at 50 to 100% profit. The result of which is, that whilst the Planter is compelled to give an exorbitant price for these necessary articles, the Americans find nearly the same demand as formerly, and consequently are only irritated, not injured by the restrictions contained in the Proclamation.". . .

So extensive became this roundabout intercourse with the United States that an act of 1787 forbade the entry of any flour, bread, rice, wheat, other grains, and lumber from the foreign West Indies into the British islands except in cases of emergency when the governor and council might permit their importation for a limited time only. This provision was continued by the statute of the following year, definitely establishing the existing restrictions on the American trade, with the further proviso that entries in such cases must be made in British bottoms.

The greater cost of supplies after 1783, the drop in the market prices of tropical produce and the continued levying of high duties in Great Britain had a withering effect on West Indian agriculture. Hopes that peace would be followed by quick recovery were rudely shattered. The decade from 1783 to 1793 brought no relief to the planters; large numbers fell beneath the weight of accumulated distress.

Great dissatisfaction and apprehension were felt in Jamaica at the closing of the American trade and the refusal of the home government to reduce the war rate on sugar. . . . A memorial and petition of the island legislature to the home government in December 1784 portrayed a melancholy state of affairs—property saddled with debts incurred in defending the colony during the late war and the owners of estates facing ruin. Freeing the American trade, reducing the duties on West Indian produce, encouraging sugar refining in the colonies by removing the prohibitive duty then levied on the finished product entering Great Britain, and permitting sugar to be bonded in warehouses where it might be held for a rise in price rather than requiring the immediate payment of duty upon unloading, were recommended as measures which would relieve their desperate situation. . . .

* * *

Further hurricanes in 1784, 1785, and 1786, making an unprecedented total of six in seven years, created a tense situation in the colony. Faced with the danger of famine and rebellion on the part of the Negroes, Lieutenant-Governor Clarke, on advice of the council in August 1784, opened local ports for the free importation of provisions and lumber and they were not again closed until the end of January 1785. Under the circumstances, this action was approved by the home government, but it failed to avert a serious food shortage. A committee of the lower house estimated the number of slave deaths from actual starvation or from diseases occasioned by scanty and unwholesome diet following these several natural disasters at no less than 15,000.[13]

Matters in the other Caribbean colonies stood no better. The closing of ports to the Americans threw the Leeward Island planters into greater distress than they had known at any stage of the war. Prices at once rose 50 percent. A petition of the assembly of Antigua to the governor, requesting a temporary suspension of the July (1783) order, was barren of results. Such quantities of rum remained unsold that by February 1784 the price had fallen as low as from 2s. 6d. to 3s. per gallon.

The raking of salt for sale to the Americans had been an important industry in Anguilla. The inhabitants now found that product wholly unsalable and suffered indescribable hardships in consequence.

Despite the illegal importations which have been noted, an acute shortage of supplies arose after the hurricane of August 1785. Appeal was made to Governor Shirley to open the ports of Antigua and St. Kitts to American vessels, but he refused. In May 1787 there was but a month's supply of provisions in Nevis; in July 1789 both St. Kitts and Nevis were left with less than a week's stock each. Importations were therefore quickly made from Antigua and the harbors of both possessions were opened to cargoes imported from the foreign West Indies in British bottoms.

By 1787 the greater part of the plantations in Antigua were under mortgage to merchants in London, Liverpool, and Bristol.[14] A succession of droughts and ravages of the cane-borer brought the island to the verge of ruin. Describing St. John's in 1792, Sir William Young wrote, "The town . . . has the appearance of ruined trade and habitancy." The distress of the planters was such that they could make but scant allowances of provisions for their Negroes.[15]

In Barbados rum became all but unmarketable following the institution of the new commercial policy toward America. In consequence, the planters engaged in extensive illicit relations with the Dutch from the Main to the south. One smuggler even went so far as to slip cable and carry off a customs officer who had boarded his vessel. A small ship was subsequently provided by the home government to break up such enterprises, but great difficulty was experienced in keeping the situation in hand. The high price of lumber prevented much-needed repairs from being made on many buildings destroyed by hurricane.

Dominica had suffered most severely of all the British islands during the war. The long-continued French occupation, during which trade had ceased and Roseau had been burned, had blasted the hopes of those engaged in developing the colony. The decade after the Revolution found them deeply involved, unable to secure further credit, and with payments due the Crown for land purchased far in arrears. A Negro revolt further complicated the situation. In despair, the planters petitioned for a remission of the balances still due on their estates and for such other relief as would seem meet. About 1790 only fifty sugar plantations were in operation; some thirty had then been abandoned.[16]

A grant of all the waste lands in St. Vincent, made by the king of France to one Madame Swinburne, a lady-in-waiting at the royal court, during the period of the war, checked the opening of new estates in that colony until 1786, when the British government regained possession of such tracts through the payment of £6,500 in compensation for her claims.[17]

Two noteworthy developments along agricultural lines marked the post-revolutionary decade—the growth of coffee culture and the attempt made to stimulate cotton cultivation. . . .

Efforts to further cotton planting were not so successful. Its cultivation in the tropical American colonies had gradually declined from the middle of the eighteenth century on, due to the competition of growers on the fresh soil of the foreign West Indies whose product was given free access to the markets of Great Britain by way of her Caribbean island ports.

The reopening of free ports in certain of the British West India possessions after the Revolution was an event of capital importance to the commercial interests, both local and in Great Britain. Attempts to secure such action were made immediately upon the conclusion of the war in 1783, at which time representations on behalf of their respective islands were sent to the home government by the legislatures of Barbados, Antigua, and St. Kitts.

But Lord Sheffield was unalterably opposed to the granting of such concessions. He declared free ports to be quite unnecessary, since the planters could secure all needed supplies upon reasonable terms without them. Their reestablishment, according to him, would be equivalent to giving the West

India trade to the Americans. A Dominican free port bill, under consideration by the government in 1785, was objected to by members of the London Caribbean/interests on the ground that it did not sufficiently guard against foreign produce being admitted into Great Britain and was subsequently dropped. Fear of losing advantages accruing to the empire from the new regime of restricted trade if free ports were again opened long delayed such action.

A bill finally passed in 1787 sought to meet the West Indians' demands while at the same time obviating this danger. Under the terms of this act cotton, indigo, cacao, drugs of all sorts, dyestuffs and dye woods, hides, skins, furs, tallow, turtle-shell, hardwood or mill timber, cabinet woods, horses, mules, and cattle, the produce of any foreign European colony in America, were admitted into Kingston, Savanna-la-Mar, Montego Bay, and St. Lucea in Jamaica, St. George in Grenada, Roseau in Dominica, and Nassau in the Bahamas in single-decked vessels of not over seventy tons burden each, owned by residents of those colonies in which the goods originated.

Such bottoms were permitted to export British plantation rum, Negroes, and all goods legally imported excepting naval stores, tobacco, and iron from the British colonies in America. . . .

Three years later this act was amended so as to remove the limitation on the burden of the vessels while still requiring them to be single-decked and, in 1792, the freedom of importation into the several ports was made perpetual. The policy thus inaugurated in 1787 was subsequently applied unchanged to other ports and colonies until the close of the century.

NOTES

1. *Editor's note:* On this subject see especially Herbert C. Bell, "British Commercial Policy in the West Indies, 1783–1793," *The English Historical Review* (July, 1916), pp. 429–41. Reprinted in *Studies in the Trade Relations of the British West Indies and North America, 1763-1793* (Philadelphia, 1917).
2. Jared Sparks, ed., *The Diplomatic Correspondence of the American Revolution,* IV (Boston, 1829–30), p. 13. 12 volumes.
3. Charles F. Adams, ed., *The Works of John Adams,* VIII (Boston, 1853–56), pp. 74, 75. 10 volumes.
4. First issued in 1783 and elaborated in subsequent editions which appeared at short intervals. The sixth (London, 1784) contains his arguments in fully developed form. The references here given are to pages of that edition.
5. Sheffield, *Observations,* pp. 264–65.
6. *Thoughts on the Late Proceedings of Government, Respecting the Trade of the West India Islands with the United States of America,* II (London, 1784), pp. 392–425. His *History* of some years later also makes a plea for the establishment of free trade relations between the two. *Editor's note:* The complete

title is *The History, Civil and Commercial, of the British Colonies in the West Indies* (London, 1793). 2 volumes.

7. *A Free and Candid Review of a Tract Entitled* "Observations on the Commerce of the American States" (London, 1784).

8. *A Letter from an American . . . on Lord Sheffield's . . . Commerce of the American States* (Philadelphia, 1784).

9. *A Report of the Lords of the Committee of Privy Council . . . on the Commerce and Navigation between His Majesty's Dominions, and the United States of America* (London, 1791). A summary of this document appears in Worthington C. Ford, ed., *Report of a Committee of the Lords of the Privy Council on the Trade of Great Britain with the United States* (January 1791). (Washington, 1888). *Editor's note:* The committee also conducted a long investigation in 1784, producing a wealth of material of considerable value for the study of the West Indian trade both before and during the Revolutionary War.

10. *American State Papers,* (Commerce and Navigation), II, p. 251. For a detailed discussion of the orders, see John Reeves, *A History of the Law of Shipping and Navigation* (Dublin, 1792).

11. For an exhaustive and scholarly study of such legislative measures, see Albert A. Giesecke, *American Commercial Legislation Before 1789* (New York, 1910).

12. For Nelson's years in the Caribbean, see Robert Johnstone "Nelson in the West Indies," in *Journal of the Institute of Jamaica* (December 1897), pp. 380 ff., and (March 1899), pp. 521 ff.

13. Report of the committee, quoted in Bryan Edwards, *History . . . of the British Colonies in the West Indies,* II (London, 1793), p. 415.

14. John Luffman, *Brief Account of the Island of Antigua* (London, 1789). *Editor's note:* Luffman's book, one of the best descriptions of plantation life, is really a series of 40 letters written between 1786 and 1788.

15. "A Tour," in Bryan Edwards, *Historical Survey of . . . St. Domingo. Editor's note:* This was written after the first edition of his *History . . . of the British Colonies in the West Indies,* and was not included until the expanded editions of 1801 and 1819, which were to also include Young's account.

16. Thomas Atwood, *A History of Dominica* (London, 1791), p. 72.

17. C. P. Lucas, *A Historical Geography of the British Colonies,* II (Oxford, 1888–1920), p. 214, note 2. 7 volumes. *Editor's note:* Volume II, on the West Indies, was revised by C. Atchley, and was published separately in 1905.

CHARLES W. TOTH

AMERICA AND THE BRITISH WEST INDIES: THE POST-REVOLUTIONARY DIALOGUE

From the previous selections the interdependency of the mainland colonies with the islands of the West Indies, both on the eve of the Revolution and during the war for independence, has been clearly traced in all of its ramifications. The British hardly had time to digest the significance of Yorktown when the Americans started the drumbeat with regard to a re-entry into the carrying-trade of the West Indies. Franklin, Adams, and Jay had tried, unsuccessfully, to incorporate the right for re-entry, and the presence of John Adams on the negotiating team assured that it would be discussed as a "natural right."

And there were Englishmen not unsympathetic. David Hartley, although warning that Great Britain would not alter her "ancient system," suggested that the American ministers be satisfied with the temporary expedient of returning to pre-1775 conditions. William Pitt, going even further, presented legislation in 1783 to open West Indian ports to American ships on equality with British vessels—legislation which had strong support in the islands.

But the advocates of mercantilism were to carry the day, sweeping Pitt's recommendations aside. As Fox, with a desire for friendship, remarked to Henry Laurens: "the navigation act is the vital of Great Britain, too delicate to touch." Frustrated, Adams wrote gloomily to Livingston that "our natural share in the West India trade is all that is now wanting to complete the plan of happiness and prosperity of our country."

The result was a decade of sustained diplomacy with respect to restoring

From "Anglo-American Diplomacy and the British West Indies, 1783–1789."
The Americas, XXXI (1975).

the American presence in the West Indies, and this became a chief task for John Adams, America's first minister to England after peace was established. But by 1786 he would write to the Secretary of State, John Jay, that "the King and every member of each house have entirely forgotten that there is such a place upon the earth as the United States."

* * *

The profits of the West Indian trade helped to create a reserve capital which became the mainstay of the colonial economy, thereby facilitating the payment of debts to England and Europe. "To lubricate the transatlantic trade," as Richard Pares phrased it, "a useful, indeed necessary, device for settling the balance of payments." Even before the Revolution there was a growing anxiety with regard to actions involving, or touching, the West Indian trade the residual effect of which might be negative.... Pares argues with considerable success that the American colonies were forced to take care of their remittances to Europe (England primarily) by purchasing bills of exchange in the West Indies as payment for exports, thereby attempting to gain some relief from what had become a system of chronic indebtedness.[1]

* * *

The West Indies, then, constituted a vital part of the colonial economic structure by the last quarter of the eighteenth century "from the Kennebec to the Savannah." As Herbert Bell perceptively wrote: "nor was it only love of liberty which in 1774 united Whigs of England, of America, and of Jamaica in opposition to the Intolerable Acts."[2]

The mercantilist policy, which was just beginning to be seriously challenged, had locked the external trade of the American colonies with that of England and the West Indies. And on the eve of the Revolution it was more than evident that the American colonies "had gradually circumvented the parent country in supplying the British West Indies with all the productions of agriculture."[3] This fact must be appreciated to understand the persistent diplomacy with regard to the West Indies not only in the immediate post-revolutionary period, but for several generations to come.

From the Declaration of Independence to the establishment of the Re-

197

public in 1789, the largest percentage of American trade continued to be with the West Indies. Sixty to eighty ships at one time could frequently be found in the French islands, with many of the products eventually reaching the British West Indies. As soon as the war was over, and more particularly after the peace treaty was signed, the American concern became pronounced, and the diplomatic activity of the American representatives often involved threats. A good example of this is found in a letter John Adams sent to Secretary Jay in 1785, commenting on his conversations with the Marquis of Caermarthen. After trying to frighten the Marquis about the ill effects upon British creditors by removing the islands as "a vast source of remittance," Adams warned that "when [the Americans] . . . find remittances discouraging, impeded, and even prohibited, it was natural, to expect that they would be alarmed."[4] To underscore the complicated nature of the sources of remittance, Adams remarked that "New England had no other remittance but the fishery . . . that it entered into our distilleries and West India trade as well as our European trade."[5]

The Confederation enacted a series of reciprocal treaties, the most important with France (1778), and Holland (1882). But these treaties, as well as future ones, could only enjoy partial success pending the formation of a more perfect union. England in the meantime could afford to remain largely unconcerned in the knowledge that the Confederation labored under serious handicaps. As Weeden summarized, "the chief business was done with the West Indies [and] Congress was tinkering constantly with this commerce, trying to get control, which the states as yet meant to keep for themselves."[6]

Not a few Americans beguiled themselves with the thought in the period following the hostilities that, in the words of John Adams, "England stands on the brink of a precipice [and] the only chance they have for salvation is reform, and in recovering the affection of America." By reform was meant the abandonment of what Americans considered the outdated mercantilist system. As Adams phrased it, "the commerce of the West India Islands is a part of the American system of commerce. They can neither do without us, nor we without them." In a letter to Secretary Jay, Adams had occasion to remark that "nothing is more extravagant than the confident pretensions of the French and English merchants that they can supply their own islands. It is whimsical . . . that the mercantile spirit should be most hostile to the freedom of commerce."

* * *

In his classic study, George Beer advanced the argument that after 1763 the economic factor in the British carrying-trade gave way, or was subordinated, to military considerations and related problems of strategy.[7] Yet in the 1780s the economics of the West Indian trade still provided the *raison d'être* for parliamentary legislation. Still changes were beginning to emerge. The first important modification of mercantilist policy came with the adoption of the free port system, and the Free Port Act of 1766 was the first of a series to deal with the problems of empire involving the colonial structure of the western hemisphere. The free port system, however, always remained a pragmatic, although not entirely successful, approach. But as the eighteenth century drew to a close, the free port trade formed an important part of the whole system of commerce with respect to England's foreign trade. That the free port system was not a serious departure from mercantilist practice may be observed by the fact that products would be allowed entry only if they did not compete with goods produced in England, or important segments of the empire. In the West Indies the free ports were not open to a particular island so much as to a particular nation possessing islands in the Caribbean. Important for the purpose of this study is the fact that the carrying-trade between Great Britain and its colonies remained under strict English control, much to the chagrin of American mercantile interests.[8]

The diplomatic activity on the subject of the West Indies with respect to the Treaty of 1783 is a study in itself, and clearly reveals American concern and frustration. For a moment, especially after David Hartley had succeeded Oswald in the negotiations, the American commissioners (Franklin, Adams, and Jay) felt that they would make a breakthrough and the West Indian carrying-trade would be secured. Although Franklin felt that "I could have been content to finish with Mr. Oswald, whom we always found very reasonable," still he and Hartley shared an old and friendly correspondence. Besides, Hartley had been a staunch friend of American independence, and had urged in Parliament the formation of an Anglo-American alliance based on commercial reciprocity "to proceed upon the same terms it would have done if the political separation had never taken place."[9]

Hartley's arrival, then, as Minister Plenipotentiary, understandably produced both momentary confusion as well as hope with respect to all questions. The English government was being racked by resignations and death during this delicate period of negotiations, and the American delegation was hard bent at times to keep up with the swift-moving developments. But they soon learned that the coalition of Fox and North would act as a brake upon the enthusiasms of David Hartley. Indeed, they understood the situation quite realistically, and were quick to report that ". . . his zeal for systems friendly to us constantly exceeded his authority. . . ."

The importance of the West Indies in the thinking of the American delegates is highlighted by the fact that only two days after the arrival of Hartley they went straight to that subject with the suggestion that the products (and subjects) of both countries be admitted freely into each other's ports.

As John Jay told Hartley "we have received particular instructions on the business of commerce . . . of our readiness to add to the provisional treaty an article for opening and regulating the trade between us on principles as liberal and reciprocal as you please."[10] . . .

Hartley obviously did not enjoy the stature in England which could bring any concessions with regard to the West Indies, and asked the American ministers not to complicate the matters with their requests. In any case, he anticipated correctly, for on the very day that he spoke optimistically that the West Indian trade would be open to both parties (June 14, 1783), Fox sent Hartley a message (based on the Order in Council of May 14, 1783) that products from the islands could not be picked up by American vessels. The American reaction can be imagined. Only a few days earlier, Adams had received a letter from Francis Dana strongly suggesting that "the West India trade, as tendered by Mr. Pitt's bill . . . be secured." Dana continued: "In this quarter of the world I see the whole importance of it . . . I proposed to [Livingston] the same plan . . . with the difference, that we should have full liberty to export the West India commodities to *all parts* of the world. . . ."[11] The Order in Council of May appeared to Englishmen as generous, but of little comfort to American commercial interests. Writing many years later, John Adams remarked that this Order was "the first link in that great chain of *Orders in Council,* which has been since stretched and extended, till it has shackled the commerce of the whole globe; that of Great Britain herself."

The Fox declaration was formalized on July 2, 1783, by an Order in Council in which the carrying-trade was restricted to British ships. American vessels would now be excluded from the British islands for an entire decade, and such staples as fish, beef, pork, butter, and lard were generally not permitted entry even in British ships. However, British vessels could carry any naval stores, grain, livestock, and lumber from the United States. All West Indian products going to the United States, of course, would be carried in British ships.[12]

The importance of the West Indies in the whole process of peace-making in 1783 was made evident by the remark of John Adams the day following the first Order in Council. Writing to Richard Livingston, Adams stated that "the West India commerce now gives us the most anxiety . . . [this] commerce falls . . . into the natural system of the commerce of the United States." Since Adams came from New England he had an immediate concern with the West Indies, whose trade had a more intimate relationship with the economy than any other section of the country. The shipping interests also included the ship-builders. Adams became so agitated that he wrote the Duc de la Vanguyon that "the English were a parcel of sots to exclude us." Vanguyon answered quite prophetically: "Yes, I think you will have another war with the English."

The Provisional Treaty was signed on September 3, 1783. Although historians have generally agreed that the Treaty of Paris has been the most successful ever signed by the American people, John Jay was not without anger and frustration, remarking that "the British ministry amuse [Hartley] and us, and deceive themselves."[13] Sensing the chagrin of the American ministers, and influenced by wishful thinking, Hartley wrote to Benjamin Franklin a few weeks later that the Cabinet would probably come up with a temporary convention "nearly on the ground of my memorial (May 19, 1783), that American ships were not to bring foreign manufactures into Great Britain, nor to trade directly between the British West Indies and Great Britain." Otherwise, Hartley concluded, "all should rest as before the war." As to further propositions, Hartley doubted whether anything could be done "before the next meeting of Parliament." But Hartley was closer to the truth of the matter in his letter of June 14, 1783, when he told the American delegation that "the British navigation acts were not likely to be suddenly altered in favor of the United States."

The events of 1783 helped to set into motion a long history of diplomacy with respect to the West Indies. Even while waiting for congressional ratification of the Paris Treaty, a series of attempts were made to produce some system of commercial reciprocity. Adams clearly defined the situation with the remark that "we have not to this hour agreed upon one proposition, nor do I see any probability that we shall at all, respecting commerce." Writing gloomily to Livingston, Adams bemoaned that "our natural share in the West India trade is all that is now wanting to complete the plan of happiness and prosperity of our country. Deprived of it we shall be straightened and shackled. . . ."

. . . In March of 1783, in the very midst of the peace negotiations, William Pitt had submitted a bill to allow American ships into the West Indies on equality with British vessels, provided Oswald and the American ministers reached some agreement on commercial reciprocity.[14] Pitt's action was not only a gesture of goodwill. It was also an early attempt to provide England relief from some of the growing burden of the navigation laws. The bill had strong support in the West Indies. As one eighteenth-century source summarized, "the necessity of allowing free enterprise . . . in American bottoms, had been very much insisted on by many of the West India planters and merchants. . . . It appeared that the West Indies could not be wholly supplied with provisions and lumber without the aid of American shipping."[15]

Indeed, Pitt was sincere during the Shelburne administration to open trade, but that was before he had to face Parliament as prime minister. . . . Henry Laurens, writing to Paris, informed the ministers that Fox had told him that "the navigation act is the vital of Great Britain, too delicate to touch." "England," remarked Fox, "could not give up her whole navigation law by allowing American vessels to bring other than American goods to Great Britain—that was allowed to no nation."

. . . The reaction, outside as well as inside Parliament, represented the first important polemical confrontation on the validity of the navigation acts. For such as Adam Smith and his disciples, the acts were regarded as a distorted view of economics. But in the eighteenth century, any attempt to adopt a more liberal approach to the economics of empire could only be soundly defeated. . . .

The spearhead of the attack against Pitt's proposal was led by the Earl of Sheffield, and his *Observations,* published in 1783, became a bible for those who saw only tragedy in any relaxation of the mercantilist system. For Sheffield the navigation laws represented nothing less than the guardian of British prosperity. As for the United States, Sheffield strongly felt that "by asserting their independence, the Americans have at once renounced the privileges, as well as duties, of British subjects."[16]

The most bellicose reaction came from the pen of Thomas Paine. Accusing Sheffield of being primarily responsible for getting Parliament all worked up and thereby blocking American ships from the West Indies, Paine declared that "America would be foolish . . . were she to suffer so great a degradation on her flag, and such a stroke on the freedom of her commerce."[17] John Adams was furious with Parliament, referring to the English approach as "a mean, contemptible policy." Richard Livingston, writing from America, expressed the feeling of his contemporaries by remarking that "we are very angry here with Great Britain, on account of her West India restrictions, and [Congress] in fulminating resolutions to prohibit all intercourse with her. . . ."[18]

On January 24, 1785, Congress nominated John Adams Minister Plenipotentiary to England, and in a resolution adopted the following month (from a draft drawn up by Adams), advised him "to represent to the British ministry a strong and necessary tendency of their restrictions on our trade [and] that you will manage your conferences . . . as to discover whether [they] are inclined to a commercial treaty with us. . . ."

Neither Jay nor Adams hesitated to suggest, as an ultimate recourse, the adoption by the United States of its own navigation law. Already in 1783 Jay wrote that "It is in our power finally to make a navigation act . . . if Britain should adopt and persist in a monopolizing system, let us retaliate fully and firmly." Congress did assign a special committe to the task of looking into "all such proceedings as might prove injurious to the United States," and it reported to Congress on April 13, 1784, that Great Britain had already taken action "destructive of our commerce with the West India islands. . . . It would be the duty of Congress . . . to meet [these] attempts

... with similar restrictions on her commerce."[19] The committee also noted in its report that the powers of Congress were not explicit enough, and that a greater sense of union had to develop before any positive action could be taken. Thus the question of the West Indian trade was a factor in the move to alter, or strengthen, the Confederation. In the meanwhile the committee recommended to Congress that imports and exports be strictly regulated by treaties of commerce.

After John Jay had been elected by Congress as secretary of Foreign Affairs, Jefferson was sent to Europe to join Adams in the effort to negotiate such treaties. The instructions Jefferson brought with him stipulated that with those European nations holding territorial possessions in America, a reciprocal intercourse be admitted (e. g., each party should have the right to carry their own bottoms, and duties should be on the basis of favored nation).[20] Congress also stipulated, as an alternative, direct and similar intercourse between the United States and certain free ports within these possessions; or, the permission to bring from such possessions, in American vessels, the produce of foreign states, together with the right for the United States to carry their own products in their vessels to stipulated free ports. But the going was slow since London felt no sense of urgency in the matter. . . .

The attitude which prevailed in American thinking was based, ultimately, on two major themes. The first involved the more immediate question of West Indian commerce in relation to the total American trade. The second, and pervasive factor, was the continuing abstract argument of "natural right." Here one finds a parallel with another contemporary question—the extension of the American frontier. John Jay, for example, was delighted by the suggestion of Lafayette that the Mississippi belonged to the United States "by the laws of nature." For decades Americans would continue to claim a "natural right" with respect to their place within the framework of the British West Indian Empire.

In the meantime, Jefferson searching for a *quid pro quo,* felt that since the United States allowed British vessels in all American ports, this was "more quid than pro." John Adams, suspicious though more receptive than Jefferson, remarked that "if Congress should recommend to . . . the States to lay . . . heavy duties upon all British vessels . . . especially upon all vessels coming from or bound to the West India Islands . . . by this means the [British] would be compelled to enter into an equitable treaty."[21] . . .

By the summer of 1785 it was more than evident that England was cool to any sort of arrangement, whatsoever, with respect to the West Indies. Thomas Jefferson commented realistically to Secretary Jay that "it is difficult to say what the United States had to offer any country for an admission into the West Indies." Adams, also writing to Jay, suggested that England relied upon the fact that the United States could never act in concert. "It cannot, therefore, be too earnestly recommended," wrote Adams, "in giving to Congress full power to make treaties of commerce, and, in short, to govern all our external commerce." And with a true New Englander's eye, Adams later wrote to Jay that "We should stipulate for the admission of all our produce, and should agree upon a tariff of duties on both sides." Adams continued: "We should insist upon entire liberty of trade and navigation, both in the East and West Indies, and in Africa. . . ."

* * *

On July 25, 1785, Adams submitted to Lord Caermarthen a proposal for "a fair and equitable treaty of commerce," with the object of returning the trade between the two countries "to its old channels and nearly under the same regulations," avoiding especially those which "are destructive of the trade with the British West Indies Islands."[22] There were, of course, the usual warnings that the American Congress was growing impatient. But Secretary Jay harbored no illusions remarking that "although a disposition prevails to enable Congress to regulate trade. . . . Yet I am apprehensive." This inability of Congress to get united action was well understood in Europe, a fact eventually made more glaring by the failure of the Annapolis convention. In April 1786, for instance, the American ministers reported from Paris that Lord Dorset, "after harping a little on the old string, the insufficiency of the powers of Congress to treat and compel compliance with treaties, said he would lay the matter [the West Indies] before the ministry and the King."

* * *

Still no progress. During the previous December (1785), Adams strongly reiterated to Secretary Jay that perhaps it might well be more convenient to wait until the parliamentary session was finished "to better discern English designs." Adams also warned that the United States would become a nation of mere husband-men, fleeced almost at pleasure by rapacious foreign countries. He then posed the question: "Will you be your own carriers?" Adams answered his question with the recommendation that the United States "prohibit and exclude in turn, and confine [its] exports to [our] own ships, or, at least, exclude the ships of Great Britain."

The Confederation had already acted on April 26, 1784, stipulating that no imports or exports be carried on foreign ships belonging to countries without a commercial treaty with the United States. Congress had been encouraged by similar action already taken by individual states, but it could not really assert itself fully under the existing constitution. The activity of the individual states made Adams momentarily optimistic, and he wrote to Jay in the summer of 1785, that if Congress should recommend to the legislatures of the states the adoption of a policy of heavy duties on all British vessels, entering or leaving American ports, *especially from the West Indies,* "every legislature would immediately comply." Adams's optimism could only be momentary not only because of the lack of concerted American effort, but, as he wrote to Arthur Lee, "the national sense and public voice [of England] is decidedly against us in the . . . ship trade, and they are as yet but feeble parties for us in the West India trade. . . ." Adams finally concluded that "they now have evidence, they think, that their commerce flourishes, and their credit is established without a treaty . . . and without opening the West Indies."

*   *   *

By the end of January 1786, America's Minister Plenipotentiary had lost most of his confidence, writing to Jay that "they think America may have whatever she desires except a free trade with the West India Islands. . . ." With increasing frustration, Adams later complained that "the most remarkable thing in them is that the King and every member of each house have entirely forgotten that there is such a place upon the earth as the United States."

But Secretary Jay had the responsibility of office, and he gently guided his emissaries in London and Paris. Jefferson's hostility toward England had already become chronic, and had reached the point where he was unwilling to pay just any price for entry into the West Indies. However, in July of 1786, Jay reminded Jefferson that countries other than England "do not regard us entirely without jealousy," and Jay concluded by pointing out that "the Dutch obviously were beginning to resent America's presence in China, and that will doubtless be more or less the case with every nation with whose commercial views we may interfere."

In the meantime the impatience of Adams continued to grow. Already in October of 1785, he wrote John Jay that "if the States do not make haste . . . it will be to no purpose to continue here and I . . . shall wish myself any where else rather than here." Secretary Jay, of course, was well aware of the fact that not only the question of the West Indies but of commerce in general, would necessitate exhaustive diplomacy. Writing to Lord Lansdowne in April of 1786, Jay expressed the wish that all civilized people would consider and treat each other like fellow citizens, and strive to admit each other "to a perfect freedom of commerce." But he concluded realistically by remarking that "it is pleasant, my Lord, to dream to these things. . . .

205

Yet the passions and prejudices of mankind forbid us to expect it."

Still Adams and Jefferson were basically realists, and it was this ability to combine idealism with practicality which helped nurture the growing success of America at the end of the eighteenth century. John Adams, although steadily pushing the idea of an American system of navigation laws as a possible form of retaliation, could also warn Jay that if the United States resolved to prohibit all foreign vessels from American ports, and attempted to confine all exports and imports to American ships, the results could only be disastrous ultimately to all of America.[23]

In March of 1786, at the request of Adams, Thomas Jefferson visited England to join in a mission which was to prove fruitless for American diplomacy. Both sought to get an Anglo-American commercial treaty, but met with nothing but delay and indifference. This experience not only embittered Jefferson further, but later was a factor in widening the gap between himself and Hamilton with respect to England. As for Adams, the most sobering fact was that the balance in the trade with Great Britain was becoming increasingly more favorable for Massachusetts.[24]

Until 1786 Alexander Hamilton apparently did not concern himself with the subject of the American carrying-trade, evidently satisfied that American commerce with Great Britain was rapidly increasing. Hamilton did suggest that Congress seek the funds necessary to strengthen the navy to bargain for commercial privileges from a greater position of strength. But Hamilton appeared skeptical of any restrictions upon England in order to force concessions in the West Indies. His argument for a position of strength was based in part upon his concern for a neutrality which would be respected. As Hamilton wrote: "A nation despicable by its weakness, forfeits even the privilege of being neutral."[25] And many of Hamilton's fellow Americans quickly learned during the period of the Confederation that a Congress which was largely impotent could not wield any influence in foreign affairs, nor could American officials carry out their functions properly. But the attitude of such as Jefferson and Madison, in confrontation with Hamilton, appears to highlight more a difference in approach. "Realpolitik versus excess idealism," as Paul Varg emphasized.[26]

But to return to the efforts to secure rights for American shipping in the West Indies. In the midst of this diplomacy, several factors should not be overlooked. First of all, the fruits of proximity which the Americans enjoyed prior to the Revolution were not entirely lost in the period after 1781; secondly, the Order in Council of 1783 allowed the importation of stipulated American products (in British vessels, of course); thirdly, the hurricanes of 1784, 1785, and 1786, causing vast damages across the West Indies, not only increased the demand for American products but also temporarily opened scattered ports to American ships.

Officially, however, the policy of the Committee on Trade (formerly the board of trade), remained intact: the privilege of supplying the islands belonged to the United Kingdom and the loyal colonies. This policy was rigidly adhered to in the period after 1784 through a succession of Enabling Acts, with that of 1788 showing no response to the attempts at American negotiation.[27] . . .

Yet American negotiations continued in the attempt to convince London to open the West Indian ports on a permanent basis. The diplomacy proceeded along several lines of argument: (1) that although the export trade from Great Britain to the West Indies showed a progressive increase (especially true after 1786), the increase was not sufficient to supply the demands of the islands, thereby justifying a policy of keeping island ports open to American products carried in American ships; (2) the triangular trade (England-British North America-West Indies-England) was not successful, and that the imperial policy of encouraging direct trade from English ports to the West Indies was not succeeding; (3) that the system of navigation laws was now obsolete, and that the English had best listen to Adam Smith and not Lord Sheffield, and abandon the obsolete mercantile system for free trade.[28]

In addition to the above was the underlying theme, increasingly used, and perhaps best defined by Henry Bliss in his excellent review of British-American commercial relations published under the title *On Colonial Intercourse*. Bliss remarked that "the Americans seem always to have considered the West India trade as theirs of right . . . which they apparently interpret to be the law of nature and of nations."[29]

In the meantime the English leaders watched American leadership trying to form a more perfect union, and they could afford to dictate the terms. Although a bill was introduced in Parliament (February 12, 1788) "to settle the commercial intercourse between the United States of America and the British West India Islands on a more permanent footing," at the same time Grenville, now vice-president of the Committee of Trade, also introduced legislation to make permanent the policy as expressed by the Enabling Acts.[30]

But hardly had the new republic been established under the leadership of Washington, when diplomacy was inaugurated with renewed vigor. The Crown's official representative to the United States, Phineas Bond (later to become consular-general), wrote to the Duke of Leeds in 1789 that "the present views and objects of those who look forward to . . . a commercial treaty with England extend no further . . . than to the opening of trade to the West Indies."[31] Bond was quite accurate in his observation. For in October of 1789, President Washington delivered an "unofficial" commission to Gouverneur Morris in Paris to sound out the British Cabinet with respect to a mutual treaty of commerce. In addition, Morris was instructed to "let it be strongly impressed on your mind, that the privilege of carrying our productions in our vessels to the [West Indies] , and of bringing in return the productions of those islands to our own ports . . . is regarded here of the highest importance; and you will be careful not to countenance any idea of our dispensing with it in a treaty."[32]

But the ports of the British West Indies were to remain closed to American ships until England went to war with France in 1793. And the new president was well aware of the long road ahead in the area of negotiations, writing to John Jay before the new government was established, that "toleration in commerce like toleration in religion gains ground . . . but I am sanguine in my expectations that either will soon take place in their due extent."

NOTES

1. For a good introduction to the international aspects before the Revolution, see Richard Pares, *War and Trade in the West Indies, 1739-1763* (Oxford, 1936).
2. Note that this time about one-half of the trade with the BWI involved the island of Jamaica. For an interesting study on Whiggism and indebtedness, see George H. Guttride, *English Whiggism and the American Revolution* (Berkeley, 1942).
3. Adam Anderson, *The Origin of Commerce,* IV (London, 1787-89), p. 519. 4 volumes. Sometimes referred to as *Anderson's History of Commerce.*
4. *The Diplomatic Correspondence of the United States of America, 1783-1789,* II (Washington, 1855), p. 382. 3 volumes. Originally published in 7 volumes, (Washington, 1833-34).
5. L. H. Butterfield, ed., *Diary and Autobiography of John Adams,* III (Cambridge, 1961), p. 77. 4 volumes.
6. William B. Weeden, *Economic and Social History of New England, 1620-1789,* II (New York, 1890), p. 232. 2 volumes. For an excellent review of the situation in the 1780s see Albert A. Giesacke, *American Commercial Legislation Before 1789* (Boston, 1910).
7. George L. Beer, *The Commercial Policy of England Toward the American Colonies* (New York, 1893, 1948), pp. 144 ff.
8. For a good survey of the free port as practiced over a long span of time, see Frances Armytage, *The Free Port System in the British West Indies, 1766-1822* (London, 1953).
9. So reasonable did Franklin find Oswald that he made the audacious suggestion that all of Canada and Nova Scotia be awarded to the United States. See George H. Guttridge, *David Hartley M.P., An Advocate of Conciliation, 1774-1783* (Berkeley, 1926). Especially chapter 9.
10. Francis Wharton, ed., *The Revolutionary Diplomatic Correspondence of the United States,* VI (Washington, 1889), p. 688. 6 volumes. Reprinted in 1968.
11. Charles F. Adams, ed., *The Works of John Adams,* VIII (Boston, 1850-56), p. 66. 10 volumes.
12. An excellent survey of the Order in Council can be found in Gerald S. Graham, *Sea Power and British North America, 1783-1820* (Cambridge, 1941). On December 26, 1783 an Order continued the previous declaration, and this policy

of exclusion of American ships was to be continuously reaffirmed until embodied in an Act of Parliament in 1788 which remained in force until 1793.

13. Henry P. Johnston, ed., *The Correspondence and Public Papers of John Jay*, III (New York, 1890–93), p. 66. 4 volumes.

14. Edmund Fitzmaurice, *Life of William Shelburne*, II (London, 1876), pp. 253. 3 volumes. Second revised edition (London, 1912). 2 volumes.

15. Adam Anderson, *The Origin of Commerce*, IV (London, 1787–89), pp. 554, 675. 4 volumes.

16. The complexities of English politics with regard to American commerce, especially the West Indian trade, is excellently reviewed by Clarence Alvord, in *Lord Shelburne and the Founding of British-American Goodwill* (London, 1926).

17. William Van der Weyde, ed., *The Life and Works of Thomas Paine*, III (New York, 1923), p. 251. 10 volumes.

18. Henry P. Johnston, ed., *The Correspondence and Public Papers of John Jay*, III (New York, 1890–93), p. 109. 4 volumes.

19. *The Diplomatic Correspondence of the United States, 1783-1789*, I (Washinton, 1855), pp. 76 ff. 3 volumes.

20. The full text of the *Instructions* may be found in Paul L. Ford, ed., *The Works of Thomas Jefferson*, IV (New York, 1904–05), pp. 353–58. 12 volumes.

21. Quoted in Lester J. Cappon, ed., *The Adams-Jefferson Letters*, I (Chapel Hill, 1959), p. 86. 2 volumes.

22. *The Diplomatic Correspondence of the United States, 1783-1789*, II, p. 406. The full draft of the *Treaty of Amity and Commerce* is composed of twenty-seven articles, and should rank as a major document in the history of American diplomacy. See pages 406–17.

23. Adams remarked: "We should have the most luxurious set of farmers that ever existed [but we] should not be able to defend our coasts." The reader will note that, not unlike his British contemporaries, Adams viewed the merchant fleet as a training ground and source for naval power.

24. By 1788 the balance of trade was solidly in favor of Massachusetts. See Ian Christie, *Crisis of Empire, Great Britain and the American Colonies, 1754-1783* (London, 1966).

25. Harold G. Syrett, ed., *Papers of Alexander Hamilton*, IV (New York, 1961–   ), pp. 341–42.

26. Paul A. Varg, *Foreign Policies of the Founding Fathers* (East Lansing, 1963), p. 73.

27. For an excellent review of the enabling legislation, see Herbert C. Bell, "British Commercial Policy in the West Indies, 1783-1793," *English Historical Review* (July, 1916), pp. 429–47. The Committee on Trade conducted a long investigation in 1784, producing a wealth of material of considerable value for the study of West Indian trade both before and during the Revolutionary War.

28. Graham clearly shows that the arguments in favor of a British monopoly of the West Indies carrying-trade would have lost their weight had there been any serious doubt of retaining the American market. The relaxation of the navigation laws within the next two decades was to prove that conclusively. See Gerald S. Graham, *Sea Power and British North America, 1783-1820* (Cambridge, 1941).

29. Henry Bliss, *On Colonial Intercourse* (London, 1830), p. 12.

30. Herbert C. Bell, "British Commercial Policy in the West Indies, 1783-1793," *English Historical Review* (July, 1916), p. 441.

31. J. Franklin Jameson, ed., "Correspondence of Phineas Bond," *American Historical Review* (Annual Report), I (1896), p. 611.

32. John C. Fitzpatrick, ed., *The Writings of George Washington*, XXX (Washington, 1939), p. 441. 39 volumes.

WILBUR H. SIEBERT

LOYALIST EXODUS
TO THE WEST INDIES:
LEGACY OF REVOLUTION

Historians frequently ask the question: How revolutionary was the American Revolution? Suffice it to say that the founding fathers fought the war for independence while subscribing to principles and ideas some of which were indeed revolutionary but, unlike the French Revolution (and others to follow), the revolt in America did not devour either its direct participants, or the non-participating public. This is not to say that certain individuals and groups were not roughly treated. But the almost 100,000 "British Americans" who left the thirteen colonies were not fleeing from terror; rather these Loyalists were departing since they could no longer accept, in good conscience, the idea of separation from England. And most left after the fighting was over.

This was especially true for those who left for the West Indies. Although the largest number of Loyalists were to go back either to England or to British North America, many from the southern states found the West Indies to be at least the most convenient stepping-stone to freedom, including the freedom from Spanish control in the Floridas. For example, the evacuation of Savannah in 1782 sent some 7,000 exiles temporarily into East Florida, and the more desperate of them, especially those with slaves, sought refuge primarily in Jamaica or the Bahamas. The Crown not only provided transportation, but forty acres in the Bahamas to every head of a family, plus twenty acres for each black—and this land "to be delivered free and exempted from the burden of quit rents for ten years." For the two year

---

From *The Legacy of the American Revolution to the British West Indies and Bahamas.* The Ohio State University, 1913.

period 1783-1785 it has been estimated that over 6,000 refugees of both races sailed into the Bahamas. Needless to say cotton was quickly introduced as a crop and the institution of slavery securely established by the end of the century.

In the West Indies proper, Jamaica was the most popular with the exiles because of its size and cosmopolitanism. Besides, Jamaica offered the convenience of proximity. In addition the assembly of Jamaica "felt bound by every principle of humanity" to assist the refugees, which added to its attraction. In retrospect, the story of the American exile is sad, and not without tragedy, but it offers at the same time many happy endings.

East Florida escaped subjugation by the Spaniards, but nevertheless shared the fate of the adjoining district when England made peace with Spain. By the Treaty of Versailles, the latter country gained both provinces, but the Loyalists preferred the hardships of another removal rather than submit to Spanish rule. During the earlier years of the Revolution, refugees had taken shelter under the British flag in Jamaica and the Bahamas. In October 1775, one of the London papers gave currency to the item that several American families had arrived in Jamaica with their effects "on account of troubles in their own country." When Sir James Wright, governor of Georgia, fled to England in March 1776, a considerable number of Georgia Loyalists took their departure to the West Indies and Bahamas. It is true that some of these returned after Governor Wright resumed his office in the spring of 1777, but not all of them did so.

When, in July 1782, Savannah was evacuated, less than half of the 7,000 persons who withdrew from that port went to East Florida; Governor Wright, with some of the officers, civil and military, and part of the garrison, disembarked at Charleston; Brigadier-General Alured Clark and part of the British regulars went to New York; and the remainder—described as inhabitants and their effects—sailed to Jamaica under convoy of the frigate *Zebra*. Doubtless, these effects were mostly slaves, for Mr. Wright and some of his fellow Loyalists had no less than 2,000 for shipment to the island.[1] The governor explained afterwards that he considered Jamaica the best market for his Negroes, and that they were in danger of being stolen at Savannah. Probably, much more of the same kind of property was transported to the same destination. At any rate, Bridges tells us in his *Annals of Jamaica* that the island gained nearly 5,000, besides 400 white families, by the evacuation of Savannah.[2]

When, in December 1782, Charleston was surrendered to the Americans, 3,891 persons embarked for Jamaica, of whom 1,278 were whites and 2,613 were blacks.[3] At the same time, 20 whites and 350 blacks sailed for St. Lucia. It will be remembered that the number carried from Charleston to East Florida was almost equal to that destined for Jamaica. Of the remainder, 240 sailed for New York, 470 for Halifax, and 324 for England.[4]

What the result of the exodus from East Florida may have been for Jamaica and the other West Indies is not clear. At the end of July 1782, some of the Georgia refugees at St. Augustine memoralized Carleton, informing him that there were at least 4,000 people of both races from their colony in their neighborhood, and that they regarded the West Indies as the only region where they could employ their slaves to any advantage. But we have no means of ascertaining how many of these people found their way to the desired destination. The same uncertainty appertains to the various families in New York City who were seeking conveyance to these islands during the years 1782 and 1783. That a considerable proportion of them succeeded in reaching their goal admits of little doubt. Sabine gives several instances of Massachusetts Tories who settled in Antigua and St. Christopher.[5] Near the close of May 1783, eighty-five persons registered at St. Augustine to go to Jamaica, and a ship with these refugees, and probably others, sailed from that place for the island named about the twenty-fifth of the following month.

Some of the new settlers in Jamaica came also from Honduras and the Mosquito Shore, where the British had colonists engaged in cutting logwood and mahogany. The Spanish had long regarded these people as intruders in Central America, and during the later years of the Revolution attacked them with such persistence as to drive them out.[6] Their certificates of loyalty are still to be found among the official records of their chosen retreat, and show that they arrived at various times during the year 1783, some being accompanied by their slaves. Their numbers were sufficiently large to cause them to be mentioned in certain acts passed by the assembly of Jamaica in 1783 and 1784. The certificates also bear testimony to the fact that Loyalists continued to come to this island down to 1788 from both northern and southern states, albeit in very small numbers. Doubtless Jamaica profited also by the dispersion of the 10,000 refugees who were sent from New York to Shelburne, Nova Scotia, in the spring and fall of 1783. This dispersion took place during the years from 1785 to 1788, inclusive; and we are told by Mr. T. Watson Smith, author of "The Loyalists at Shelburne," a paper showing careful and extensive investigation, that numbers of these exiles found their way not only to the Canadas and Great Britain, but also the West Indies.[7] The above facts help to explain the remarkable increase in population of Jamaica between the years 1775 and 1787. The census for the former year showed 18,500 whites, 3,700 free colored people, and 190,914 slaves; while for the latter year the figures are 30,000 whites, 10,000 free colored people, and 250,000 slaves. By 1785 the number of slaves had already reached from 220,000 to 240,000.[8]

* * *

We have already seen that a single ship was sufficient to carry those who embarked at St. Augustine near the end of June 1783, for Jamaica. It may be added that two vessels sufficed for those taking passage for England, and that while ninety signed to go to New Providence, no reference is made to their departure at this time. This disinclination on the part of the Loyalists to proceed to the Bahamas was due to a lack of information about the conditions obtaining there. Hence, some of the intending settlers of New Providence went to find out what they could about these conditions, and were soon followed by Lieutenant Wilson, of the Engineers, who was officially dispatched from St. Augustine for the same purpose. The report made by the former was not very favorable; it represented that the soil was rocky and that there were "no tracts of land contiguous where any considerable number of negroes could be employed."

Although we catch but few glimpses of what was taking place in East Florida during the remainder of the time allowed for its evacuation, we can scarcely doubt that parties of varying size, some in small vessels supplied by themselves, were embarking from time to time for the Bahamas and the neighboring islands. This exodus was encouraged . . . by the means of transportation provided by the Crown, [and] also by the favorable conditions offered to those who wished to settle in the achipelago. According to instructions issued to Lieutenant-Governor Powell, September 10, 1784, he was to grant unoccupied lands in the Bahamas as follows: "To every head of a family, forty acres, and to every white or black man, woman or child in a family, twenty acres, at an annual quit rent of 2s. per hundred acres. But in the case of the Loyalist refugees from the continent such lands were to be delivered free of charges, and were to be exempted from the burden of the quit rents for ten years from the date of making the grants."

These instructions were issued none too soon, for only fifteen days afterwards a number of transports and ordinance vessels arrived at Nassau with the garrison and military stores of St. Augustine. With this fleet came McArthur, whom Carleton had placed in command of the Bahamas for the time being. Within a few days there arrived also "seven ships and two brigs crowded with refugees." We are told that the stream of Loyalists continued to pour into the islands during the early months of the following year, Spain having extended by four months the period allowed for the withdrawal of

213

British subjects from Florida. Even this concession proved barely sufficient, for Governor Tonyn appropriated a few days of grace by making announcement that the last transport would leave the port of St. Mary's River, on March 1, 1785. He advised all persons of English blood to leave East Florida for the Bahamas before the Spanish governor took possession.[9]

But East Florida was not the only important source of the multitudes coming to settle in the Bahama Islands during our period. From New York City, Carleton sent more than 1,400 persons, who had associated themselves to colonize the Island of Abaco.

Other refugees embarked at the same time for Cat Island. Carleton now shipped provisions for an additional six months, and instructed McArthur to do everything in his power for the exiles. During the month of October, two additional contingents of the associators got ready to sail, one of those numbering 509 persons. All told, 1,458 Loyalists embarked at New York for Abaco, according to an official return of the commissary-general, dated two days before the British troops evacuated that port. This number does not include eight companies of militia sent from New York to the Bahamas in October 1783. That Abaco derived part of its settlers from East Florida is indicated by a memorial, addressed to Carleton in June of the year just named, by some of the New York associators. This memorial stated that many persons from St. Augustine were expected to join the new colony, and another memorial, published in New York about the same time, announced more explicitly that the number of loyal inhabitants of East Florida who had actually engaged to take part in the settlement of Abaco was upwards of 1,500.

It is difficult to estimate the increase in population of the Bahamas due to the immigration of the Loyalists. Bryan Edwards, writing at the beginning of the nineteenth century, does not attempt it, but contents himself with telling us that the inhabitants who in 1773 numbered 2,052 whites and 2,241 blacks were "considerably augmented" by the emigrants from North America.[10] Northcroft, writing in 1900, is more positive: he states that before the emigration there were only 1,750 white people in the colony and 2,300 colored; but that the influx of refugees raised the number of the former to 3,500 and the latter to 6,500.[11] Dr. Wright, who investigated the subject in 1905, seems to accept these figures.[12] But, according to a census of 1782, in which seven of the islands are named, the total number of inhabitants was 4,002, less than one quarter being Negroes. In the light of the evidence presented in this paper, it seems safe to say that the Bahama Islands gained between 6,000 and 7,000 inhabitants of both races from June 1783 to April 1785.

Abaco, which probably received a greater share of the immigrants than any of the other Bahamas, is the largest island of the group, and one of the most fertile. Philip Dumaresq, who remained there as commissary for more than a year and half . . . found the climate delightful, but noted that the soil was so shallow that in a dry season the sun heated the rock underneath and burned up any vegetables that had been planted. He also recorded that an unusual drought had prevailed almost from the time the Loyalists had arrived there. . . . He and his family did not find the people of Abaco at all congenial, and he speaks of them in no complimentary terms in the letter to his father-in-law, Dr. Sylvester Gardiner, the Boston Loyalist, from which we glean our informant's impressions of the island and its occupants; on the other hand, the commissary had nothing but good words for the treatment accorded him by John Maxwell, governor of the Bahamas, and General McArthur. These gentlemen, he testified, treated him only with the greatest politeness, and the former appointed him a magistrate in order, he declared, to keep him from being "insulted by the Abaco Blackguards."[13]

If, however, Governor Maxwell showed himself kindly disposed towards this lone Loyalist officer, he yet exhibited an unmistakable prejudice, which he shared with the older inhabitants, towards the new element in the colony. The coming of the Loyalists thus brought with it factional feeling—feeling that grew so pronounced ere long as to lead the new settlers to disavow openly any responsibility for an address of regret presented to the governor when he surrendered his office, and returned to England in the summer of 1785. The Americans promptly became the party of opposition to the existing government in the islands: they criticized the administration, accused Governor Maxwell of attempting to withhold from them the right of trial by jury, and of other conduct which they characterized as tyrannical. They also found fault with some of the laws, on the ground that they were repugnant to those of the mother country, and they demanded reform. The elections of 1785 gave the Loyalists some members in the House of Assembly, but the native population was still in control there; and when several members, who favored the new party, withdrew from the House and persisted in absenting themselves against the House's orders, they were declared to be no longer eligible to seats in that body. The Loyalists sent a petition to the assembly asking for its dissolution, which, after being read, was handed over to the common hangman to be burned before the door of the House.

By the latter part of 1786, the Americans had become the stronger party in the Bahamas; but the Earl of Dunmore, who succeeded to the governorship at this time, pursued the same policy as his predecessor. He received petitions from New Providence, Abaco, Exuma, and Cat Island, again praying that the assembly be dissolved; but, as he declined to accede to them, that body lasted about eight years longer, or until the end of Dunmore's administration. Then, finally, an act was passed that limited the life of a legislature to seven years.

Besides affecting political conditions in the colony, the influx of the Loyalists had a marked effect upon the commercial, agricultural, and social conditions of the archipelago. By 1800 the town of Nassau alone had a population—a little more than 3,000—equal to the whole population of the only islands inhabited thirty years before, namely, New Providence, Eleuthera, and Harbor Island. . . . McKinnen, who made a tour of the Bahamas in 1802 and 1803, reports that six square-rigged vessels were seen at one time in Nassau Harbor laden with cotton for London, and tells us that during many years previous the exports of this commodity amounted to several hundred tons per annum. He also notes that the town was frequently visited while he remained there by African slave-ships, some of which disposed of their cargoes on the island. The principal trade of Nassau, McKinnen says, was carried on with England, the southern islands in the West Indies, and the United States, whence it derived continual supplies of livestock and provisions. The same authority states that the exports from the islands included salt, turtles, mahogany, dye, and other woods and barks. Wrecking was also a source of considerable income, since wrecks were continually occurring among the Bahamas.[14]

Agriculture, even more than commerce, was given a new impetus by the American refugees, many of whom were planters from the South, accompanied by a considerable number of their slaves. It did not take these experienced cotton raisers long to clear lands and plant their crops. "It is said that fifteen years after their arrival, forty plantations, with between 2,000 and 3,000 acres in cotton fields, had been established on Crooked Island alone, and that on Long Island, which was settled at an earlier date, and which had been more extensively improved, there were in 1783 nearly 4,000 acres in cultivation. The combined yield from Long Island and Exuma for one year was estimated at over 600 tons." McKinnen found that the planters—most of whom came from Georgia, according to his account—had brought with them different varieties of seed, especially the Persian, but that Anguilla cotton was being more generally cultivated at the time of his visit.

The presence of the American refugees affected more or less the social conditions in the Bahamas, for the newcomers soon outnumbered the older inhabitants, and they introduced their own conceptions of plantation life and of the relations of master and slave. Many of the new whites were persons of energy, and we have McKinnen's word for it that the blacks in general possessed "more spirit and execution" than those in the southern parts of the West Indies. The planters assigned the various tasks to their Negroes, "daily and individually" according to their strength; and if the latter were so diligent as to have finished their labors at an early hour, the rest of the day was allowed them for amusement or their private concerns. Another feature that tended to soften the system of slavery in the islands was the absence of the overseer from most of the estates. The master usually acted as his own superintendent; and it rarely happened, therefore, according to McKinnen, that the Negroes were so much subject to the discipline of the whip as was the case where the gangs were large, and the direction of them was entrusted to agents or overseers. It was, nevertheless, true that some planters were brutal, that female slaves as well as males were sometimes flogged, and that masters "had the right practically to punish their slaves at their own discretion," without being held accountable for their acts of cruelty.

The immigration to the Bahamas probably trebled the number of blacks, and raised the relative majority of blacks over whites by more than twenty percent. It is not surprising, therefore, that the stringency of the laws regulating slaves should have been increased. The sentiments and fears of the ruling class, which arose out of the changed situation, appear in the legislation enacted by the General Assembly of the colony in 1784. This legislation provided for the punishment of assault on a white by a slave with death; it provided that other abuse of a white person should be atoned for by a fine of £15, or by corporal punishment, not limited in amount or character; it provided that "whites could disarm not only slaves but also free coloured persons whom they found at large with arms in their hands;" it imposed a tax of £90 on any one manumitting a bondman, and gave validity to the evidence of slaves against manumitted persons in all trials for capital or criminal offenses; while against white persons only Christian Negroes, mulattos, mustees, or Indians were allowed to testify at all, and they only in suits for debt.[15]

While we know far less of the life of the Loyalists in Jamaica and the other British West Indies than of the life of those who settled in the Bahamas, the general conditions amidst which they settled are clearly distinguishable. . . .

Jamaica was receiving considerable numbers of Loyalists and Negroes from the mainland, the great convoy from Charleston arriving on January 13, 1783. Six weeks later, the assembly of the island passed an act for the benefit of all white refugees who had already come in, or should follow later, with the intent of becoming inhabitants. This act was made applicable to former residents of North and South Carolina and Georgia, the Bay of Honduras, the Mosquito Shore, and other parts of North America, who were paying the price of exile by being forced to relinquish their dwellings, lands, slaves, or other property. It exempted these persons for seven years after their arrival from the payment of imposts on any Negroes that accompanied them, as well as from all manner of public and parochial taxes, excepting the quit rents on such lands as they might purchase or patent. It also released them from all services, duties, and offices, except the obligations to serve in the militia, and decreed that the charges for patenting their lands should be borne at the public expense. . . . Loyalists who patented lands were obliged to settle and plant at least a part of these, and proceed with their improvements without intermission within two years from the date of their patents, and in default of so doing were to lose their lands. The reasons for the enactment of the above measure, which were embodied in its preamble, were that the assembly of Jamaica felt bound by every principle of humanity to relieve and assist the suffering refugees, and that, it was only good policy to give them all due encouragement, inasmuch as nothing could tend more to the security, wealth, and prosperity of the island than the increase of the inhabitants.

These reasons, however, did not prevent a protest against the new law on the part of some of the older inhabitants. While applauding the law and the motives from which it sprang, the justices and vestry of Kingston presented a petition to the assembly, November 30, 1784, calling attention to the effects of the measure upon their parish, which, they claimed, was more burdened by its provisions than all the other parishes combined. The petition explained that there were nearly seventy housekeepers in the town of Kingston who were refugees, and hence were exempt from parochial taxes, although many of these were apparently wealthy and were engaged in commerce to a considerable extent. Others were tradesmen or mechanics in the exercise of lucrative employments. Some of these persons were occupying fine houses in the best situations in the town. Thus, the petitioners were deprived of the taxes that might have accrued from the "opulent refugees," and were also burdened with a numerous poor of the same description, who came from the Mosquito Shore, the Bay of Honduras, and all parts of North America. . . .

Other parishes in which Loyalists are known to have settled were Port Royal, St. Thomas-in-the-Vale, and Trelawney. But, as was asserted by the justices and vestry of Kingston, the proportion of newcomers in these parishes was small in comparison with those in Kingston, probably between eight and nine percent of the latter number. The writer has in his possession copies of 174 of the certificates that were issued to refugees, in accordance with the act of 1783. These show that 145 of the recipients chose Kingston as their place of abode. Eighteen others, whose locations are given, distributed themselves over the other parishes. Sixty-one of the 145 were accompanied by slaves, to the number of 881. Of the 18 others, only 9 had slaves, who numbered all told 568. While fully a fourth of these certificated Loyalists had but few Negroes, the rest had anywhere from 5 up to 200 and over. One refugee was in charge of 202 blacks, including 89 of his own, who had been employed for some time on the public works, but were afterwards engaged in "jobbing" in different parts of the county of Surrey. Another refugee had brought over 412 blacks, of whom more than half were the property of Sir James Wright, recently governor of Georgia, while another was in charge of 181, nearly two thirds of these belonging to the Honorable William Bull, late lieutenant-governor of South Carolina. Since their arrival, the last named group of 181 slaves had been employed on the public works and in "jobbing" in several parishes.

A few of the exiles came from Connecticut, Massachusetts Bay, New York, and Pennsylvania, a few also from Maryland, and Virginia, but by far the greater number came from the other southern states. Out of the 174 certificated Loyalists, referred to above, 66 were from South Carolina, the most of these having come at the time of the evacuation of Charleston. Fifty-four gave the Bay of Honduras and the Mosquito Shore as their former places of residence. Among the new settlers there was a sprinkling of "gentlemen," surgeons, tradesmen, Quakers (from Philadelphia), widows, and men who had served in Loyalist corps. The Quakers had been driven southward being threatened with trials for treason. William Roach, a refugee from New York, in making affidavit before the magistrate of his parish, told of having raised a company in the corps of Loyal American Rangers, commanded by Colonel William Odell. That there were many planters among these people goes without saying. As early as January 1784, accounts of the success of some of these Loyalists in raising large crops of indigo were circulating in St. Augustine. One surviving record shows that lands were granted to no less than 183 refugees in the parish of St. Elizabeth. We are informed that the region in which these grants were made was little better than a morass, and that a claim for payment by the persons who surveyed and apportioned the tract led to an inquiry on the part of the House of Assembly, "when it was stated in evidence that none but amphibious creatures, such as fishes, frogs, and 'Dutchmen' could live there." It chanced that one of the Loyalists who tried the experiment bore the appropriate name of Frogg, but reported in sorrow that he had buried most of his family in consequence, and that his case was only one of many.

Among the refugee families that settled in Jamaica was that of Dr. William Martin Johnston, the son of Dr. Lewis Johnston, for some years treasurer and president of the King's Council of Georgia. While in the North, William became a captain in the New York Volunteers, or Third Loyal American Regiment. In 1779 Captain Johnston married Elizabeth Lichtenstein of Savannah, in whose *Recollections,* written in 1836, is preserved a record of experiences that may fairly be regarded as typical for a large class of island settlers. ... When Charleston was evacuated, Mrs. Johnston and her children took passage to St. Augustine to join her father-in-law's family, while her husband accompanied his regiment to New York City. Mrs. Johnston relates that she was conveyed to her destination by a small schooner, and arrived there safely "with many more Loyalists," although she saw "many vessels lying stranded along the shore that had been wrecked on the sand bar." It may have been that she was writing of this dismal sight, when she remarked in a letter of January 3, 1783, to her husband: "Out of the last fleet from Charleston there have been sixteen sail of small vessels lost on and about the Bar. There are six or eight high on the beach." At any rate, she reported that no lives had been lost at the time of her own landing, although "much of the poor Loyalists' property" was destroyed.

Mrs. Johnston found St. Augustine occupied by many Greeks from Smyrna and Minorca, who had been brought there by a Dr. Turnbull to cultivate his lands on the Metanges, some miles from the city. Inasmuch as these people had failed to get along well with their employer, they had left his estates and come into town. The Johnstons remained in St. Augustine for sixteen months, during which period fish proved to be their "chief dependence and ration." With the announcement that East Florida had been ceded to the Spaniards, and that St. Augustine was soon to be evacuated, Dr. Lewis Johnston was granted a transport for his sole use "to go wherever he wished in the British Dominion." . . . Captain Johnston had sailed in advance, with the intention of pursuing medical studies in Edinburgh and London. About the same time Brigadier-General Alured Clark, formerly commandant of Savannah, was appointed governor of Jamaica. This circumstance with others led the captain to decide on locating in Kingston, which he accordingly did in the autumn of 1785. However, his family continued in Scotland until some time in October 1786, and did not arrive in Jamaica until the middle of the following December. The Elder Dr. Johnston spent the remainder of his life in Edinburgh, and died there, October 9, 1796.[16]

The first large companies of Loyalists who resorted to Jamaica were furnished provisions by the British government, but the supply soon proved inadequate. A memorial dated April 8, 1783, was forwarded to Sir Guy Carleton at New York. . . . requesting a further allowance until they could find "lands or employment, especially for their negroes." Some of these Loyalists secured the desired employment for their slaves, as we have already seen, by hiring them out to labor on the public works, or sending them out "jobbing," that is, to perform the heavy work on sugar and other plantations, such as digging the cane holes and planting. To the extent of being able to call on the British authorities in the United States for provisions, the Loyalists were fortunate; but unless their appeal was promptly answered they had to endure not only the hardships peculiar to their own lot, but also the visitations of famine and hurricane that prevailed during the early years of their residence in the islands. In part, the prospect of starvation that confronted new and old settlers alike at this time was due to the destructive effects of the hurricanes of 1780 and 1781; in part, however, it was also due to the War of Independence, to which they owed their banishment from the states. Despite the proclamation of peace, the home government adopted the policy of restricting trade with the neighboring continent. An Order in Council was promulgated, July 2, 1783, limiting the importation of American products (livestock, grain, lumber, etc.) into the West Indies, to British vessels, and prohibiting entirely salt beef, pork, and fish.

Whether this policy of commercial hostility towards the revolted states met with the approval of the Loyalist element in the West Indies or not, it led most of the islands to send remonstrances and petitions to the British Parliament in 1784, on the score that they were dependent on America for supplies. The legislature of Jamaica advocated free trade with the United States as the only means of affording a chance of carrying on the island estates, of supplying their families with bread, and of averting "impending ruin."[17] These protests were given added emphasis by a destructive storm, which occurred July 30, 1784. This storm either sank, drove ashore, or dismasted every vessel in Kingston Harbor. It blew down public buildings in or near Kingston, and caused the loss of many lives. . . . The immediate effect of all this was to induce the planters to increase their acreage in corn and other farm produce. Scarcely had they harvested their crops when another hurricane swept over Jamaica, August 27, 1785; and the governor found it necessary to prohibit the exportation of provisions to other suffering colonies as an alternative to opening the ports once more to American ships. Even this measure did not prevent scarcity of food during the remainder of the year, but "the climax of misery seemed to be reached" when still another storm "burst upon the land," October 20, 1786. Under the drastic stimulus of these years of disaster, supplemented by the severities of the navigation laws, the islanders came to depend more on themselves, not only in raising their own provisions, but also in hewing their own staves. The navigation laws ceased to be enforced after 1792, and were rescinded by Parliament a few years later.

It should be noted, however, that the increased production of foodstuffs was not accomplished at the expense of the sugar and coffee crops, which in 1787 exceeded those of any former year. We have no means of learning how far the Loyalists and their slaves contributed to these various results. Probably, they contributed their share, especially in the cultivation of coffee, inasmuch as this industry was rapidly growing in favor with the island planters at the time the exiles began to arrive. While some refugees were early reported to have raised large quantities of indigo, they must have found, as did the other cultivators, that this crop was unprofitable in the absence of protection; although it was well suited to men of moderate means owning but few Negroes. The growing of cotton, to which many of the Americans had been accustomed, proved to be only partially successful in the West Indies, on account of the variable climate of these islands.

It has been truly said that in no colony did the system of slavery run

221

more thoroughly its baneful course than in Jamaica, and in none did it die harder. As most of the Loyalists who established themselves here were, or had been, slaveowners, there can be no doubt that they held the same views on the abolition of the slave-trade, the compulsory improvement of the slave code, and emancipation as did their fellow-colonials in the Bahamas. Moreover, they were (in the year 1800) fully identified with a population of 30,000 whites, who were the proprietors of 300,000 Negroes. . . .

The losses of real and personal property sustained by many of the Loyalists who fled to the West Indies and Bahamas were liberally compensated by the British government, as were the losses of those adherents of the Crown who settled in other parts of the British Empire. That the newcomers in these islands had relinquished a great amount of property is shown by the certificates issued to those who landed in Jamaica and avowed their intention of remaining as residents. As previously remarked, the writer has copies of 174 of these certificates; and in 158 of them he finds evidence of the losses sustained by their possessors, definite amounts being given in 111 certificates, while only general statements regarding the losses appear in the other 47. The amounts reported range all the way from £15 up to £12,000, not a few running from £1,000 to £5,000. James Cotton of North Carolina reported the largest loss mentioned, namely, £12,000; while James Cary tells of having left Charleston "under the necessity of abandoning all his property that he could not carry off with him, which property, so left, was confiscated by an Act of the Rebel Legislature and was of the value of £6,000 and upwards." Taking into account only the definite estimates contained in these certificates, the total amount of the losses would be £115,051, although doubtless some of the estimates were exaggerated.

A large class of claimants among the island settlers had suffered the deprivation of their property in consequence of the cession of East Florida to Spain. Four months before the definitive treaty was signed confirming this cession, the East Florida *Gazette* published a communication from Governor Tonyn in which the intended surrender of the province was announced. The communication also gave assurance that the government of Great Britain would pay every attention to the welfare of the refugees in the province, and that the governor would exert himself in "cooperating with them to obtain a compensation for their great losses and suffering."

The wretched condition of these unhappy people, for whom East Florida would soon cease to be an asylum, caused a stir in London, where the members of the Cabinet thought the matter sufficiently grave to warrant a special meeting, July 24, 1783. The purpose of this meeting was to discover some expedient for giving relief to the large number of Loyalists then assembled at St. Augustine. The London papers reported that 5,000 of these people had transmitted a memorial of their distresses to the government; but that the mode of alleviation to be adopted had not yet been made known.

Despite the commendable promptness of the Cabinet in considering this matter, Parliament appears to have taken no action for the financial relief of these Loyalists until 1786, when it passed an act designating two commissioners to investigate the losses of such of the East Florida sufferers as might submit their claims for liquidation. For the benefit of those "proprietors" of the province who had already removed to the Bahama Islands, or other British colonies in America, the act provided that the governor, lieutenant-governor, or commander-in-chief, and council of such islands or colonies might act in place of the commissioners for East Florida, and that these officials should report their findings to the regular commissioners to be laid in turn before the lords of the treasury and the secretaries of state. It was further provided that no claim should be received in Great Britain after January 1, 1787, or in the Bahama Islands or other colonies after March 1, of the same year. This act was to continue in force for two years after the time of its passage. Early in June of the next year, however, the same measure was reenacted for an additional twelvemonth.

In the meantime, the House of Commons adopted a resolution, May 8, 1787, recommending the granting of a sum not to exceed £13,600 to be applied in payment "for present relief and on account" to persons who gave satisfactory proof of their losses to the commissioners of investigation for East Florida, this sum to be paid in proportion not exceeding 40 percentum.

However, as we have already seen, the claim of large numbers of other Loyalists were paid in money on a liberal scale. Still others received compensation in the form of appointments to offices of emolument and honor under the Crown. Various executive, judicial, and fiscal positions in the Bahamas, Lesser Antilles, and Bermudas were filled in this way. Thus, in 1781, William Browne of Salem, Massachusetts, then an exile in England, was appointed governor of Bermuda. Previous to the Revolution, Mr. Browne had been a man of note in his native province, having served as colonel of the Essex regiment, judge of the Supreme Court, and a mandamus counselor. It is said that the revolutionary committee of safety offered him the governorship on condition that he support the American cause; but the Loyalist declined and retired to England. His administration as governor of Bermuda began January 4, 1782, his reception by the islanders being most cordial. He conducted the business of the colony successfully and in harmony with the local legislature, greatly improved the finances, and left the island in a prosperous condition when he withdrew to the mother country in 1788. Another Massachusetts man who held office in Bermuda was Daniel Leonard of Taunton. A member of the general court, he was appointed a mandamus counselor in 1774, although he never served in that capacity. In 1776 he accompanied the British army to Halifax, and doubtless went thence to England. In recognition of his past services and sacrifices he was made chief justice of the Bermudas.

In the Lesser Antilles, the Virgin Islands, St. Christopher or St. Kitts, and Antigua had Loyalists among their officials. In Antigua the post of attorney to the Crown was held for some years by Samuel Quincy of Massachusetts. Like his fellow-colonials, Leonard and Browne, Quincy went to England after the evacuation of Boston, having previously been solicitor-general. He held the attorneyship of Antigua until his death in 1789. Another fugitive from Boston, Nathaniel Coffin, was appointed collector of customs in St. Christopher's, a station worth £1,500 per annum, and occupied by Mr. Coffin for thirty-four years. James Robertson, attorney-general of Georgia before 1779, and later a member of the House of Assembly and the council in that province, went from New York to London in the fall of 1782, and about a year later was appointed chief justice of the Virgin Islands.

In the Bahamas at least three Loyalists held offices of more or less importance. One of these was William Wylly [who] ... had been a resident of Georgia, although he spent a considerable period in New Brunswick before going to the islands. In New Brunswick, Mr. Wylly served as the first Crown counsel and registrar to the court of vice-admiralty, but in 1787 he removed to the Bahamas with his family. In the following year, he was appointed solicitor-general and surrogate of the court of vice-admiralty. In 1804 he became advocate-general of the vice-admiralty court. By 1812 he was chief justice, and two years later exchanged with the attorney-general. In 1822 he was transferred to the chief justiceship of St. Vincent, one of the islands of the Windward group.[18] Another refugee who served as chief justice of the Bahamas was Stephen De Lancey, formerly lieutenant-colonel of the first battalion of the New Jersey Volunteers. William Hutchinson of Massachusetts also held an office in these islands. Isaac Hunt of Philadelphia, after being carted through the streets of that city by a mob, departed for the West Indies, where he took church orders. Subsequently, he removed to England, and became tutor in the family of the Duke of Chandos. It may be added that he was the father of Leigh Hunt, one of the most eminent literary men of England in the first half of the nineteenth century.

NOTES

1. *Editor's note:* Major General Campbell, writing to Lord Shelburne, estimated the number as 1,400. For supplementary material, see Lowell J. Ragatz, *The Fall of the Planter Class in The British Caribbean, 1763-1833* (New York, 1928), pp. 194 ff.

2. Rev. George W. Bridges, *The Annals of Jamaica* (London, 1828). 2 volumes.
3. *Editor's note:* This group disembarked at Port Royal on January 13, 1783.
4. *South Carolina Historical Magazine* (January, 1910).
5. Lorenzo Sabine, *The American Loyalists* (Boston, 1847). *Editor's note:* The volume is primarily composed of biographical sketches, alphabetically presented. An expanded two volume edition was published in 1864, entitled *Bibliographical Sketches of Loyalists of the American Revolution.*
6. Sir Daniel Morris, *The Colony of British Honduras* (London, 1883).
7. See article by T. Watson Smith, *Collections of the Nova Scotia Historical Society* (1787–88), IV, pp. 57, 63, 65, 85, 86, 88 (Halifax, 1888).
8. W. J. Gardner, *A History of Jamaica*, (London, 1873), p. 221.
9. Richard L. Campbell, *Historical Sketches of Colonial Florida* (Cleveland, 1892), p. 142.
10. Bryan Edwards, *History of the British Colonies in the West Indies*, II (London, 1793), pp. 199, 200. 2 volumes. Expanded edition of 1819 published by AMS Press (New York, 1966).
11. George J. Northcroft, *Sketches in Summerland* (Nassau, 1900), p. 282.
12. J. M. Wright, *History of the Bahama Islands*, p. 425. *Editor's note:* This work will be found in George B. Shattuck, ed., *The Bahama Islands* (Baltimore, 1905).
13. The Gardiner, Whipple, and Allen Letters, Vol. II. p. 49. (In the Library of the Massachusetts Historical Society.)
14. David McKinnen, *A Tour Through the British West Indies, 1802-1803* (London, 1804).
15. See George J. Northcroft, *Sketches in Summerland* (Nassau, 1900), p. 288.
16. See Elizabeth L. Johnston, *Recollections of a Georgia Loyalist* (New York, 1901). Reprinted by Spartansburg Reprint, South Carolina (1972). *Editor's note:* An excellent general history is E. Merton Coulter, *Georgia, A Short History* (Chapel Hill, 1947).
17. *Editor's note:* Perhaps this is one of the reasons why many hundreds of Loyalists used Jamaica as a stepping-stone to migrate to Honduras Bay. When Great Britain renounced her territorial claims there, many finally migrated to Dominica. This subject has yet to be thoroughly researched.
18. John W. Lawrence, *Footprints* (St. Johns, 1892), p. 107.